William Crookes, Adolphe Wurtz

An Introduction to Chemical Philosophy According to the Modern Theories

William Crookes, Adolphe Wurtz

An Introduction to Chemical Philosophy According to the Modern Theories

ISBN/EAN: 9783337070229

Printed in Europe, USA, Canada, Australia, Japan

Cover: Foto ©Thomas Meinert / pixelio.de

AN INTRODUCTION TO

CHEMICAL PHILOSOPHY

ACCORDING TO THE

MODERN THEORIES.

BY

DR. ADOLPHE C. WURTZ, F.R.S.

Translated from the French, by permission of the Author, by
WILLIAM CROOKES, F.R.S.

LONDON:
J. H. DUTTON, "CHEMICAL NEWS" OFFICE,
1, WINE OFFICE COURT, FLEET STREET.

1867.

INTRODUCTION.

At a time when the philosophy of chemistry is becoming more and more clearly apprehended, we need to be reminded of its historical development. The more acute and profound our co-ordination and interpretation of phenomena, the more careful should be our scrutiny of the successive views regarding them, which have been previously held. Such a scrutiny will serve two useful purposes, for it will correct two common and erroneous modes of thought. Thus, the technical terms finally adopted in the expression of chemical facts will cease to be vague—they will acquire a constant as well as a definite meaning; and at the same time, that narrowness of vision, which sees everything in one aspect only, will be duly enlarged.

For these reasons the appearance in an English dress, and in a separate volume of Professor Wurtz's "Introduction to Chemical Philosophy," must be regarded as peculiarly seasonable. Many other chemical books have, indeed, been published within the last year or two—in some cases, original works of great merit and usefulness—but the progress of the science has not been recorded lately in a systematic form. Dr. Hofmann's "Modern Chemistry," for example, enounces in the fullest terms the laws of combination by volume, the functions of radicals, and the dependence of chemical types upon the different equivalencies of the elements. Dr. Frankland's "Lecture Notes," on the other hand, develope very amply the equations of chemical changes, and, more especially, the constitution of compounds as made up of atoms bonded together in diverse but systematic modes. But Dr. Wurtz's compact volume fulfils most of the intentions of the works just named, and yet does something more. It traces in sufficient detail the varying opinions of chemical philosophers as to the laws of chemical combination, and the nature of chemical structures. Thus the reader is led gradually to the study of the newest system, while on his way the errors and the glimpses of truth in the older systems are clearly pointed out.

For breadth of view, lucidity of expression, orderly arrangement of facts, shrewdness and fairness in reasoning, Dr. Wurtz's treatise appears to be singularly distinguished. The dates and references will be found of the utmost value, while the justice which marks his attribution of discoveries to their true originators is not the least agreeable feature of the work.

CONTENTS.

PART I.

EQUIVALENTS, ATOMIC WEIGHTS AND MOLECULAR WEIGHTS.

Section I.

Section II.

PART II.

THEORY OF TYPES AND ATOMICITY.

Section I.

Section II.

Section III.

Section IV.

PART III.

CONNECTION BETWEEN ORGANIC AND INORGANIC CHEMISTRY.

Section I.

Section II.

Section III.

Section IV.

Section V.

CONCLUSION.

AN INTRODUCTION

TO

CHEMICAL PHILOSOPHY.

PART I.

EQUIVALENTS, ATOMIC WEIGHTS AND MOLECULAR WEIGHTS.

SECTION I.

Historical Development of the Ideas, Equivalent, Atom, Molecule.

THAT bodies combine in definite proportions is one of the fundamental truths of chemistry. The notions of equivalents, of atomic weights, and of molecular weights are a consequence of it, and the idea of regarding chemical compounds as molecules formed of a juxtaposition of atoms is its theoretical representation. These ideas are involved in all that appertains to chemistry, and are the basis of all discussions connected with the science. It is important, therefore, to look for their origin and development, and to examine how, from being for a long time ill defined and confused, they have ultimately assumed the definite forms which they now possess.

Definite Proportions.—Equivalents.—The ideas of definite proportions have become introduced into science by researches into the composition of salts. It was found that, in order to saturate a definite weight of alkali with an acid of known strength, it was necessary to employ an invariable weight of the latter; and it was observed that the formation of a neutral salt depended upon the existence of a fixed relation between the amounts of real alkali and acid present, the least excess of one or the other being sufficient to destroy the neutrality.

In 1699 Homberg* undertook some experiments on this point which deserve to be mentioned. He found that 1 ounce of salt of tartar (carbonate of potash) required to saturate it,—

14 ounces of the best vinegar.
2 ounces 3 drachms of spirit of salt (hydrochloric acid).
1 ounce, 2 drachms, 36 grains of aquafortis (nitric acid).
5 drachms of vitriolic acid.

After evaporating the saturated liquids the increase in weight of the solid matter was,—

3 drms.	36 grs.,	after saturation with	vinegar.
3 "	14 "	" "	hydrochloric acid.
3 "	36 "	" "	nitric acid.
3 "	6 "	" "	sulphuric acid.

It is seen that these experiments have for their object the determination of the quantities of different acids which are required to saturate the same weight of base. Inaccurate as are their results, they amount to an attempt, crude, indeed, but the earliest, to determine what we to-day call the equivalents of acids.

Nearly a century elapsed before the question of the composition of neutral salts, started by Homberg, received a satisfactory solution. Bergmann and Kirwan examined it with but moderate success, and it is some-

* Hermann Kopp, *Geschichte der Chemie,* ii. 355.

what remarkable that it was reserved for one of the last upholders of alchemy—Wenzel*—to settle this point.

The work written by this chemist in 1777, under the title of "Vorlesungen über die Chemische Verwandschaft der Kœrper" (Lessons on the Chemical Affinity of Bodies), is even now remarkable for the accuracy of the analyses there described, and for the justness of the conclusions which the author knew how to deduce from them. The starting point of these researches was the following phenomenon, which was then well known, and which had already been observed by chemists:—

When concentrated and neutral solutions of sulphate of potash and nitrate of lime are mixed together, there are formed, by double decomposition, sulphate of lime which is precipitated, and nitrate of potash which remains in solution. The two newly formed salts are neutral, like the former, and it is the permanency of this neutrality which requires explanation.

Wenzel found this explanation in the composition of the four salts under examination. Having analysed the nitrate of lime, he found that 363 parts of this salt contained 123 parts of lime and 240 parts of nitric acid. He then tried how much sulphate of potash he should have to take for the lime to be completely precipitated by the sulphuric acid. Experiment had shown him that 162·5 parts of lime neutralised 240 parts of sulphuric acid, and he concluded from this that 123 parts of lime ought to require 181·5 parts of sulphuric acid.

On the other hand, he found that 240 parts of sulphuric acid required for neutralisation 290·4 of potash; 181·5 of sulphuric acid should therefore require 220 parts of potash; and to completely precipitate the lime from 363

* Charles Frederick Wenzel was born at Dresden in 1740 and died in 1793, being at that time the director of the famous mines of Freiberg, in Saxony. He published in 1773 a work entitled "An Introduction to the Higher Chemistry" (Einleitung zur Höheren Chemie), and devoted it to the defence of alchemical ideas.

parts of nitrate of lime it would be necessary to take 181·5 + 220, or 401·5 parts of sulphate of potash.

The 304·5 parts of sulphate of lime (containing 123 parts of lime and 181·5 parts of sulphuric acid) being precipitated, Wenzel concluded that the 240 parts of nitric acid originally combined with 123 parts of lime, ought, in order to form a neutral salt, to unite with the 220 parts of potash originally combined with the 181·5 parts of sulphuric acid. An analysis of nitrate of potash proved that his conclusion was correct; for he showed experimentally that 240 parts of nitric acid united with $222\frac{2}{3}$ parts of potash, an amount differing very little from 220.*

The important deduction from these researches is this: when nitrate of lime and sulphate of potash are mixed together in such proportions that the lime of the first salt will be neutralised by the sulphuric acid of the second, the nitric acid left by the lime is *precisely the amount* necessary to neutralise the potash abandoned by the sulphuric acid.

In other words, when two neutral salts mutually decompose each other, the neutrality is maintained for the reason that the amount of base which is neutralised by a certain weight of one acid, is also neutralised by a definite weight of another acid.

Hence arises the idea of equivalency. We have here two acids and two bases. The same quantities of each base neutralise successively a given weight of each acid, and are consequently *equivalent* to each other; thus:—

123 parts of lime 222 parts of potash	severally neutralise 240 parts of nitric acid,

* 363 parts of nitrate of lime contain 123·9 of lime and 239·1 of nitric acid; these figures are almost identical with the figures 123 and 240 obtained in Wenzel's analysis.

401·5 parts of sulphate of potash contain 184·5 parts of sulphuric acid and 217 of potash. Wenzel found in it 181·5 of sulphuric acid and 220 of potash. A comparison of these numbers will give a good idea of the accuracy of his analyses.

and are, consequently, equivalent in relation to this weight of nitric acid.

123 parts of lime 222 parts of potash	neutralise also 181·5 parts of sulphuric acid.

and are, therefore, equivalent in respect to this weight of sulphuric acid.

It suffices, therefore, to determine the proportions in which two bases combine with an acid, to know also the proportions in which these bases will unite with another acid.

In these memorable experiments it was necessary to determine the composition both of nitrate of lime, and of sulphate of potash; also to find what quantity of sulphuric acid was necessary to saturate the lime in the nitrate, and then to know how much nitric acid was necessary to saturate the potash in the sulphate. The composition of nitrate of potash was then foreseen by theory; 240 parts of nitric acid required 220 of potash. This is the amount predicted theoretically; 222·5 is the experimental quantity. Thus, Wenzel not only introduced into chemistry the idea of equivalency, but, at the same time, he foresaw and predicted the conclusions that could be drawn from it respecting the theoretical calculation of the composition of salts and the control of analyses.

Researches so exact and so important were scarcely noticed by chemists at that time, and were soon quite forgotten. The time for Wenzel had not yet arrived; his contemporaries were discussing theoretical ideas of a higher order; the chemical world was excited by the teachings and astonishing discoveries of Lavoisier.

Nearly twenty years passed over before this question of the proportion between the weights of acids (or bases) saturating a definite amount of a base (or an acid) was again taken up. Another German chemist, Richter, of

Berlin, drew attention to the subject in a work which he published in 1792 or 1794, entitled *Stœchiometry, or the Art of Measuring the Chemical Elements.** Besides this he published between 1792 and 1802 a periodical work, called *Ueber die Neueren Gegenstände in der Chemie* (Later Discoveries in Chemistry), the seventh, eighth, and ninth numbers of which are especially interesting. The author observed and explained, as did Wenzel, the phenomenon of the permanence of neutrality after the mutual decomposition of neutral salts. He determined the relative saturating capacity of acids and bases. He noticed that when a metal precipitated another metal from a solution of a neutral salt the liquid remained neutral. From this last observation he deduced a very correct explanation by showing that there existed a constant ratio between the amount of an acid saturating given weights of different bases and the quantity of oxygen contained in these bases; or, what comes to the same thing, that the quantity of oxides required to saturate the same weight of a given acid contained the same amount of oxygen.

To Richter we owe the first tables of equivalents. They are drawn up in reference to the reciprocal saturation of acids and bases, and consist of two kinds of tables.

The first shows the weight of different bases required to neutralise 1000 parts of an acid—sulphuric acid, for instance.

The second shows the quantity of acids required to neutralise 1000 parts of a base, such as potash or lime.

The figures which compose these tables are derived from analyses which are less exact than those of Wenzel, and which appear to have been subsequently corrected to

* *Stœchiometrie oder Messkunst Chemischer Elemente*, by Jeremie Benjamin Richter, in three volumes. The word stœchiometry is used in Germany at the present day to designate that branch of the science which treats of the equivalents. Richter died at Berlin in 1807.

make them agree with certain theoretical ideas which were more erroneous than the experiments themselves.*

For all that, Richter recognised this important fact, that the weights of bases forming the first series were proportional to each other, and that the same proportionality existed between the quantities of acids forming the second series; so that if he knew the quantities of all the bases which neutralised an acid A, it would be sufficient, in order to find the amount of any base which would be required to neutralise another acid A′, to determine by one experiment the weight of any one of the bases necessary to form a neutral salt with this acid A′; knowing the weight of this base, it would be easy to calculate the weight of all the others. Thus Richter showed that the composition of a great number of salts could be calculated theoretically from the known composition of certain other salts—an important deduction from the fact of the proportional relation between acids and bases which had been already established by Wenzel, and which the Berlin chemist saw the force of in all its bearings.

One thing, however, escaped him, and that was that it was useless to multiply the series so much, and that they might all have been founded on one alone. Indeed, after having determined the quantity of different bases required to neutralise 1000 parts of sulphuric acid, it would have been sufficient, instead of determining the quantity of base which would neutralise another acid, to find out how much of the other acids would be required to saturate the weight of any one of the bases neutralising 1000 parts of sulphuric acid. These amounts of acids would be equivalent to 1000 parts of sulphuric acid, and would exactly saturate the weight of base neutralised by 1000 parts of this acid. It is seen from this that

* Richter imagined that the weights of acid neutralising the same base were in geometrical progression, and that the quantities of base neutralising the same acid were in arithmetical progression.

Richter need have constructed only one table of equivalents of bases and acids, calculated in relation to 1000 parts of sulphuric acid. Fischer calculated a table of this kind from Richter's data, and published it in 1802.* The following is a copy of it:—

Bases.	Fischer's numbers.	Theoretical numbers.
Alumina	523	428
Magnesia	615	500
Ammonia	672	
Lime	793	700
Soda	859	775
Strontia	1329	1295
Potash	1605	1177
Baryta	2222	1912
Acids.		
Sulphuric	1000	1000
Hydrofluoric	427	500
Carbonic	577	550
Hydrochloric	712	912
Oxalic	755	900
Phosphoric	979	887†
Formic	988	925
Succinic	1209	1224
Nitric	1405	1350
Acetic	1480	1275
Citric	1683	1375
Tartaric	1694	1650

It will be noticed that for many bodies Fischer's numbers are widely different from the theoretical figures, and consequently the analyses of Richter, from which

* Hermann Kopp, *Geschichte der Chemie*, vol. ii., page 364.

† This number is half of 1775, which represents the weight of PO_5, if 1000 represents that of SO_3. But it must be noticed that to *neutralise* PO_5, that is to say, to form $2NaO,HO,PO_5$, there must be twice as much soda as is required to neutralise SO_3. The quantity of phosphoric acid strictly equivalent to SO_3 is therefore half PO_5 under the circumstances in which Richter was placed.

they are calculated were not nearly so accurate as those of Wenzel. The inaccuracy of these analyses, and the obscurity of a perplexed explanation, have not been much noticed in giving credit to Richter and some authority to his works.

One thing, however, remains established: Wenzel and then Richter introduced into the science the notion of equivalents.

Multiple Proportions.—Atoms.—The idea of atoms arises from a fundamental discovery which was made about 1804 by Dalton, and which depends upon facts entirely distinct from those observed by Wenzel and Richter. Having studied the composition both of olefiant and of marsh gas, Dalton perceived that for the same quantity of carbon, the latter contained exactly double the quantity of hydrogen which was contained in the former. He made analogous observations concerning the composition of carbonic oxide and carbonic acid, and of the compounds of oxygen and nitrogen. In this way he discovered the *law of multiple proportions.*

The following is the explanation of this law:—When two bodies, either simple or compound, form several combinations with each other, if the weight of one of them be taken as constant, the weight of the other varies in a very simple ratio. Thus, nitrogen forms five combinations with oxygen. If we take quantities of these compounds containing the same weight of nitrogen, the weight of the oxygen in them will be in proportion to the numbers 1, 2, 3, 4, 5. For example:—

		Of nitrogen.	Of oxygen.
Protoxide of nitrogen	contains for	175 parts	100 parts
Binoxide of nitrogen	,,	175 ,,	200 ,,
Nitrous acid	,,	175 ,,	300 ,,
Hyponitric acid	,,	175 ,,	400 ,,
Nitric acid	,,	175 ,,	500 ,,

The acute intellect of Dalton did not stop at facts,

but sought to explain them by devising a theory. Reviving an idea of Leucippus and a statement of Epicurus, he supposed that bodies were formed of small indivisible particles which he called atoms. To this old and vague notion he gave a distinct meaning by admitting, on the one hand, that for every kind of matter the atoms possess a uniform weight, and, on the other, that combination between different kinds of matter is the result of the juxtaposition of their atoms. This fundamental hypothesis being admitted, the fact of definite proportions and of multiple proportions finds a simple and satisfactory explanation. The definite proportions according to which bodies combine represent the unvarying relations between the weights of the atoms which are in juxtaposition; and if a body can combine with another in several proportions, such multiple combinations can only be effected by the juxtaposition of 1, 2, 3, 4, &c., atoms of one body, and one or several atoms of another body. The evident result is, that if the weight of this latter body is constant, the weights of the other in the different combinations must be multiples of one another.

As immediate consequences of these propositions, Dalton inferred that the atomic weight of a compound body was formed by adding together the atomic weights of its elements, and that the definite proportions according to which compound bodies, such as acids and bases, combine, represent merely the uniform relation between their atomic weights. Thus the laws of Wenzel and Richter are seen to be only particular cases of a general law which governs the composition of all bodies. The atomic hypothesis explained them at once.

But these atomic weights have no absolute value; they only represent the proportions according to which bodies combine. An unit must be chosen as a term of comparison. Dalton referred all the atomic weights to that of hydrogen, which he called 1. In a work entitled *A New System of Chemical Philosophy*, published in 1808, he gave the numbers shown in the following table:—

	Dalton's atomic weights.	True numbers.
Hydrogen . . .	1	1
Nitrogen . . .	5	7
Carbon	5	6
Oxygen	7	8
Sulphur	13	16
Magnesia . . .	20	20
Lime	23	28
Soda	28	31
Potash	42	47·1
Strontia	46	51·8
Baryta	68	76·5
Iron	38	28
Zinc	56	32·6
Copper	56	31·7
Lead	95	103·5
Silver	100	108
Platinum . . .	100	98·7
Mercury	167	100

Thus, for a certain number of bodies, Dalton's numbers come very near to theory. This accordance is still closer in a table published by Wollaston in 1814,* in which the atomic weights, or rather the equivalents (to use Wollaston's term), are referred to that of oxygen, which is taken as 10.

Law of Gay-Lussac.—Difference between Atoms and Equivalents.—In the early part of this century most chemists recognised the fact both of definite proportions and of multiple proportions. Some stopped there, and by preference used the terms *equivalents* or *proportional numbers;* whilst others, advocates of Dalton's theory, assumed that the proportional numbers

* *Annales de Chimie*, xc., 138.

represented the relative weights of the atoms, and called them *atomic weights*. But the terms equivalents and atomic weights had then the same meaning: they represented the same proportions. According to Dalton, as seen by the table just given, water was composed of one atom of hydrogen (1) and one atom of oxygen (7), whilst according to Wollaston it was formed of one equivalent of hydrogen and one equivalent of oxygen.

In reality the two words meant one and the same thing: the true atomic theory was not yet conceived.

And yet in Wollaston's time the facts had already been discovered which should have led chemists to separate these two ideas one from the other. In 1808 Gay-Lussac propounded his memorable laws of the combination of gases by volume. After having found in 1805, with A. Von Humboldt, that hydrogen and oxygen would combine in the exact proportion of two volumes of the first gas to one volume of the second, he generalised from these observations, and showed that there exists a simple relation not only between the volumes of two gases which combine, but also between the sum of the volumes of gas which enter into combination and the volume which this combination occupies when in the gaseous state. Thus:—

I. Two volumes of hydrogen combine with one volume of oxygen to form two volumes of aqueous vapour.

II. Two volumes of nitrogen combine with one volume of oxygen to form two volumes of protoxide of nitrogen.

It is seen in these two cases that the three volumes of combining gas are reduced to two volumes by the act of combination. There is a condensation of one-third. In ammonia there is a condensation to half the original volume; on the contrary, in the case of binoxide of nitrogen and of hydrochloric acid equal volumes of the two gases combine without condensation. Thus:—

III. Three volumes of hydrogen are combined with one volume of nitrogen in two volumes of ammoniacal gas.

IV. One volume of nitrogen is united with one volume of oxygen in two volumes of binoxide of nitrogen.

V. One volume of hydrogen is united with one volume of chlorine in two volumes of hydrochloric acid gas.

The discovery of Gay-Lussac was of immense importance. In the first place it gave a striking confirmation to the law of definite proportions, which was thus demonstrated, not only in reference to weights, but also to volumes: and it must be remembered that an independent proof was by no means superfluous, for the law to which it referred had even at this period some opponents. Berthollet even in 1808 took great pains to demonstrate that the proportions according to which bodies combined are not absolutely invariable. But even his great authority was of no avail against the power of facts. The opposite theory was victoriously upheld by Proust.

But there is another consequence of the discovery of Gay-Lussac. If we can admit with Dalton that the definite proportions according to which bodies combine represent the weights of their atoms, and if we are to agree with Gay-Lussac that the volumes according to which gases unite bear to each other simple and invariable proportions, it is clear that the relative weights of these volumes—that is to say, their densities—ought to represent the relative weights of the atoms. Thus, the atomic weights of gases ought to be proportional to their densities (or should at least bear a simple proportion to them). It therefore follows that to find the relative atomic weights of simple gases it is sufficient to determine and compare their densities. This is an immediate consequence of Gay-Lussac's law, and it is important from two points of view—first, in giving a new means for the determination or control of atomic weights, and then in leading chemists to realise a distinction between the notion of atomic weights and of equivalents. Hitherto they had been confounded, but henceforth a similar confusion was not possible. This is an important point, and it must, therefore, be clearly explained.

We have seen that Dalton, taking the atomic weight of hydrogen as unity, adopted for that of oxygen the figure 7 (the exact figure is 8); and that he looked upon water as formed of one atom of hydrogen and one atom of oxygen. But, as hydrogen combines with oxygen in the proportion of two volumes to one volume, if it be admitted that the atomic weights are in proportion to the densities, it must also be admitted that combination takes place in the proportion of two atoms to one atom. In fact, the densities of hydrogen and oxygen are in the ratio of 1 to 16, and not as 1 to 8, as would be required by Dalton's atomistic hypothesis of the composition of water. If, then, 1 is the atomic weight of hydrogen, that of oxygen will be 16; and since the combination of the two bodies takes place in the proportion of 1 to 8, or of 2 to 16, it evidently follows that water is composed of two atoms of hydrogen and one atom of oxygen. This is an inevitable consequence if we allow a proportionality between atomic weights and densities.

In respect to simple gases chemists have been led to admit this proportion, and to regard their volumes as representing atoms; and this conclusion has been strengthened by considerations drawn from the physical properties of gases. When examined at a moderate distance from their liquifying point, they dilate or compress in appreciably the same manner under the influence of the same variations of temperature and pressure.

It has therefore been admitted, Ampère being the first,* that equal volumes of two gases contain the same

* The same idea was expressed by the Italian chemist, Avogadro.

number of atoms, and that consequently the atomic weights of simple gases are proportional to their densities.

Thus, the discoveries of Gay-Lussac became one of the fundamental bases of the atomic theory. In regard to this, Berzelius wrote as follows* :—"If we say atom instead of volume, and if we view bodies in the solid state instead of taking them in the gaseous state, we find in Gay-Lussac's discovery one of the most direct arguments in favour of Dalton's hypothesis."

It is a remarkable fact, that this latter philosopher opposed in principle Gay-Lussac's ideas; this singular opposition may be explained if we remember that Dalton had stated that when two bodies form only one combination, this is effected atom by atom. The law of volumes upset this hypothesis, which, moreover, rested on no solid foundation. This law was soon admitted by all chemists; and among those who used it largely in the development of the atomic theory, Berzelius stands first.

Berzelius's Atomic Weights and Notation.—The important researches of this Swedish chemist, on equivalents and atomic weights, date from almost the same period as do those of Dalton. In 1807, whilst he was preparing the first edition of his *Traité de Chimie*, he happened to read Richter's forgotten work, and called the attention of chemists to the laws which govern the composition of salts.

Richter had stated that for the same class of salts there existed a constant relation between the proportion of acid and the amount of oxygen in the base. Berzelius confirmed this statement, and put it in a simpler form by proving that for the same class of salts there existed an uniform and simple relation between the

* "Traité de Chimie," French edition, 1831, iv. 532.

amount of oxygen in the acid and of oxygen in the base. Thus he showed that in neutral sulphates this proportion was as 3 to 1; in nitrates as 5 to 1; and in neutral carbonates as 2 to 1.

Here the principal achievement is less, perhaps, in propounding a law than in the superiority of the analyses. Bergmann had made several analyses, and Wenzel had made some tolerably exact ones, but no one had yet arrived at the same degree of accuracy as did Berzelius, the father of our modern analytical processes. He commenced his works in 1808, and in 1815 he was enabled to give a table of atomic weights based upon his own determinations, and much more accurate than those of his predecessors. He compared the atomic weights with that of oxygen, which he called 100; that of hydrogen was 6·24. The influence of Gay-Lussac's discoveries on fixing the atomic weights is here clearly shown. In fact, the ratio of the atomic weights, 100 to 6·24, or 16 to 1, is that of their densities. Wollaston had given for the *equivalents* of hydrogen and oxygen numbers which were not very different from those of Dalton. These numbers, which represented the proportions by weight according to which oxygen combines with hydrogen, are true equivalents, whilst Berzelius's numbers, which express the proportions by weight which exist between equal volumes of hydrogen and oxygen, are true atomic weights. But this distinction is shown still more clearly in the chemical notation which Berzelius brought into use. Dalton represented the composition of water by the symbol ⊙○, in which ⊙ represented one atom of hydrogen and ○ one atom of oxygen. Berzelius expressed this composition by the formula H_2O, in which H_2 represented two atoms of hydrogen and O one atom of oxygen. He also made use of an abridged notation. Thus the formula of water was written Ħ̇, the letter Ħ representing two atoms of hydrogen and the dot one atom of oxygen. Moreover, Berzelius attached a particular meaning to these barred symbols; they represented what he termed double atoms. According to him, two atoms of hydrogen $\bar{H}$, or two atoms of chlorine $\bar{C}l$, were looked upon as inseparable, as they entered together into combination. Thus, one double atom of hydrogen (two atoms) entered into combination with one single atom of oxygen. One double atom of hydrogen entered into combination with one double atom of chlorine. Berzelius wrote the formula of water $\dot{\bar{H}} = H_2O$; that of hydrochloric acid $\bar{H}\bar{C}l = H_2Cl_2$; that of ammonia $\bar{N}\bar{H} = N_2H_6$; that of chloride of calcium $Ca\bar{C}l = CaCl_2$. In certain cases, therefore, the double atoms represented the quantities which entered into combination—that is to say, the equivalents. The idea of double atoms is not now adopted in the sense in which Berzelius used it. But it is necessary to observe one thing, which is, that having taken as unity one atom of oxygen, he admitted that the atoms of hydrogen, chlorine, nitrogen, phosphorus, arsenic, &c., only represented half equivalents, and that it was necessary to take a double atom (or two atoms) of these bodies to make one equivalent. This conclusion was perfectly logical. In the tables which the illustrious Swedish chemist gave, there are seen, besides the simple atomic weights, certain double atomic weights, which represent the proportions according to which bodies enter into combination, or their equivalents. These are the numbers given by Berzelius:—

	Atomic Weights.		Equivalents.	
	Symbols		Symbols	
Oxygen . .	O	100	O	100
Hydrogen . .	H	6·24	$\bar{H}$	12·48
Nitrogen . .	N	87·53	$\bar{N}$	175·06
Fluorine . .	Fl	117·717	$\bar{F}l$	235·435
Chlorine . .	Cl	221·64	$\bar{C}l$	443·28
Bromine . .	Br	499·81	$\bar{B}r$	999·62

	Atomic Weights.		Equivalents.	
	Symbols		Symbols	
Iodine	I	792·996	~~I~~	1585·992
Sulphur	S	200·75	S	200·75
Selenium	Se	495·285	Se	495·285
Tellurium	Te	801·76	Te	801·76
Phosphorus	P	196·0205	~~P~~	392·041
Arsenic	As	469·40	~~As~~	938·80
Carbon	C	75·12	C	75·12
Boron	Bo	136·204	Bo	136·204
Silicium	Si	277·778	Si	277·778
Potassium	K	488·856	K	488·856
Sodium	Na	289·729	Na	289·729
Lithium	Li	81·66	Li	81·66
Calcium	Ca	251·651	Ca	251·651
Barium	Ba	855·29	Ba	855·29
Strontium	Sr	545·929	Sr	545·929
Magnesium	Mg	158·14	Mg	158·14
Aluminium	Al	170·90	~~Al~~	341·80
Glucinum	Gl	87·124	~~Gl~~	174·248
Zirconium	Zr	419·728	~~Zr~~	839·456
Magnesium	Mn	344·684	Mn	344·684
Chromium	Cr	328·87	Cr	328·87
Uranium	U	742·875	U	742·875
Iron	Fe	350·527	Fe	350·527
Cobalt	Co	368·65	Co	368·65
Nickel	Ni	369·33	Ni	369·33
Zinc	Zn	406·591	Zn	406·591
Cadmium	Cd	696·767	Cd	696·767
Copper	Cu	395·60	Cu	395·60
Lead	Pb	1294·645	Pb	1294·645
Bismuth	Bi	1330·377	~~Bi~~	2660·754
Tin	Sn	735·294	Sn	735·294
Titanium	Ti	301·55	Ti	301·55
Tungsten	W	1188·36	W	1188·36
Molybdenum	Mo	596·10	Mo	596·10
Antimony	Sb	806·452	~~Sb~~	1612·903
Mercury	Hg	1251·29	Hg	1251·29
Silver	Ag	1349·66	Ag	1349·66
Rhodium	R	651·692	~~R~~	1303·924
Palladium	Pd	665·477	Pd	665·477
Platinum	Pt	1232·08	Pt	1294·645
Iridium	Ir	1232·08	Ir	1232·08
Osmium	Os	1242·624	Os	1242·624
Gold	Au	1129·165	~~Au~~	2458·33*

* The numbers here given are not those which appeared in the first

The principles which guided Berzelius in the determination of the atomic weights are simple, and his processes are exact. The latter he varied and controlled by one another. He thus learnt, as he modestly said,* to discover the faults that he had at first committed, and at last had the satisfaction of finding an accurate agreement between the results of analysis and theoretical calculations.

In general he considered the atomic weight of a metal to be the quantity of this metal which combined with 100 of oxygen to enter into the first degree of oxidation. He deviated from this rule, however, in certain cases.

Thus he considered that the atomic weights of copper and of mercury were represented by the amounts of these metals which combined with 100 of oxygen to arrive at the second degree of oxidation. Since 1826† he represented the composition of the oxides of copper and mercury by the formulæ

Cu_2O,	CuO;	Hg_2O,	HgO.
Cuprous oxide.	Cupric oxide.	Mercurous oxide.	Mercuric oxide.

Amongst the reasons which led him to deviate from

tables of Berzelius. We have thought it best to give the atomic weights which he finally adopted, and we have extracted them from the last German edition of his great work (Appendix to vol. iii. "Tabulæ Atomicæ"). Amongst the equivalents of the metals, it will be remarked that those of aluminium, glucinum, bismuth, antimony, rhodium, and gold are double their atomic weights. Berzelius supposed that the combination of these bodies contained at least two atoms of metal. Thus he wrote—AlO_3, $AlCl_3$, BiO_3, $BiCl_3$, SbO_3, $SbCl_3$, RCl (protochloride of rhodium), $AuCl$ (protochloride of gold), $AuCl_3$, &c. It is seen that in all these compounds the amount of metal which enters into combination (improperly termed its equivalent) is represented by two atoms.

* *Lehrbuch der Chemie*, 1845, iii., 1160.

† In 1815 he took for certain metals double the atomic weights that he adopted later; thus, at this period he wrote:

FeO_2,	FeO_3;	CuO,	CuO_2;
Ferrous oxide.	Ferric oxide.	Cuprous oxide.	Cupric oxide.
HgO,	HgO_2;	PbO_2;	AgO_2, &c.
Mercurous oxide.	Mercuric oxide.	Plumbic oxide.	Argentic oxide.

the above rule may be given two which possess considerable importance.

In 1819 and 1820 were announced two great discoveries which have exercised a marked influence over the development of the atomic theory.

The first according to date is that of Dulong and Petit, concerning the relations which exist between the specific heats of simple bodies and their atomic weights; the second, which is due to Mitscherlich, is that of isomorphism.

Law of Specific Heats.—Dulong and Petit have shown that the specific heats of simple bodies are in inverse ratio to their atomic weights, in such a manner that if the two quantities are multiplied together the product is constant.

This is equivalent to saying that the atoms of simple bodies, so different from each other in their relative weights, possess appreciably the same specific heat. This is an unexpected result, which may be regarded as a striking confirmation of the atomic hypothesis:—

The following are the results obtained by Dulong and Petit:—

Simple bodies.	Specific heat.	Atomic weight.	Product of atomic weight by the specific heat.
Sulphur . .	0·1880	201·15	0·3790
Gold . .	0·0298	1243·0	0·3704
Platinum .	0·0314	1215·2	0·3816
Tin . .	0·0514	735·3	0·3779
Bismuth .	0·0288	1330·4	0·3835
Copper . .	0·0949	395·7	0·3755
Lead . .	0·0293	1294·5	0·3793
Zinc . .	0·0927	403·2	0·3738
Nickel . .	0·1035	369·7	0·3826
Iron . .	0·1100	339·2	0·3731

Some few exceptions to the law of specific heats have been observed. Among the simple bodies experimented on by Dulong and Petit, arsenic, antimony, silver, tellurium, and cobalt have not shown this remarkable relation between the atomic weight and the specific heat. But these exceptions may be attributed, on the one part, to our ignorance of the real atomic weights, and on the other to errors in the determination of the specific heat —errors which the classical researches of M. Regnault have since entirely overcome. We shall return to this subject.

In order to appreciate the assistance to the atomic theory rendered at that time by the law of specific heat, it is enough to remark that in the case of copper and of some other metals it has helped to make the true series of oxidation of these metals known, and to decide in favour of the atomic weights which have been generally adopted.* Thus the atomic weight of copper compared with that of oxygen (100) is not 791·4, but 395·7, a number which agrees with the law of specific heats.

Isomorphism.—The grand discovery of Mitscherlich has rendered similar service. It may be thus explained. Bodies composed of an equal number of atoms arranged in the same manner, crystallise in forms identical, or almost so. The resemblance of the exterior forms results from the similitude of their atomic structure; and isomorphous bodies offer this remarkable peculiarity, that they can mix in indefinite proportions in crystals without the form being sensibly changed.

But it is a necessary consequence of this law that whenever two bodies are really isomorphous they possess similar atomic structure. Their composition ought then to be expressed by analogous formulæ. Sulphate of copper and sulphate of iron when mixed can crystallise together, and the form of these crystals

* Berzelius, *Traité de Chimie*, French edition of 1831, iv., 601 (see also the note, p. 19).

remains that of sulphate of iron whenever the proportion of sulphate of copper is less than $\frac{19}{20}$. These mixed crystals contain seven molecules of water, like crystals of green vitriol. If, on the contrary, the proportion of sulphate of copper exceeds $\frac{19}{20}$, the mixed salt takes the form of blue vitriol (unsymmetrical prisms), and like it contains five molecules of water. These two vitriols, which can crystallise together, must then possess the same atomic structure, and if green vitriol contains one atom of iron, blue vitriol ought to contain one atom of copper. It follows, therefore, that oxide of iron and oxide of copper each contain one atom of metal and one atom of oxygen, and we must take for the atomic weight of copper the quantity of this metal which combines with one atom of oxygen (100 of oxygen) to form the second oxide of copper—that is to say, cupric oxide.

Isomorphism and the law of specific heats agree, then, in the adoption of the formula CuO for this oxide, a fact which fixes the atomic weight of copper. We know, on the other hand, that the two oxides in question are isomorphous with the protoxides of nickel, cobalt, and manganese, oxide of zinc, and magnesia. All these oxides possess the same atomic composition. The following is another example:—Iron alum and ordinary alum will crystallise together, and whatever be the proportions of the mixture the form of the crystals is always that of a regular octahedron. The double sulphate of alumina and potash is thus isomorphous with the sulphate of iron and potash. The two sulphates and the two oxides should therefore possess the same atomic composition, and if ferric oxide contains two atoms of iron and three atoms of oxygen, alumina must be composed of two atoms of aluminium and three atoms of oxygen.

Such is the assistance that the law of isomorphism affords in the construction of formulæ and the determination of atomic weights.

Equivalent Notation.—The discoveries of Gay-Lussac, of Dulong and Petit, and of Mitscherlich proved to be a strong confirmation of Dalton's ideas, and the enormous labours of Berzelius had given a solid basis to them. For twenty years the system of atomic weights and notation of the great Swedish chemist were paramount in science, owing to the legitimate and incontestable authority of his name. Nevertheless, some objections were raised against this notation, and the idea of double atoms met with a certain amount of opposition. Why should we admit, said Gmelin,* that the equivalents of hydrogen, chlorine, bromine, nitrogen, &c., are formed of double atoms, when the simple atoms of these bodies do not in reality exist in any combination? An atom is the smallest quantity of a body which enters into combination. The equivalents of the preceding bodies represent, therefore, their atoms, and it will be much better to take for their atomic weights numbers double those which Berzelius has given in conformity with the theory of volumes. The formulæ of water, of hydrochloric acid, and of ammonia, become therefore HO, HCl, NH_3.

To raise these objections was to revive afresh the ideas of Dalton and Wollaston; it was in reality making a step backward, for no importance was attached to the discoveries of Gay-Lussac, and, in consequence, this notation by equivalents which was thus inaugurated, finished by acquiring, during the years 1843-1844, the unanimous assent of chemists. The idea of atoms, said they, and atomic notation, are undoubtedly based upon an hypothesis; equivalents represent a reality. Equivalent notation is, therefore, preferable, as it only involves facts.

It was in this manner that the objections raised against the idea of double atoms, which constituted, in fact, the weak part of Berzelius' doctrine, were the cause

* *Handbuch der Chemie.* Fourth edition. I. 47.

of the abandonment of atomic notation and the adoption of equivalent notation—a system which is even now employed by many chemists. The equivalents which form the basis of this latter notation are, with few exceptions, those given in the fifth column of the table on page 18, with the exception that it is now considered more convenient to compare them with hydrogen, taken as unity.

The following is the table, so modified:—

Table of the Equivalents of Simple Bodies.

Aluminium	13·7	Nickel	29·5
Antimony	122	Niobium	48·8
Arsenic	75	Nitrogen	14
Barium	68·5	Osmium	99·6
Bismuth	210	Oxygen	8
Boron	10·9	Palladium	53·3
Bromine	80	Phosphorus	31
Cadmium	56	Platinum	98·7
Cæsium	130	Potassium	39·1
Calcium	20	Rhodium	52·2
Carbon	6	Rubidium	85·4
Cerium	46	Ruthenium	52·2
Chlorine	35·5	Selenium	39·7
Chromium	26·7	Silicium†	14
Cobalt	29·5	Silver	108
Copper	31·7	Sodium	23
Didymium	48	Strontium	43·8
Fluorine	19	Sulphur	16
Glucinum*	4·7	Tantalum‡	68·8
Gold	197	Tellurium	64
Hydrogen	1	Thallium	204 (?)
Iodine	127	Thorium§	59·6
Iridium	99	Tin	59
Iron	28	Titanium	25
Lanthanum	46·4	Tungsten	92
Lead	103·5	Uranium	60
Lithium	7	Vanadium	68·6
Magnesium	12	Yttrium	?
Manganese	27·5	Zinc	32·6
Mercury	100	Zirconium ‖	44·8
Molybdenum	48		

* Oxide of glucinum, GlO. † Silicic acid, SiO_2.
‡ Tantalic acid, TaO_2 § Thorina, ThO.
‖ Zirconia, ZrO_2.

It should be remarked that this notation was never applied in a very rigorous manner; and, moreover, the progress of science soon rendered it insufficient, and involved those chemists who persevered in its employment in singular inconsistencies.

In the first place, let us observe that the composition of the poly-acid bases, such as alumina or ferric oxide, has almost always been expressed by molecular formulæ and not by equivalent formulæ. It was known that one molecule of alumina would saturate three molecules of sulphuric acid, and this quantity of alumina was wrongly termed an equivalent of alumina. The true equivalent of alumina—that is to say, the quantity of alumina which corresponds to one molecule of potash or of oxide of silver—is the quantity of alumina which contains an equivalent of oxygen. It is this quantity which saturates an equivalent of sulphuric acid. In notation by equivalents the alumina ought, then, to be represented by the formula $Al_{\frac{2}{3}}O$, and sulphate of alumina by the formula $Al_{\frac{2}{3}}O,SO_3$, or $SAl_{\frac{2}{3}}O_4$. Thus wrote Gay-Lussac.* The general formula used, $Al_2O_3,3SO_3$, did not express an equivalent of sulphate of alumina, but a molecule of sulphate of alumina.

Analogous remarks apply to the poly-basic acids, discovered by Mr. Graham, which have clearly defined the notion of poly-atomic molecules. Mr. Graham has shown that common phosphoric acid will saturate three equivalents of a base RO. From that it is evident that one molecule of phosphoric acid saturating three equivalents of oxide of silver cannot correspond to one molecule of acetic acid which only saturates one. The equivalent of phosphoric acid is the quantity of this acid which saturates one equivalent of oxide of silver, and its equivalent formula is therefore $\frac{1}{3}PO_5$. Gay-Lussac, with that rigid accuracy characteristic of his mind, employed such formulæ.

* *Cours de Chimie*, 1828, 8e lecon, page 16.

Moreover, Richter was not deceived by this, and the number given in his tables well represents the quantity of this acid which saturates one equivalent of soda in bi-sodic phosphate. (See the note on page 8.)

Should we, then, say that this equivalent notation adopted by Gay-Lussac is preferable to the molecular notation employed by other chemists less scrupulous than he? This must be answered in the affirmative if chemical formulæ only serve to represent equivalents between bodies. But it is not so. Their language is higher and more significant. They are employed to show the complication of molecules, and when they are made use of to depict a reaction, they ought to represent both the bodies which enter and those which are removed—to show, in short, their molecular movements. Equivalent notation is of no use in this respect. It hides very important points in reactions or in the constitution of bodies. When it represents sulphate of alumina by the formula $Al_{\frac{2}{3}}O,SO_3$, it does not express the polyacid character of alumina; when it represents phosphate of silver by the formula $AgO,\frac{1}{3}PO_5$, it hides the tribasic nature of phosphoric acid. This is why chemists have instinctively preferred molecular notation to equivalent notation for the salts in question.

It is seen from the above that, after having pointed out a difference between atoms and equivalents, the progress of science leads to the separation of the idea of molecule from that of equivalent of a compound body. Molecules, in fact, are not always equivalent among each other. One molecule of phosphoric acid is not the equivalent of one molecule of acetic acid, and one molecule of alumina is not equivalent to one molecule of oxide of silver.

The distinctions here spoken of were not established in a day. They are ideas which long fermented in chemists' minds before they found expression. The merit of having clearly defined the words atom, equivalent, and molecule belongs principally to Gerhardt, whose researches we will now briefly explain.

Gerhardt's Atomic Weights and Notation.— Gerhardt returned to the atomic notation, but he introduced important modifications into it. At first he met with the inconveniences of the system of equivalents when he attempted to formulate the composition and reactions of organic bodies. By adopting for carbon, hydrogen, and oxygen the equivalents 6, 1, and 8, the formulæ of organic compounds became such that the number of equivalents of carbon was always divisible by two; or, in other words, the organic molecules always increased by double equivalents of carbon; moreover, when these molecules were destroyed, or by any energetic action lost carbon as carbonic acid, or hydrogen as water, there was never disengaged one equivalent of carbonic acid CO_2, or one equivalent of water HO, but two, or a multiple of two equivalents of carbonic acid or water.

Gerhardt was led to *this* strange result of equivalent notation. Why, said he, should no reaction in organic chemistry give rise to one equivalent of carbonic acid or one of water? This is apparently caused by some fault committed in the determination of the atomic weight of carbon and of oxygen. In fact, if the smallest quantity of carbonic acid which is produced by one molecule is C_2O_4, this amount undoubtedly represents one molecule of carbonic acid. This, therefore, contains 12 of carbon and 32 of oxygen, and it will be more convenient to represent this by the formula CO_2, in which C represents 12 of carbon and O 16 of oxygen. On the other hand, if the smallest quantity of water produced by a reaction is H_2O_2, this quantity represents a molecule of water, and it had better be expressed by the formula H_2O, in which H represents 1 of hydrogen and O 16 of oxygen. This was returning to the atomic weights given by Berzelius for hydrogen, oxygen, and carbon; for the numbers 1; 16; 12 are proportional to the numbers 6·28; 100; 75. It was likewise coming back to the atomic notation which is founded on the considerations of volumes—that is to say, to the law of Gay-Lussac. To my mind, Gerhardt did not insist on this double characteristic. If he had invoked in favour of the reform he was endeavouring to inaugurate the two great names of Gay-Lussac and Berzelius, he would have easily quieted the mistrust of some and the opposition of others. "See," a diplomatist would have said, "I am returning to the notation with which you have been quite familiar; I merely introduce into it certain changes rendered necessary by the progress of science." But the strength of his conviction and the warmth of his character led him to less moderate and admissible expressions.

In fact, the alterations in the system of atomic weights and of notation which he introduced into Berzelius' notation were really insignificant. Like him, he doubled the equivalents of hydrogen, chlorine, bromine, iodine, fluorine, nitrogen, phosphorus, and arsenic to convert them into atomic weights.* But he extended to the metals themselves this reduction of the equivalents to one half. Adopting and developing an

* Gerhardt said:—We must either double the equivalents of hydrogen, chlorine, bromine, iodine, fluorine, nitrogen, phosphorus, arsenic, and the metals, or else we must retain the ordinary equivalents for these, and double those of oxygen, carbon, sulphur, and selenium. In either case we get the same result. This will be seen by looking at the following table, in which are given the numbers obtained in each of these two cases:—

	H.	Cl.	Br.	I.	N.	P.	As.	K.	Hg.	O.	C.	S.	Se.
Equivalents	1	35·5	80	127	14	31	75	39	100	8	6	16	40
Atomic weights I.	½	17·75	40	63·5	7	15·5	37·5	18·5	50	8	6	16	40
Atomic weights II.	1	35·5	80	127	14	31	75	39	100	16	12	32	80

Gerhardt thought that it would be more convenient to adopt the latter idea first started by Laurent, he compared the oxides, RO, with water, and assumed that they contained two atoms of metal to one of oxygen. The density of mercury vapour (6·9) compared with that of oxygen (1·1056) furnished him with a powerful argument in favour of this theory. To form oxide of mercury would require two volumes of mercury vapour and one volume of oxygen, for

$$\frac{2 \times 6{\cdot}9}{1{\cdot}1056} \text{ is practically} = \frac{100}{8}.$$

If the atomic weight of oxygen is 8, that of mercury would be 50, and the formula of oxide of mercury Hg_2O. Analogy leads to classifying the other protoxides under the general formula R_2O, and to doubling the equivalents of the metals contained in them.

Such are the fundamental points of Gerhardt's system of atomic weights, and of the notation which springs from it.

For certain bodies this notation is similar to that of Berzelius, but for others it is very different. In all cases it is developed from an obvious consequence of the theory of volumes. With few exceptions the formulæ of volatile compounds answer to two volumes of vapour. In the notation of Berzelius, the same formulæ answer sometimes to two, sometimes to four, volumes of vapour, as may be seen by the following table:—

Names of the Compounds.	Berzelius's Notation.		Gerhardt's Notation.	
Water	H_2O	= 2 vols.	H_2O	= 2 vols.
Sulphuretted hydrogen	H_2S	= 2 vols.	H_2S	= 2 vols.
Hydrochloric acid .	H_2Cl_2	= 4 vols.	HCl	= 2 vols.
Hydriodic acid . .	H_2I_2	= 4 vols.	HI	= 2 vols.
Ammonia . . .	N_2H_6	= 4 vols.	NH_3	= 2 vols.
Phosphurettedhydrogen	P_2H_6	= 4 vols.	PH_3	= 2 vols.

numbers, compared with hydrogen taken as unity. He called these numbers equivalents, out of habit, no doubt, for they are not really equivalents, as Gmelin well remarked in 1844 (*Handbuch*, 4th Ed., iv., 26). But in such a case as this, an error of language does not detract from the value of the ideas.

Names of the Compounds.	Berzelius's Notation.		Gerhardt's Notation.	
Arseniuretted hydrogen	As_2H_6	=4 vols.	AsH_3	=2 vols.
Hypochlorous acid gas .	Cl_2O	=2 vols.	Cl_2O	=2 vols.
Hypochloric acid gas .	Cl_2O_4	=4 vols.	ClO_2	=2 vols.
Protoxide of nitrogen .	N_2O	=2 vols.	N_2O	=2 vols.
Binoxide of nitrogen .	N_2O_2	=4 vols.	NO	=2 vols.
Hyponitric acid . .	N_2O_4	=4 vols.	NO_2	=2 vols.
Nitric acid N_2O_5,H_2O =	$N_2H_2O_6$	=4 vols.	NHO_3	=2 vols.
Nitrates N_2O_5,RO =	N_2RO_6	—	NRO_3	—
Anhydrous sulph. acid	SO_3	=2 vols.	SO_3	=2 vols.
Sulph. acid SO_3,H_2O =	SH_2O_4	—	SH_2O_4	—
Sulphates SO_3,RO =	SRO_4	—	SR_2O_4	—
Carbonic oxide .	CO	=2 vols.	CO	=2 vols.
Carbonic acid . .	CO_2	=2 vols.	CO_2	=2 vols.
Carbonates CO_2,RO =	CRO_3	—	CR_2O_3	—
Cyanogen . . .	C_2N_2	=2 vols.	C_2N_2	=2 vols.
Hydrocyanic acid. .	$C_2N_2H_2$	=4 vols.	CNH	=2 vols.
Acetic acid . . .	$C_4H_8O_4$	=4 vols.	$C_2H_4O_2$	=2 vols.
Alcohol . . .	$C_4H_{12}O_2$	=4 vols.	C_2H_6O	=2 vols.
Ether	$C_4H_{10}O$	=2 vols.	$C_4H_{10}O$	=2 vols.

A comparison of these two systems of formulæ will give rise to some important remarks. The proportions between the atomic weights of hydrogen, oxygen, nitrogen, chlorine, and carbon being the same in the two notations, it is evident, in the first place, that the formulæ of bodies containing these elements should be identical whenever they are represented by two volumes; in the second place, that the formulæ of Berzelius should be double Gerhardt's formulæ whenever the first represent four volumes. Thus, the formula by which Berzelius represented the composition of nitric acid is exactly double Gerhardt's formula.

It may be asked—why should the founder of atomic notation prefer these doubled formulæ corresponding to 4 volumes of vapour, to simple formulæ which would refer all volatile compounds, with few exceptions, to the same volume? He had good reasons for that. He considered that compound bodies were always formed by the addition of their elements, so that in any combination each of its ingredients occupied a distinct place. According to him, combinations might be more or less complicated, but they would always contain two elementary parts (either simple or compound) which would be in juxtaposition, and, as it were, opposed to one another. Chemical affinity would result from this opposition between two contrary forces always tending to neutralise each other; and these opposing forces which govern chemical combinations were of the nature of electricity. There are two electric fluids: every combination should therefore contain two halves—one electro-positive, the other electro-negative. Such is in a few words the system of Berzelius; the compound dualism of the electro-chemical theory.

It is now seen why Berzelius represented nitric acid by the formula N_2O_5,H_2O. In his view it was a combination of the second order, containing integrally all the elements of nitric acid on the one side, and all the elements of water on the other. The first constituted the electro-positive, the second the electro-negative element. To divide such a formula in half was to strike at the foundation of his system, for in the simplified formula there would neither be found the elements of water nor those of anhydrous nitric acid.

Again, nitrates would contain unchanged the elements both of nitric acid, and of the oxide, and if Berzelius had adopted half the atomic weights for the metals he would have written the nitrates N_2O_5,R_2O. His ideas would forbid him to simplify this or any analogous formula.

Modern chemistry has changed all that. The discovery of substitutions struck the first blow at the electro-chemical theory. This memorable discussion will long be remembered, in which a comparatively young chemist had the temerity to oppose his new theory in opposition to the one which had stood its ground for twenty years.

Chemists will recall that famous discussion in which Dumas proved conclusively that chlorine, an electro-negative element, could replace hydrogen, an electro-positive element; that chlorine could enter into organic molecules otherwise than by molecular addition. This was the commencement of the new chemistry.

Gerhardt commenced by saying:—"Combinations do not take place by molecular addition; everything is effected by substitution." The basis of this idea lies in an hypothesis formerly started by Ampère concerning the combination of chlorine with hydrogen. He regarded the formation of hydrochloric acid as due to a double decomposition. If, said he, 2 volumes of chlorine, representing 2 atoms, combine with 2 volumes of hydrogen, likewise representing 2 atoms, to form 4 volumes of hydrochloric acid, it is evident that 2 volumes of this acid should contain 1 volume or an atom of chlorine, and the other 2 volumes the other atom of chlorine; and the same in the case of the hydrogen. It is then evident that there has been a change between the atoms of hydrogen and of chlorine, that is to say, a double decomposition;

$$HH + ClCl = HCl + HCl.$$

M. Dumas expressed the same thing under another form when he said that in the combination of hydrogen and chlorine the *physical* atoms of these bodies became halved.* M. Dumas termed physical atoms what Gerhardt designated by the name of molecules. One molecule of chlorine contains two atoms and corresponds with two volumes. Free chlorine, according to Gerhardt, is chloride of chlorine; free hydrogen is hydride of hydrogen. A molecule of hydrochloric acid (HCl) contains, therefore, as many atoms as a molecule of hydro-

† Dumas. *Philosophie Chimique.* 265.

gen (HH), and if a molecule of hydrocyanic acid is HCy, a molecule of cyanogen must be represented by CyCy. Free cyanogen is, therefore, a cyanide of cyanogen.

Thus, not only do the molecules of compound bodies correspond to two volumes, but the molecules of simple bodies themselves must be similarly viewed. In their molecular complication these latter approach the nature of compound bodies, except that the elementary atoms they contain are of the same kind. Simple bodies can therefore undergo double decomposition the same as compound bodies. In all chemical reactions it is the molecules which enter into collision and exchange their atoms in such a manner as to give rise to new molecules. When hydrogen combines with oxygen it attacks a molecule of oxygen, which being defeated, becomes converted into two molecules of water; $2HH + OO = H_2O + H_2O$.

In the same manner, the combination of acids with bases depends upon double decomposition. When acetic acid combines with oxide of silver there is an exchange of elements between two molecules of acid and one molecule of oxide of silver: water and acetate of silver are formed by double decomposition;

$$2C_2H_4O_2 + Ag_2O = 2C_2(H_3Ag)O_2 + H_2O.$$

Thus acetate of silver does not contain, as Berzelius imagined, all the elements of a molecule of oxide of silver. It contains a single atom of silver, which is substituted for a single atom of hydrogen in a molecule of acetic acid.

Such are the ideas which are intimately connected with Gerhardt's system of atomic weights and notation, and which have led to a distinct separation between the notion of atoms and that of molecules.

An *atom* is the smallest quantity of an element, indivisible by chemical means, which can exist in a compound body.

A *molecule* is a group of atoms, forming the smallest quantity of a simple or compound body which can exist in a free state, or is able to take part in, or result from, a reaction.

SECTION II.

New System of Atomic Weights.

GERHARDT'S system of atomic weights and notation never received the unanimous assent of chemists; and the discoveries since made seem to show that their author went too far in the reform which he inaugurated. It has been previously shown that he compared the protoxides to water, and attributed to them the general formula R_2O, and that the equivalents of the metals were, in consequence, doubled. The density of mercury vapour *seemed* to furnish an argument in favour of such a reduction, but this argument is really of little value. The vapour-density of mercury is evidently an anomaly, which we will endeavour to define and explain further on. The vapour-densities of chloride, bromide, and iodide of mercury assign to this element an atomic weight double that which is deduced from the anomalous density of its own vapour.

The reduction of the atomic weights of most of the metals as proposed by Gerhardt would be contrary to the law of Dulong and Petit, to which the accurate researches of M. Regnault have latterly drawn attention.

M. Regnault remarked that, as early as 1849,* the law

* *Annales de Chimie et de Physique*, 3rd series, xxvi. 261. See also *Premiers Elements de Chimie*, by M. Regnault. 1850, p. 544.

of Dulong and Petit applied, with a few exceptions, to all the elements; and that to bring these under the influence of the same general law it was only necessary to double the equivalents of hydrogen, nitrogen, chlorine, bromine, iodine, phosphorus, arsenic, potassium, sodium, and silver; "for," said he, "the equivalents of these bodies, as given by their specific heats, are half those which have been fixed upon from chemical considerations." He said justly that the numbers so obtained no longer represented equivalents, and he proposed to term them *Thermic proportional numbers.*

To double the equivalents of hydrogen, nitrogen, chlorine, bromine, iodine, phosphorus, and arsenic was to return in the case of these metalloids to the atomic weights of Berzelius.

Gerhardt had already done this, but while the latter chemist proposed for all metals atomic weights half as great as their equivalents, Regnault confined this reduction to the equivalents of potassium, sodium, and silver, to which he has lately added lithium. Gerhardt supposed that all the protoxides, R_2O, possessed the atomic composition of water, H_2O. In adopting the numbers proposed by M. Regnault, this supposition is confined to the oxides of the alkali metals and to oxide of silver, the formulæ of which become—

	Of potassium.	Of sodium.	Of lithium.	Of silver.	
Oxides .	K_2O	Na_2O	Li_2O	Ag_2O	analogous to H_2O.
Hydrates .	$(KH)O$	$(NaH)O$	$(LiH)O$		

The other oxides, in which one atom of oxygen is united with one instead of two atoms of metal, have their composition expressed by the general formula RO. Each atom of one of these latter metals corresponds, therefore, to two atoms of potassium or two atoms of hydrogen; this is at present expressed by saying that they are diatomic. The following oxides are of this class:—

$Ba''O$, $Sr''O$, $Ca''O$, $Mg''O$, $Mn''O$, $Fe''O$, $Zn''O$, $Pb''O$, $Hg''O$.*

The idea of diatomic metals was first announced by M. Cannizzaro†; the principal argument in favour of this view being founded on the existence of diatomic radicals‡ in organic chemistry—an idea which was introduced into science by my own experiments on the formation of glycol with diniodide or dibromide of ethylene. These experiments showed that ethylene or propylene, which combine with two atoms of bromine or chlorine, can also replace two atoms of silver or hydrogen, and are consequently equivalent to two atoms of a monatomic element.§

But organic radicals are the representatives of the elements in the mineral kingdom, and the existence of polyatomic organic radicals constitutes a powerful argument in favour of the polyatomicity of certain metals. It must be mentioned that this idea of the polyatomicity of certain elements dawned upon chemistry slowly and by degrees. This is too important a point to be passed over slightly; we will return to it again, merely mentioning at present that Dr. Odling first suggested that those metals should be considered as triatomic which are in combination with three atoms of oxygen in the sesquioxides R_2O_3.

It has been already mentioned that the atomic weights deduced from the law of Dulong and Petit, and which represent the thermal equivalents of simple bodies, are

* The accents ′ ″ ‴, the employment of which in chemistry was introduced by Dr. Odling, show atomicity or substitution value; Ba'', is equivalent to $2H'$ in respect to O'' in the combinations $\left.\begin{matrix}H'\\H'\end{matrix}\right\} O''$ and $Ba''O''$.—(*Quarterly Journal of the Chemical Society*, 1856, vii., 1.)

† *Sunto di un corso di filosofia chimica fatto nella R. Università di Genova*, dal Prof. S. Cannizzaro. Pisa. 1858, p. 35.

‡ *Ibid*, page 34.

§ *Leçons professées à la Société Chimique de Paris*, i. 108.

the same as the atomic weights of Berzelius, except in the case of the alkali metals and silver. This will be seen by the following table, in which the new atomic weights are compared with those of Berzelius and of Gerhardt. To assist comparison, all these atomic weights have been reduced to the same standard (hydrogen = 1). The numbers in the third column have been obtained by dividing by 6·24—that is to say, by the atomic weight of hydrogen on the O = 100 scale,—the atomic weights of Berzelius as given in the table on pages 17 and 18.

Names of the Elements.	New Atomic Weights.	Atomic Weights of Berzelius.	Atomic Weights of Gerhardt.
Hydrogen	1	1	1
Oxygen	16	16	16
Nitrogen	14	14·02	14
Chlorine	35·5	35·52	35·5
Bromine	80	80·09	80
Iodine	127	127·08	127
Fluorine	19	18·70	19
Sulphur	32	32·17	32
Selenium	79·5	79·37	79·5
Tellurium	129	128·48	129
Phosphorus	31	31·41	31
Arsenic	75	75·22	75
Carbon	12	12·04	12
Boron*	11	21·82, of which $\frac{1}{2}$=10·91	11
Silicium	28	44·51, of which $\frac{2}{3}$=29·66	,,
Zirconium†	89·6	67·26, of which $\frac{4}{3}$=89·6	,,
Potassium	39·1	78·47	49
Sodium	23	46·43	23
Lithium	7	13·08	7
Silver	108	216·29	108

* Berzelius wrote boric acid BoO_3, and chloride of boron $BoCl_3$, or $BoCl_6$, whilst he represented the composition of silicic acid and chloride of silicium by the formulæ SiO_3 and $SiCl_6$. According to the vapour densities of chlorides of boron and silicium, it is better to represent their composition by the formulæ $BoCl_3$ and $SiCl_4$, and consequently that of boric and silicic acids by the formulæ Bo_2O_3 and SiO_2. The atomic weight which Berzelius attributed to boron must, therefore, be reduced one-half, and that of silicium two-thirds.

† Berzelius represented zirconia by the formula Zr_2O_3. By adopting the formula ZrO_2, the atomic weight of zirconium is increased by $\frac{4}{3}$.

Names of the Elements.	New Atomic Weights.	Atomic Weights of Berzelius.	Atomic Weights of Gerhardt.
Barium .	. 137	137·06	68·5
Strontium	. 87·5	87·48	43·75
Calcium.	. 40	40·32	20
Magnesium	. 24	25·34	12
Aluminium	. 27	27·39	13·75
Manganese	. 55	55·23	27·5
Chromium	. 53·5	52·70	26·25
Uranium	. 120	118·88	60
Iron .	. 56	56·17	28
Cobalt .	. 59	59·07	29·5
Nickel .	. 59	59·19	29·5
Zinc .	. 65·2	65·16	32·6
Cadmium	. 112	111·66	56
Copper .	. 63·5	63·39	31·75
Lead .	. 207	207·47	103·5
Bismuth	. 210	213·20	210
Tin .	. 118	117·83	59
Titanium	. 50	48·3	25
Tungsten	. 184	190·44	92
Molybdenum	. 96	95·53	48
Vanadium*	. 68·6	137·32	,,
Antimony	. 122	129·24	122
Mercury	. 200	200·52	100
Rhodium	. 104·4	104·48	,,
Palladium	. 106·6	106·64	,,
Platinum	. 197·5	197·44	98·5
Iridium .	. 198	197·44	98·5
Ruthenium	. 104·4	,,	,,
Osmium	. 199·2	199·13	,,
Gold .	. 197†	196·98	,,

It will be seen that with few exceptions the new system of atomic weights is almost identical with that of Berzelius; and that in respect to the metals, the new atomic weights are double those which Gerhardt

* Berzelius wrote perchloride of vanadium VCl_6.

† A description and discussion of the analytical methods by which these numbers have been obtained would be beyond the domain of this work. The reader may consult with advantage on this subject the numerous memoirs of M. Dumas and the classical researches which have been lately published by M. Stas (*vide* CHEMICAL NEWS, vol. iv. pp. 181, 206, 215, 228, 243, 257, 270, 282, 297, 307, 324, 335, and vol. v. pp. 1, 15, 29, 57)

adopted, except those of the alkali metals, and silver, bismuth, and antimony.

It now remains to demonstrate that this system of atomic weights is in better harmony than any other; first, with the physical data which serve for the control and determination of atomic weights, and second, with the chemical facts.

The physical data made use of are:

1. The law of specific heats.
2. Isomorphism.
3. Vapour densities.

1. The new atomic weights are identical, with about three exceptions, with those deduced from Dulong and Petit's law. It follows from M. Regnault's researches that the anomalies observed in this law (pointed out at p. 21) were owing to inaccurate determinations of the specific heat of many bodies. But, on the other hand, M. Regnault has found that this law does not yield results of that rigorous accuracy which it was at first supposed to do, as may be seen by the following table:—

Names of solid elements.	Specific heats.	Atomic weights.	Product of specific heat multiplied by atomic weight.
Sulphur (between 0° and 100°)	0·2026	32	6·483
Selenium	0·0762	79·5	6·058
Tellurium	0·0474	129·	6·115
Bromine (between −78° and −20°)	0·08432	80	6·746
Iodine (between 0° and 100°)	0·05412	127	6·873
Phosphorus (between 10° and 30°)	0·1887	31	5·850
Arsenic	0·08140	75	6·095
Carbon { graphite	0·200	12	2·400
Carbon { diamond	0·147	12	1·764
Crystallised boron	0·250	11	2·750
Silicium (mean)*	0·176	28	4·928

* Regnault, *Annales de Chimie et de Physique*, 3rd series, lxiii. 24.

Names of solid elements.	Specific heats.	Atomic weights.	Product of specific heat multiplied by atomic weight.
Potassium	0·1695	39·1	6·500
Sodium (between $-34°$ and $+7°$)	0·2934	23	6·748
Lithium	0·9408		6·586
Thallium	0·03355	204	6·844
Magnesium	0·2499	24	5·998
Aluminium	0·2143	27	5·786
Manganese	0·1217	55	6·693
Iron	0·5138	56	6·115
Zinc	0·09555	65·2	6·230
Cadmium	0·05669	112	6·349
Cobalt	0·1068	59	6·301
Nickel	0·1089*	59	6·424
Tungsten	0·0334	184	6·146
Molybdenum	0·0722	96	6·931
Lead	0·0314	207	6·450
Bismuth	0·0308	210	6·468
Copper	0·09515	63·5	6·042
Antimony	0·05077	122	6·118
Tin	0·05623	118	6·635
Mercury (between $-77°5$ & $-44°$)	0·03247	200	6·494
Silver	0·05701	108	6·157
Gold	0·0324	197	6·383
Platinum	0·03293	197·5	6·487
Palladium	0·0593	106·5	6·315
Osmium	0·03063	199·2	6·101
Rhodium	0·05803	104·4	6·058
Iridium	0·03259	198	6·453

It is seen that the only exceptions to Dulong and Petit's law are carbon, silicium, and boron. This circumstance is doubtless due to some peculiarity in the molecular constitution of these bodies in the free state, and which is connected with the many allotropic states which they can assume. Let us take carbon as an instance. The different modifications of this element possess different specific heats, and consequently different thermal equivalents; and whilst in the case of

* Mean of M. Regnault's determinations, *Annales de Chimie et de Physique*, 3rd series, lxiii. 23.

other elements the thermal equivalents are identical with the atomic weights obtained by chemical means, this is not the case with carbon. It is also to be remarked that there exists no simple relation between the thermal equivalents of carbon and its atomic weight, 12. In the following table these thermal equivalents have been obtained by dividing the constant product 6·4 * by the specific heats:—

	Specific heats.	Thermal equivalents.	Atomic weight of carbon.
Animal charcoal .	0·26085	24·5	
Graphite . .	0·200	32·0	12
Diamond . .	0·147	43·5	

Experience, moreover, has shown that carbon in combination possesses a different specific heat from that which it has in its different modifications. If, therefore, Dulong and Petit's law were rigorously exact, one ought to say that, as carbon possesses different specific heats according as it is free or combined, and according to its different allotropic states, so also does it possess different atomic weights; these atomic weights being identical with the thermal equivalents given above. This conclusion appears strange at first sight. It is, however, strengthened by the interesting facts which Mr. Brodie † has discovered relative to the oxidation of graphite. In treating this body with nitric acid and chlorate of potash he obtained a certain acid, graphic acid, in which he proves the existence not of carbon, but of graphite itself. He represents the composition of this acid by the formula $Gr_4H_4O_5$, in which the graphite possesses the atomic weight 33, which approaches closely to the thermal equivalent 32 indicated above.

Thus, chemical facts and theoretical considerations

* Mean of the product of atomic weights by specific heats.

† *Philosophical Transactions*, 1859, p. 249.

respecting specific heat lead us to look upon free carbon as forming in its various states aggregations of matter differing from the chemical atom which exists in the combinations of this body. These aggregations which are governed by heat differ in relative weights according to the allotropic states of carbon. They represent the physical atoms of free carbon, and for graphite at least it would appear that these atoms are capable of forming special combinations.

Such is the interpretation which the facts at present known allow us to give to the anomalies which are presented by the specific heats of carbon. There is nothing to prevent the same interpretation being extended to boron and silicium, which are similar to carbon in the number of their allotropic states.

As to the other elements, it is seen by the preceding table that the product of their specific heats by their atomic weights are practically equal, which is the same thing as saying that the specific heats of their atoms are sensibly identical. They are not absolutely the same, to judge by the results of experiment; but the differences which are shown in this respect may be due to certain disturbing causes.

In reference to this subject, it must, in the first place, be considered that the atomic weights of some elements are not determined with all the accuracy which is desirable, and the same, perhaps, may be said of the specific heats of some simple bodies which it is difficult to isolate in a state of perfect purity. On the other hand, as M. Regnault has observed,* the determination of the specific heats of solid bodies involves some uncertainty, "for it includes many other elements which have not yet been successfully separated, especially the latent heat of dilatation, and a portion of the latent heat of

* *Annales de Chimie et de Physique*, 3rd series, xxvi. 262.

fusion which bodies successively absorb as they soften, frequently long before the temperature which is regarded as their fusing point."

Similar disturbing influences naturally interfere with the specific heat of compound bodies. It has been observed that, in general, equivalent quantities of substances which possess a similar atomic composition have also the same specific heat: the product of the specific heat of these substances by their atomic weights is sensibly equal; and if this product is called *atomic heat* we may say with Hermann Kopp "that these bodies possess the same atomic heat."*

This latter physicist has, however, pointed out several exceptions to this law. Whether they be due to the above-named disturbing influences, or to some other cause, it is not less true that the law in question is worth attention, for it is verified in the case of many groups of analogous bodies, provided the new atomic weights are adopted for the elements. Thus the carbonates†

$$RCO_3 = RO,CO_2$$

and the silicates—

$$RSiO_3 = RO,SiO_2$$

have the same atomic heat, provided the atomic weight 12 is taken for carbon, and 28 for silicium.

M. Regnault observed some time ago that the chlorides of tin, titanium, and silicium possessed sensibly the same atomic heat, provided the composition of chloride

* M. Regnault has put this law in the following manner:—"*The specific heats of compound bodies having the same chemical formulæ are to one another in the inverse ratio of their equivalents.*"—*Annales de Chimie et de Physique*, 3rd series, xxvi. 264.

† It is the same according to Hermann Kopp in the case of nitrates and chlorates $RN\Theta_3$ and $RCl\Theta_3$, perchlorates and permanganates $RCl\Theta_4$ and $RMn\Theta_4$, sulphates and chromates $RS\Theta_4$ and $RCr\Theta_4$.

of silicium were expressed by the formula $SiCl_4$, and the atomic weight of silicium were consequently taken at 28*. The following figures demonstrate this:

	Specific heat.	Molecular weight.	Product.
Chloride of tin . .	0·1413	260	36·7
Chloride of titanium .	0·1813	192	34·8
Chloride of silicium .	0·1907	170	32·4

It is thus that theoretical considerations respecting the specific heat of some compounds of carbon and silicium justify the atomic weights assigned to these elements, which, in the free state, form exceptions to Dulong and Petit's law.

Upon comparing the atomic heats of a large number of compound bodies, it is observed that they are formed of the sum of the atomic heats of their elements. Indeed, the product (CA) of the specific heat multiplied by the atomic (molecular) weight is practically equal to $n \times 6{\cdot}4$; n being the number of elementary atoms contained in a compound having the specific heat C, and the molecular weight A; and 6·4 being the mean atomic heat of simple bodies as derived from the table on pages 40 and 41. We thus get the formula† $n \times 6{\cdot}4 = CA$.

In some cases this relation may serve for the indirect verification of an atomic weight. As an example:—Is the atomic weight of mercury 100 or 200?

In the former case if we represent 100 of mercury by the symbol Hg, the mercurous and mercuric chlorides, bromides, and iodides contain—

Mercurous compounds.	Mercuric compounds.
Hg_2Cl	$HgCl$
Hg_2Br	$HgBr$
Hg_2I	HgI

* *Annales de Chimie et de Physique*, 3rd series, ix. 341.
† Hermann Kopp, *Comptes Rendus*, lvi. 1254.

In the latter case, if we represent 200 of mercury by the barred symbol Hg,* they become—

Mercurous compounds.	Mercuric compounds.
Hg_2Cl_2 †	$HgCl_2$
Hg_2Br_2	$HgBr_2$
Hg_2I_2	HgI_2

Judging from the specific heats of these compounds, it is the second of the formulæ which expresses the atomic composition of these chlorides; for in this case we have $n = 4$ for the mercurous compounds, and $n = 3$ for the mercuric compounds; and the atomic heats, which can be calculated according to the preceding formula, are practically the same as those directly deduced from experimental data.

Formulæ.	Specific heats.	Molecular weights. — Hg=200	Product of molecular weight by specific heat. — Experimental atomic heats.	Calculated atomic heats. — $n \times 6{\cdot}4$.
$Hg\,Cl_2$	0·0689	271	18·67	19·2
$Hg\,I_2$	0·0420	454	19·06	19·2
Hg_2Cl_2	0·05205	475	24·51	25·6
Hg_2I_2	0·0385	654	25·83	25·9

It must be mentioned that this very simple relation between the atomic heat of a compound and the atomic

* The barred symbols represent bodies whose atomic weights are double their equivalents, as explained further on.

† Or HgCl, HgBr, HgI. These are the latest formulæ adopted by M. Cannizzaro. We prefer the doubled formulæ, for reasons to be given hereafter. It is evident, besides, that if arguments based on the specific heat of the compound bodies in question are allowed to decide in reference to the atomic weight of mercury, they throw no light whatever on the question as to doubling or not the formulæ of mercurous compounds. If they are doubled, as we have written them, each side of the equation—

$$n \times 6{\cdot}4 = CA$$

must be multiplied by 2.

heats of the elements which it contains does not hold good, according to M. Hermann Kopp, for all compounds. It is accurate in the case of chlorides, bromides, and iodides. It has just been shown, for instance, that the iodine and the mercury possess, in the form of iodide of mercury, the same atomic heat which they have in the free state. But this is not always the case. The preceding rule, therefore, will not bear general application.

2. The new system of atomic weights is in harmony with the law of isomorphism.—Isomorphous bodies are, in fact, represented by analogous formulæ. Thus cuprous sulphide, which is isomorphous with sulphide of silver, Ag_2S, is represented by the formula Cu_2S,* whilst Gerhardt gives it the formula Cu_4S.† Sulphate of silver and anhydrous sulphate of sodium receive the analogous formulæ

$$SAg_2O_4 \text{ and } SNa_2O_4.$$

The isomorphous sulphates of the magnesian series are represented by the formula

$$SMO_4 + 7H_2O.$$

The double sulphates of the same series receive the formula

$$SMO_4 + SR_2O_4 + 6H_2O$$

Lastly, the composition of alums is represented by the formula

$$S_3R_2O_{12} + SR_2O_4 + 24H_2O.$$

3. The new system of atomic weights is in harmony with the relations existing between the densities of gases and vapours, and their mole-

* Cu=63·5; S=32.

† Cu=31·75; S=32.

cular weights.—1. Let us first consider the relations discovered by Gay-Lussac between the densities of simple gases and their atomic weights. With some exceptions these densities are proportional to the atomic weights, in such a manner that if, instead of being compared with air, they are compared with hydrogen taken as unity, the same numbers will express their densities and atomic weights. The following table will show this *:—

Names of Simple Bodies.	Densities of gases and vapours compared with air.	Densities compared with hydrogen.	Atomic weights.
Hydrogen . .	0·0693	1	1
Oxygen . .	1·1056	15·9	16
Nitrogen . .	0·9714	14·0	14
Sulphur (at 1000°)	2·22	32·0	32
Chlorine . .	2·44	35·2	35·5
Bromine . .	5·393	77·8	80
Iodine . . .	8·716	125·8	127

It was upon the remarkable relation between the densities and atomic weights that this celebrated proposition of Ampère and Berzelius was chiefly founded: *equal volumes of gases contain the same number of atoms.* One atom of the preceding gases corresponds to one volume. We shall see that, slightly modified, this proposition is also applicable to compound gases.

But we ought not to pass over in silence the exceptions which have been discovered to the preceding law. Phosphorus, arsenic, mercury, and cadmium diverge from it. The densities of their vapours compared with that of hydrogen are not the same as their atomic weights. They only present a simple relation with their atomic weights, as shown by the following figures:—

* To reduce the densities of gases to that of hydrogen, it is only necessary to multiply them by $14·44 = \frac{1}{0·0693}$, which is the ratio between the density of air and that of hydrogen.

Names of Simple Bodies.	Vapour densities compared with air.	Vapour densities compared with hydrogen.	Atomic weights.
Phosphorus . .	4·42	63·8	31
Arsenic . .	10·6	153·0	75
Cadmium . .	3·94	56·9	112
Mercury . .	6·976	100·7	200

It is seen that the vapour densities of phosphorus and arsenic lead to double the atomic weights assigned to these elements, whilst, on the contrary, the vapour densities of cadmium and mercury give atomic weights half as great as those which belong to them. In other words, the first two vapour densities are twice as large as they should be; the second are half as large, and whilst the atoms of other gases correspond to one volume, those of phosphorus and arsenic correspond to half a volume, and those of mercury and cadmium correspond to two volumes.

With phosphorus and arsenic the anomaly is of the same character as that presented by the vapour of sulphur at 500°, but the vapours of the former two elements do not appear to expand like that of sulphur at higher temperatures so as to be brought to their normal densities. It is, however, possible that this phenomenon of expansion does not commence, in the case of these very dense vapours, except at temperatures inaccessible to our means of investigation.

Mercury and cadmium, to which must probably be added zinc, present an inverse anomaly; their vapours, in the free state, are too little condensed. We will endeavour presently to explain this fact by comparing these metals with certain organic radicals which offer analogous phenomena. At present it remains for us to show that these exceptions do not embarrass the theory. They are apparent when the bodies in question are examined in the free state, but they disappear when the most definite compounds of these same bodies are taken. When combined with hydrogen, chlorine, bromine, iodine, and with organic radicals, the bodies in question, that is to say, phosphorus, arsenic, mercury, and zinc, possess their normal vapour density. To show that this is so, it is necessary to recall and to accurately define the relations which exist between the atomic composition of compound bodies and their densities in the state of gas or vapour.

II. These relations are of the most simple character, and it may be expressed by saying that *equal volumes of gases contain the same number of molecules* under identical conditions of temperature and pressure, and that consequently the *molecular weights of compound bodies are proportional to their densities in a state of gas or vapour.* This is the proposition of Ampère and Berzelius slightly altered in its wording, and applicable in its new form to simple as well as to compound gases. It here refers to molecules, and not to atoms, for it is evident that compound gases do not always contain, for the same volume, the same number of atoms, in the sense in which we have used this word.

In fact, we know that 2 volumes of hydrochloric acid contain 1 volume or 1 atom of chlorine, and 1 volume or 1 atom of hydrogen—that is to say, 2 elementary atoms; whilst 2 volumes of ammonia contain 1 volume or 1 atom of nitrogen and 3 volumes or 3 atoms of hydrogen—that is to say, altogether 4 elementary atoms. Experience teaches us, on the other hand, that 2 volumes of hydrochloric acid combine with 2 volumes of ammonia. We are, therefore, led to regard the quantity of hydrochloric acid which contains 1 atom of chlorine and 1 atom of hydrogen (and which corresponds to 2 volumes) as representing 1 molecule of this acid; and to look upon the quantity of ammonia which contains 1 atom of nitrogen and 3 atoms of hydrogen (and which orresponds to 2 volumes) as representing 1 molecule of ammonia. Thus hydrochloric acid and ammonia contain for the same volume an equal number of molecules, and it is the same with the other compound gases.

In the case of hydrochloric acid and ammonia, which we will continue to take as examples, their molecular weights correspond in consequence to weights of two volumes of each gas—that is to say, to their double density, for the density represents the weight of one volume (or unit of one volume). If, therefore, the densities of these two gases were expressed in relation to hydrogen, which represents unity in the system of atomic weights, it would be sufficient to double the numbers expressing these densities to obtain their molecular weights. That is to say, to obtain the latter, the densities found in relation to air must be multiplied by twice the ratio of the density of air to the density of hydrogen, or by—

$$2 \times \frac{1}{0{\cdot}0693} = \frac{2}{0{\cdot}0693} = 28{\cdot}88.*$$

Let us, therefore, make the calculations we have just given, not only for compound bodies, but also for the elements, and let us group the bodies in such a manner as to bring out certain analogies. We shall thus find the

* This fact may be established in another way; equal volumes of simple or compound gases contain the same number of molecules, the molecular weights of which are in proportion to their densities. Thus the density of hydrochloric acid is to the density of hydrogen as the molecular weight of hydrochloric acid is to the molecular weight of hydrogen: this latter is = 2, for it corresponds to two atoms. The molecular weight of hydrochloric acid is obtained, consequently, by the following proportion:—

$$\frac{1{\cdot}247}{0{\cdot}0693} = \frac{x}{2}, \text{ whence } x = 1{\cdot}247 \times \frac{2}{0{\cdot}0693}$$

Thus, to find the molecular weight, it is only necessary to multiply the densities by the constant ratio $\frac{2}{0{\cdot}0693} = 28{\cdot}88$ The numerator 2 thus represents the molecular weight of hydrogen. We have given above the reasons which have induced MM. Dumas and Gerhardt to look upon free hydrogen—that is to say, one molecule of hydrogen—as formed of 2 atoms. Other simple bodies have been regarded in the same light.

molecular weights of all these bodies; we can construct their formulæ, and can verify if the atomic weights deduced from the vapour-densities of compound bodies are identical with those we have already given. In the following table the numbers inscribed in the third column represent the double densities of volatile substances compared with hydrogen; these numbers agree sensibly with those given in the fourth column, and which represent the molecular weights deduced from chemical considerations.

Names of bodies.	Densities.	Double densities, as compared with hydrogen.	Molecular weights.	Formulæ.
Hydrogen . . .	0·0693	2·0	2	H_2
Chlorine . . .	2·44	70·5	71	Cl_2
Bromine . . .	5·54	159·0	160	Br_2
Iodine . . .	8·716	251·7	254	I_2
Cyanogen . . .	1·806	52·1	52	Cy_2
Methyl . . .	1·0365	29·9	30	Me_2
Hydride of methyl .	0·558	16·1	16	MeH
Ethyl . . .	2·0462	59·09	58	Et_2
Oxygen . . .	1·1056	31·9	32	O_2
Sulphur . . .	2·22	63·5	64	S_2
Water . . .	0·6235	18·	18	H_2O
Sulphuretted hydrogen	1·1912	34·4	34	H_2S
Sulphurous acid .	2·234	64·5	64	SO_2
Sulphuric acid . .	2·763	79·8	80	SO_3
Nitrogen . . .	0·9714	28·0	28	N_2
Protoxide of nitrogen	1·527	44·1	44	N_2O
Binoxide of nitrogen.	1·038	29·98	30	NO
Hyponitric acid .	1·72	49·5	46	NO_2
Methylamine . .	1·08	31·19	31	$NMeH_2$
Ammonia . . .	0·591	17·07	17	NH_3
Phosphorus . .	4·42	127·6	62	P_4*

* It is seen that the molecular weights of phosphorus and arsenic, as deduced from their vapour densities, are double those which their analogy to nitrogen would cause to be given to them. Whilst the molecule of free nitrogen is N_2 = 2 vols., the molecules of free phosphorus and arsenic are P_4 and As_4 = 2 vols.

Names of bodies.	Densities.	Double densities, as compared with hydrogen.	Molecular weights.	Formulæ.
Phosphuretted hydrogen	1·184	34·2	34	PH_3
Protochloride of phosphorus	4·742	136·9	137·5	PCl_3
Oxychloride of phosphorus	5·3	153·1	153·5	$POCl_3$
Arsenic	10·6	306	150	As_4*
Arseniuretted hydrogen	2·695	77·8	78	AsH_3
Chloride of arsenic	6·3006	181·9	181·5	$AsCl_3$
Iodide of arsenic	16·1	464·9	456	AsI_3
Triethylarsine	5·61	162·0	162	$AsEt_3$
Kakodyle (arsen-bimethyl)	7·1	205·0	210	As_2Me_4
Oxide of carbon	0·967	27·9	28	CO
Carbonic acid	1·529	44·1	44	CO_2
Marsh gas	0·559	16·1	16	CH_4
Chloroxycarbonic gas (chloride of carbonyl)	3·399	98·2	99	$COCl_2$
Chloride of carbon	5·415	156·4	154	CCl_4
Sulphide of carbon	2·645	76·4	76	CS_2
Chloride of silicium	5·939	171·5	170	$SiCl_4$
Silicium-ethyl	5·13	148·1	144	$SiEt_4$
Fluoride of silicium	3·600	103·9	104	$SiFl_4$
Tetrethylic silicate	7·325	211·5	208	Si(EtO)
Perchloride of tin	9·199	265·7	260	$SnCl_4$
Stannotetrethyl (stannethide)	8·021	231·6	234	$SnEt_4$
Stannodiethyl-dimethyl	6·838	197·5	206	$Sn\begin{cases}Et_2\\Me_2\end{cases}$
Chloride of Stannotriethyl (of sesquistannethyl)	8·430	243·4	240·5	$Sn\begin{cases}Et_3\\Cl\end{cases}$
Bromide of stannotriethyl	9·924	286·6	285	$Sn\begin{cases}Et_3\\Br\end{cases}$
Iodide of stannotrimethyl	10·32	298	290	$Sn\begin{cases}Me_3\\I\end{cases}$
Dichloride of stannodiethyl	8·710	251·5	247	$Sn\begin{cases}Et_2\\Cl_2\end{cases}$

* See note, preceding page.

Names of bodies.	Densities.	Double densities, as compared with hydrogen.	Molecular weights.	Formulæ.
Dibromide of stanno-diethyl	11·64	336·1	336	$Sn \begin{cases} Et_2 \\ Br_2 \end{cases}$
Chloride of zirconium	8·15	235·4	331	$ZrCl_4$
Chloride of titanium.	6·836	197·4	192	$TiCl_4$
Chloride of boron .	3·942	113·7	117·5	$BoCl_3$
Bromide of boron .	8·78	253·6	251	$BoBr_3$
Fluoride of boron .	2·3694	68·4	68	$BoFl_3$
Boracictriethyl .	3·4006	98·2	98	$BoEt_3$
Boracictrimethyl .	1·9314	55·8	56	$BoMe_3$
Trimethylic borate .	3·59	103·7	104	$Bo(MeO_3)$
Triethylic borate .	5·14	148·4	146	$Bo(EtO_3)$
Chloride of vanadium	6·14	177·3	175	VCl_3
Chloride of antimony	7·8	225·3	228·5	$SbCl_3$
Triethylstibine (stibethyl)	7·23	208·8	209	$SbEt_3$
Chloride of bismuth.	11·35	327·8	316·5	$BiCl_3$
Oxychloride of chromium . . .	5·5	158·8	156·5	CrO_2Cl_2
Chloride of aluminium	9·34	269·7	268	Al_2Cl_6
Bromide of aluminium	18·62	537·7	535	Al_2Br_6
Iodide of aluminium.	27·0	779·8	817	Al_2I_6
Perchloride of iron .	11·39	328·9	325	Fe_2Cl_6
Osmic acid . .	8·89	256·7	263·2	OsO_4
Zinc-ethyl . .	4·259	123	123	$ZnEt_2$
Mercury . . .	6·976	201·4	200	Hg''
Chloride of mercury.	9·8	283	271	$HgCl_2$
Bromide of mercury.	12·16	351·2	360	$HgBr_2$
Iodide of mercury .	15·9	459·2	454	HgI_2
Mercuric dimethyl .	8·29	239·4	230	$HgMe_2$
Mercuric diethyl .	9·97	287·9	258	$HgEt_2$
Mercurous chloride .	8·21	237·1	235·5	$HgCl$
Mercurous bromide .	10·14	292·8	280	$HgBr$
Ethylene . . .	0·9784	28·2	28	$[C_2H_4]''$
Chloride of ethylene.	3·4434	99·4	99	$[C_2H_4]''Cl_2$.

The results which are given in the preceding table suggest the following remarks :—

Firstly, if the law of Ampère is applicable to simple as well as to compound bodies, either in the state of gas or vapour, it will be seen that the molecules of both correspond to two volumes of vapour.

Secondly, the exceptions to this law, which are apparent in the case of several simple bodies, will not apply to volatile compounds of the same bodies. Phosphorus, arsenic, mercury, cadmium, and zinc, in their combinations with hydrogen, chlorine, bromine, iodine, and organic radicals, give such vapour-densities that the atomic weights deducible from them, conformably to the law of Ampère, are the same as the atomic weights founded upon chemical considerations.

Thirdly, the molecular weights which may be deduced, conformably to this law, from the densities of a great number of combinations, are identical with the molecular weights deduced from chemical considerations, provided that numbers which agree with the law of Dulong and Petit are taken for the atomic weights of a great number of elements.

Let us examine these points further.

I. The molecular weights of all these bodies are comparable with that of hydrogen, which is 2 The molecule of hydrogen is, therefore, formed of two atoms, and it is the same with the molecules of chlorine, bromine, iodine, oxygen, sulphur, and nitrogen. Each of these bodies in the free state consists of combinations of one atom with another atom of the same kind; their molecular formulæ are—

$$H_2 \quad Cl_2 \quad Br_2 \quad I_2 \quad O_2 \quad S_2 \quad N_2.$$

This is a development of the hypothesis which Ampère and Dumas applied to hydrogen and chlorine, and which is based upon an ingenious interpretation of the reaction by which these two elements combine to form hydrochloric acid. We have already described this hypothesis (page 32), which was adopted and developed by Gerhardt, and as it is of great importance, it is necessary to strengthen it by other considerations, drawn from the domain of pure chemistry.

Some chemists refuse to admit that a body may combine with itself; that pure hydrogen in the free state may be a hydride of hydrogen. Nothing is, however, more in harmony with certain reactions, of which this hypothesis alone is able to give a satisfactory explanation. Let us first take the case of hydrogen. In 1843 I discovered a combination of this body with copper—a combination which gives, with hydrochloric acid, a curious reaction; cuprous chloride being formed, whilst there is a tumultuous disengagement of hydrogen. But it is known that hydrochloric acid is not decomposed by copper; how, then, can it be by a combination of copper with hydrogen, unless the affinity of copper for chlorine were not supplemented by the affinity of hydrogen for hydrogen? Thus regarded, this reaction becomes a double decomposition of remarkable simplicity:

HCu^*	+	HCl	=	$CuCl$	+	HH
Hydride of copper.		Chloride of hydrogen.		Cuprous chloride.		Hydride of hydrogen.

On the other hand, this reaction is inexplicable if free hydrogen is considered as formed of a single atom. In fact, if copper by itself is incapable of decomposing hydrochloric acid, this would be still more the case with hydride of copper; for, in the former case, in order to decompose the hydrochloric acid, there would be only one affinity to conquer—that of chlorine for hydrogen: whilst in the second case there are two; for to this first affinity must be added that of copper for hydrogen, and however small this latter may be, it must be considered as a new obstacle. In a word, if copper does not decompose hydrochloric acid, hydride of copper should have still less tendency to decompose it.

* $Cu = 63{\cdot}5$.

But, it may be said, the hypothesis of the duality of the molecule of hydrogen is insufficient to explain the difference between the two reactions in question; for if hydrogen, in order to be disengaged in the free state, requires to combine with itself, why is not this affinity of hydrogen for hydrogen exerted in the case of hydrochloric acid? It would only require that two molecules of hydrochloric acid should act upon the copper:—

$$Cu_2 + 2HCl = Cu_2Cl_2 + HH.$$

Such is the objection; it is removed by taking into consideration the polarity of elements—a subject first brought forward by Mr. Brodie,* and to which M. Schönbein has devoted great attention of late years.

The hydrogen in hydride of copper shows so great a tendency to unite with the hydrogen of the hydrochloric acid, because it finds itself in these two combinations in a state of opposite polarity. The hydrogen of the hydrochloric acid is positive in respect to the hydrogen of the hydride of copper.

$$Cu\overset{-}{H} + \overset{+}{H}Cl = \overset{-}{H}\overset{+}{H} + CuCl.$$

Analogous considerations apply to the molecule of free oxygen. There are reactions which can only be explained by admitting the duality of this molecule, formed like that of hydrogen, of two atoms. And these reactions have for their object, 1, the decomposition of the molecule of oxygen, and 2, the reconstruction of the molecule of oxygen.

1. It is known that oxygen and nitrogen combine with difficulty under the influence of the electric spark; but according to an old observation of Cavendish, confirmed by Lavoisier and Berzelius, the combination of these two bodies is easily effected in the presence of hydrogen. Thus, a notable quantity of nitric acid is

* *Philosophical Transactions*, 1850, part ii. p. 759.

formed when a mixture of hydrogen and nitrogen is burnt in oxygen. Here, I think, is the interpretation of this fact.

The molecule OO being attacked by hydrogen, one atom of oxygen, O, combines with H_2, whilst the other atom of oxygen, which may be considered in the nascent state, combines with the nitrogen.

M. Schönbein* has recently discovered the important fact that the oxidation of certain metals occasions the formation of small quantities of oxygenated water. Here again we must admit that there is a decomposition of the molecule of oxygen, and that one atom of oxygen in the nascent state fixes itself upon the water to form oxygenated water—

$$\underset{\text{Oxygen.}}{OO} + Cu + H_2O = CuO + \underset{\text{Oxygenated Water.}}{H_2OO}.$$

2. On the other hand, some remarkable reductions are known to be effected by oxygenated water. Thénard showed that oxide of silver was reduced by this singular agent. Mr. Brodie, and long after him M. Schönbein, discovered a great number of analogous reactions in which bodies saturated with oxygen are seen to reduce oxygenated water, and to be themselves reduced by it. Thus, when oxygenated water is added to a solution of permanganate of potash, a tumultuous disengagement of oxygen is observed, with the precipitation of brown hydrated manganic oxide: the oxygenated water is at the same time decomposed. A more curious reduction, perhaps, is that of ozone by oxygenated water. These facts may be interpreted by the following equations:—

$$\underset{\text{Oxide of silver.}}{Ag_2\ominus} + \underset{\text{Oxygenated Water.}}{(H_2O\oplus)} = Ag_2 + \underset{\text{Water.}}{H_2O} + \underset{\text{Free Oxygen.}}{\ominus\oplus}.$$

* *Annales de Chimie et de Physique*, 3rd series, v. lix. p. 103

$$MnKO_2\ominus_2 + 2(H_2O\oplus) = MnHO_2 + KHO + H_2O + 2\ominus\oplus.$$

Permanganate of potash.	Oxygenated water.	Hydrated manganic oxide.	Potash.	Free oxygen.

$$(H_2O\oplus) + O_2\ominus = \oplus\ominus + O_2 + H_2O.$$

Oxygenated water.	Ozone.	Free oxygen.

These latter reactions are particularly significant, for it cannot be comprehended how a body saturated with oxygen can reduce another in the same condition, unless the oxygen of the one possessed a certain affinity for the oxygen of the other.

M. Schönbein considers that oxygen is a combination of negative and positive oxygen; so far his opinion is strengthened by the observations just mentioned, but when he supposes that negative oxygen $\ominus$ constitutes in the free state ozone, and that positive oxygen $\oplus$ in the free state constitutes the body which he names antozone, he advances a hypothesis ingenious but gratuitous, for he has given no explanation of it. He has rather put himself in opposition to known facts. Messrs. Andrews and Tate have indeed demonstrated that ozone is condensed oxygen* and the most rational interpretation of their experiments is to admit with Dr. Odling† that ozone consists of oxygenated water, H_2O_2, in which the hydrogen is replaced by an equivalent quantity of oxygen. The recent experiments of M. Soret ‡ seem to confirm this manner of viewing it.

But to return to molecular weight. The arguments which have just been discussed appear to me to strengthen this important proposition, that two atoms of certain simple bodies can combine with each other to form one molecule. Here is another argument which

* *Annales de Chimie et de Physique*, 3rd series, vol. lii. p. 333, and vol. lxii. p. 101.

† "A Manual of Chemistry," by W. Odling. 1861. p. 94.

‡ "On the Volumetric Relations of Ozone."—*Bibliothèque Universelle et Revue Suisse*, vol. xviii., September, 1863.

strengthens this hypothesis, drawn from another order of facts. It is known that the radicals of organic chemistry may be considered in certain respects as the analogues of the elements in mineral chemistry. What, then, will happen when, in iodide of ethyl, the iodine is separated from the radical ethyl C_2H_5? This will combine with itself to form what has been named free ethyl,

$$C_2H_5 + C_2H_5 = C_4H_{10}.$$

Let us here recall that MM. Favre and Silbermann, in their classical researches on the heat evolved in chemical combination, were the first to suggest that the molecule of free oxygen was formed of two atoms.* On the other hand, it is known that M. Clausius has been led by mechanical considerations on the constitution of gases to admit "that the force which governs chemical combinations, and which probably consists of a kind of polarity of the atoms, exerts itself even between simple bodies, and that in these latter several atoms may combine into one molecule."

The most simple case, and consequently the one most likely to be true, says he, will be that in which two atoms form one molecule. Thus, in the case of oxygen or nitrogen, it may be imagined that the chemical force which resides in one atom is exerted on a second atom in a molecule of these gases.†

* *Comptes Rendus*, xxiii. 200, 1846, MM. Favre and Silbermann have proved that carbon when burnt in protoxide of nitrogen evolves more heat than when burnt in oxygen. According to them the most natural interpretation of this fact consists in admitting that, in each experiment, a chemical combination is destroyed whilst another is formed; and that the thermic effect produced is the difference between the amount of heat disengaged by the union of carbon with oxygen and the amount of heat absorbed by the decomposition of oxide of oxygen in the first instance, and of oxide of nitrogen in the second. And if the thermic effect is less for oxygen than with protoxide of nitrogen, that is due to the circumstance that oxide of oxygen (the molecule of oxygen OO) absorbs more heat in decomposing than does the molecule of protoxide of nitrogen.

† *Poggendorff's Annalen*, c. 369; and *Annales de Chemie et de Physique*, 3rd series, l. 505.

II. Phosphorus, arsenic, mercury, and cadmium are exceptions to the preceding rule. The weight of two volumes of vapour of phosphorus or arsenic (the double density as compared with hydrogen) represents, not two atoms, but four atoms of phosphorus or arsenic. The weight of two volumes of mercury or cadmium vapour represents not two atoms, but one atom of mercury or cadmium.

It may be asked if these exceptions are due to some anomaly, or to some error in the determination of the atomic weights? In our opinion the former is the true interpretation. The well-recognised analogy between nitrogen, phosphorus, and arsenic leaves no doubt as to the true atomic weight of these elements. Two volumes of ammoniacal gas combine with two volumes of hydriodic acid to form hydriodate of ammonia. Two volumes of phosphuretted hydrogen combine with two volumes of hydriodic acid to form hydriodate of phosphuretted hydrogen. Two volumes of ammoniacal gas are, therefore, equivalent to two volumes of phosphuretted hydrogen; and if two volumes of ammoniacal gas represent one molecule containing one atom of nitrogen, two volumes of phosphuretted hydrogen represent one molecule containing one atom of phosphorus. If ammonia is NH_3, phosphuretted hydrogen and arseniuretted hydrogen are PH_3 and AsH_3, and not $P_{\frac{1}{2}}H_3$ and $As_{\frac{1}{2}}H_3$. These latter formulæ correspond with the abnormal vapour density of phosphorus and arsenic. Everything now proves that these must be rejected and the former adopted. It follows, therefore, that in their combinations with hydrogen (and, we may add, with chlorine, bromine, iodine, and organic radicals), phosphorus and arsenic have the normal vapour density which would be in harmony with Ampère's law. This is evident from the figures given in the table on pages 51, 52, 53, where the molecular weights of the volatile combinations in question, deduced from the true atomic weights (31 and 75), are identical with their double densities compared with hydrogen.

Mercury, cadmium, and doubtless zinc exhibit a contrary anomaly in their vapour-densities : their molecules are the same as their atoms; for the weight of two volumes of mercury vapour (= 200) which ought to be the molecular weight, is really the atomic weight, deduced from the specific heat and chemical considerations; and what proves that this is the true atomic weight of mercury is the fact that it agrees with the molecular weights of a large number of volatile mercurial compounds, as deduced from their vapour-densities. (See the table at page 53.)

The same anomaly, if anomaly there be, is seen also in some organic radicals, comparable with mercury and cadmium. This deserves a word of explanation.

When iodine separates from ethyl in iodide of ethyl, an ethylic group takes the place of the iodine in the iodide, and combines with the other ethylic group, so as to constitute free ethyl, which occupies exactly the same volume as iodide of ethyl in a state of vapour.

I	C_2H_5

2 vols. of iodide of ethyl.

C_2H_5	C_2H_5

2 vols. of ethyl.

But when bromine separates from the ethylene in the bromide of ethylene, the radical ethylene set at liberty, instead of combining with another radical ethylene, dilates and occupies the space before taken up by the bromide of ethylene.*

Br_2	C_2H_4

2 vols. of bromide of ethylene.

C_2	H_4

2 vols. of ethylene.

In the same way, when bromine separates from the

* $C_2H_4Cl_2 = 99$, $C_2H_4 = 28$ } See table at page 53.

mercury in mercuric bromide, the mercury set at liberty, instead of uniting with itself like ethyl, expands like ethylene, so as to occupy the whole space previously filled by the bromide of mercury.*

The compound radicals, ethylene, propylene, &c., to which we can add carbonic oxide,† are, then, in this respect comparable to the diatomic metals, mercury, cadmium, and zinc. Between the molecular formula of ethylene and that of ethyl there exists the same difference as between the molecular formula of mercury and that of hydrogen or oxygen. The smallest quantity of these radicals which exists in a compound, and which corresponds to one atom, is the same as the smallest quantity which exists in a free state and represents a molecule. The foregoing is not an explanation; it is only a comparison; but in estimating the anomaly which the vapour-densities of certain metals present, we must take into account such anomalies as we have quoted.‡

It only remains to add a few words in order to demonstrate that the atomic weights which it is thought proper to adopt for certain simple bodies are confirmed by the vapour-densities of their volatile compounds. Thus it will be seen on referring to the table given at page 51:—

1. That the vapour-densities of the volatile compounds of carbon, silicium, and boron, leave no doubt as to the

* $HgCl_2$ = 1 molecule = 271 } See table at page 53.
Hg = 1 molecule = 200 }

† | Cl_2 | CO | — 2 vols. of chloride of carbonyle. | C | O | — 2 vols. carbonic oxide.

‡ Our present notions of the atomicity of carbon, which we shall develope presently, allow us to conceive the existence of an unsaturated molecule C_2H_4 = 2 vols. in which one atom of carbon is diatomic and the other tetratomic. When the vapour of mercury expands in giving up the bromine of the bromide (in which mercury plays the part of a diatomic element) it would seem that the metal becomes monatomic, and that its vapour is then formed of two atoms [Hg'Hg'] = 200.

atomic weights which must be attributed to these bodies.

If two volumes of hydrogen weigh 2, two volumes of chloride of silicium contain 28 of silicium; two volumes of chloride of carbon contain 12 of carbon; two volumes of chloride of boron contain 11 of boron.

So vanish the doubts which the law of Dulong and Petit might leave relative to the atomic weights of carbon, boron, and silicium.

2. That the vapour-densities of the volatile compounds of aluminium, iron, chromium, zirconium, tin, titanium, bismuth, zinc, lead, and mercury demonstrate that the atomic weights of these metals are double the equivalents now received, and are the same as the atomic weights of Berzelius, and those deduced from the law of Dulong and Petit.

If two volumes of hydrogen weigh 2:—

Two volumes of stannic chloride contain 118 of tin;

Two volumes of chloride of titanium contain 50 of titanium;

Two volumes of chloride of zirconium contain 89·6 of zirconium;

Two volumes of zinc ethyl contain 65·2 of zinc;

Two volumes of mercuric chloride contain 200 of mercury;

Two volumes of ferric chloride contain 2×56 of iron $=2$ atoms;

Two volumes of chloride of aluminium contain 2×27 of aluminium $= 2$ atoms.

In fact, with the exceptions of ferric chloride and chloride of aluminium, to which we shall return, we have no reason to suppose that two volumes of the volatile compounds mentioned contain more than one atom of metal. The numbers given thus express the atomic weights, and it is seen at once that they are double the equivalents at present admitted.

Discussion of Ampère's Law.—All the arguments used to determine the molecular weights of volatile compounds have for their basis the law of Ampère, that *equal volumes of gases or vapours contain the same number of molecules.* It is admitted that the molecule of simple and compound bodies corresponds to 2 volumes, and that consequently the molecular weight is expressed by their double density in respect to hydrogen.

There are exceptions to this law. The molecules of perchloride of phosphorus, of hydriodate of phosphuretted hydrogen, of hydrochlorate and hydrocyanate of ammonia, of monohydrated sulphuric acid, and certain other combinations, correspond to 4 volumes of vapour; their molecular weights are expressed by four times their vapour densities as compared with hydrogen.

MM. Hermann Kopp,* Cannizzaro,† and Kekulé,‡ have proposed the following interpretation in order to bring these exceptions into the general rule. At the temperature at which the vapour densities of the preceding compounds are taken, they decompose, and instead of being a homogeneous vapour, they consist, in fact, of a mixture of vapours. Thus, perchloride of phosphorus, PCl_5, splits up into protochloride $PCl_3 = 2$ volumes, and into $Cl_2 = 2$ volumes. Sal ammoniac, NH_4Cl, splits up into $HCl = 2$ volumes and $NH_3 = 2$ volumes; sulphuric acid, SH_2O_4, into $SO_3 = 2$ volumes and $H_2O = 2$ volumes, and the same with other compounds. But this decomposition is not definite; when the temperature lowers the original combination becomes re-formed in such a manner that after the condensation of the vapour there

* *Annalen der Chemie und Pharmacie*, cv. 390.

† *Nota sulle Condensazioni di Vapore.* An appendix to the above quoted work of M. Cannizzaro, *Sunto di un Corso di Filosofia Chimica.* Pisa. 1858.

‡ *Annalen der Chemie und Pharmacie*, cvi. 143.

no longer remains a trace of the *dissociation* * which it has undergone.

The idea is ingenious, but the demonstration is difficult. In fact, how can it be proved that the vapour of perchloride of phosphorus, for example, consists at 300° of a mixture of chlorine and protochloride? Shall the chlorine be absorbed by some body with which it can combine? Then another affinity comes into play, and however feeble this be, it may be thought that it plays an active part in the decomposition of perchloride of phosphorus. For this reason, M. Bunsen remarked that the question as to whether two gases existed in the state of combination or of mixture could only be settled by submitting these gases to physical tests. They might thus be allowed to diffuse into another gas—hydrogen, for instance; if they were combined, they would pass through in the proportions in which they existed in the combination; if they were mixed, they would pass, as if each were by itself, in the inverse ratio of the square roots of their densities.

These experiments have been tried. M. Pebal † was the first to show that when the vapour of sal ammoniac is diffused into hydrogen, the ammonia, being less dense than the hydrochloric acid, passes through in greater quantity.

More recently, Messrs. Wanklyn and Robinson ‡ have

* The word dissociation is due to M. H. Deville (*Comptes Rendus*, xlv. 857, 1857). In its original sense it was almost synonymous with decomposition. More recently M. Deville has employed it to indicate that partial and gradual decomposition which bodies undergo when exposed to a temperature below that at which they decompose in bulk, and which is their true temperature of decomposition. I have proposed (*Répertoire de Chimie Pure*, ii. 37, 1860) to employ this appropriate term dissociation to characterise the temporary disjunction which certain bodies undergo at elevated temperatures into elements which are readyto recombine when the temperature becomes lowered.

† *Annalen der Chemie und Pharmacie*, cxxiii. 199, and *Annales de Chimie et de Physique*, 3rd series, lxvii. 93.

‡ *Comptes Rendus*, lvi. 547.

found that when the vapour of hydrated sulphuric acid is allowed to diffuse into air through a very fine point, water escapes abundantly, whilst anhydrous sulphuric acid accumulates in the flask. Having in a second series of experiments substituted perchloride of phosphorus for sulphuric acid, they found that the flask after some time contained a small quantity of protochloride of phosphorus, the vapour of which, being denser than that of chlorine, diffused less easily. The accuracy of the hypothesis of MM. Hermann Kopp and Cannizzaro thus appeared to be demonstrated, but some new and important experiments of M. H. Deville * have reopened the question.

This physicist found that the vapour of water would decompose in small quantity at a temperature lower than that developed by the combination of hydrogen with oxygen, and therefore much lower than that at which water would decompose in quantity. He assumed, therefore, that bodies possess at temperatures below their decomposing point a certain tendency to decompose—a tension of decomposition, as he expresses it. It is this nascent decomposition which he now calls dissociation. This is an apt interpretation of the experiments of MM. Pebal, Wanklyn, and Robinson. By virtue of their tension of decomposition, sal ammoniac, sulphuric acid, and protochloride of phosphorus undergo an incipient decomposition at the temperatures at which they vaporise, and it is these minute portions so dissociated which give rise to the phenomena of diffusion just mentioned.

This was an interpretation, but the following is an experiment which carries great weight†:—

Having led ammonia and hydrochloric acid into a flask heated by the vapour of mercury and furnished

* *Comptes Rendus*, lvi. 195.

† *Comptes Rendus*, lvi. 193.

with an air thermometer, the temperature of the receptacle was seen to rise to 394·5° by the action of the combination of the two gases. M. Deville concluded from this that hydrochlorate of ammonia could exist in the state of vapour at the temperature of 350°, and even at 390°, and that this vapour does not consist of a mixture, but actually of a combination of the two gases —ammonia and hydrochloric acid.

Against this conclusion MM. Wanklyn and Robinson have raised the following objections:—As M. Deville passed the gas rapidly into the flask where they were to combine, nothing proves that at the moment of combination they had acquired the temperature of 350°. Therefore, being cooler than the receptacle, they were able to combine at a temperature below that which is needed for the dissociation of sal ammoniac; and this combination would, therefore, have produced an elevation of temperature. Quite true, replies M. Deville to this; but it must be remembered that the temperature rose to 394°. The gases combine, therefore, at 350° with development of heat. It follows, therefore, that sal ammoniac is not dissociated at 350°, but that it really exists in the state of combination, and not in the state of mixture.

There can be no mistaking the force of these arguments.* However, the ingenious theory of M. H. Deville—or rather, the conclusions which he draws from it—still leaves room for an objection which I shall here discuss.

According to Deville, sal ammoniac exists in the state of combination at 350°, because its elements, if brought

* Another argument of M. H. Deville is this:—Hydrocyanate of ammonia is a very stable body; it forms at 1000°. It can, therefore, exist at this temperature, which is above that in which ammonia is decomposed into hydrogen and nitrogen. If, then, its vapour density is determined at 100°, it is found to correspond to four volumes. Can a body then be decomposed at 100°, when it is capable of forming at 1000°?

together at that temperature disengage heat. The argument may be put as follows:—

Is the disengagement of heat which is observed upon the mixture of two bodies always the effect and the proof of a change in the chemical constitution of their molecules, or of an addition or an exchange of atoms? These are important questions, the solution of which appears to have been given by the beautiful researches of M. Favre on the thermic effects of mixtures.* Having added water to very weak sulphuric acid, M. Favre still observed a disengagement of heat. Thus the addition of four equivalents of water to sulphuric acid already diluted with fifty-six equivalents of water, still occasioned a slight increase in temperature. Who will be bold enough to affirm that the thermic effect is here due to a chemical combination giving birth to a new molecule? Can the molecule $SO_3 60 HO$ exist? If it can exist, can it assume the gaseous form? I believe not, and M. Favre considers justly that it is not affinity properly so called which comes into play in actions of the kind which he has observed. He has pointed out others which are similar. The addition of small quantities of water to concentrated solutions of certain salts, possessing their water of crystallisation, can give rise to a disengagement of heat; but if large quantities of water are added, a contrary effect takes place. The phenomenon of the diffusion of the salt in water occasions a diminution of heat.

But in the first place, the disengagement of heat is due, according to M. Favre, to a molecular attraction different from affinity. And why may not actions of this sort be observed in mixtures of gases? Why should not the molecules of hydrochloric acid and of ammonia, although they cannot combine at 350°—that is to say, unite and condense themselves into a true gaseous mole-

* *Memoires de la Société d'emulation de la Provence*, i. 117.

cule—why should they not exercise a mutual action at this temperature? And why should not such an action give rise to a disengagement of heat, although it acts at a distance, not between the atoms in a single molecule, but between two different molecules? I am aware that we are dealing here with gases, and not with liquids. But it would seem that the molecular constitution of gases does not exclude the idea of a reciprocal attraction, able to exert itself at a distance, between the atoms of two different molecules.

It may be imagined, on the other hand, that by the fact of their mixture, and by the effect of this attraction, which is perhaps only a degree of affinity, the molecules of the two gases might acquire a stability which they would not possess when isolated. Here would be an explanation of that interesting fact observed by M. H. Deville, that the hydrocyanate of ammonia, or the mixture of hydrocyanic and ammoniacal gases, remains intact at temperatures in which these bodies are themselves decomposed.

It is far from my wish to pretend to have answered the questions I have just put. But is it not allowable to believe that the known facts authorise an interpretation different from that at which MM. Deville and Troost have arrived?

But let us admit for a moment that these questions may be answered in such a way as to oppose the generality of Ampère's law; let us admit that the molecular formulæ of certain bodies, formed, like sal ammoniac, by the union of two molecules, each of which forms 2 volumes of vapour, correspond to 4 volumes of vapour; or rather (for we can make this concession) let us admit that the molecules of such bodies would not take a gaseous form without their vapour expanding, thus forming two molecules which occupy 4 volumes, but which nevertheless remain united by a mutual attraction; these facts would not in any manner weaken the arguments which vapour densities have afforded us, in favour of the new system of atomic weights. In fact, if it be possible that the molecules of certain complex bodies cannot take the gaseous form without forming 4 volumes of vapour, the known facts do not authorise us to admit that molecules of compound bodies can exist, which, in the gaseous state, would form less than 2 volumes of vapour;* and it would always be true to say that the atomic weights of the immense majority of volatile compound bodies are expressed by their double densities as compared to hydrogen, as we have before shown.

We must now sum up this long explanation. We have first investigated the origin of the doctrine of equivalents and of the atomic theory; we have followed its progress; we have shown that the notions of equivalent, atom, molecule, at first confounded with each other, have at length acquired distinct meanings; lastly we have demonstrated that of all the systems of atomic weights, that which we are seeking to establish agrees better with the data that are furnished by specific heat and isomorphism, and with the laws which govern the combinations of gaseous bodies.

But our task is not finished. Whatever may be the importance of these physical data in the subject under discussion, such an assistance would be unavailing if it were not strengthened by arguments drawn from the domain of pure chemistry. In a word, the new system of atomic weights must rely upon chemical proof. It is particularly necessary to know whether the double atomic weights, which we have adopted for most of the metals,

* Arsenious acid is alone an exception to this. Its vapour is twice too much condensed, like that of arsenic itself. The two anomalies are evidently connected together. Neither heat nor oxygen succeed in dividing the group of 4 atoms, As_4 (page 52), which forms 2 volumes of free arsenic, and which enters into 2 volumes of arsenious acid, As_4O_6.

harmonise with their chemical properties, and with the constitution of their combinations. We think that it is so, and we shall give, in the course of these pages numerous arguments in support of this opinion.

For the present, we shall confine ourselves to remarking, in conclusion, that the new notation gives, for a very large number of bodies, formulæ identical with those which Berzelius* used for twenty years.

We will give some examples of them :—

	Formulæ of Berzelius.	New Formulæ.
Oxide of calcium .	CaO	$= Ca\Theta$
Chloride of calcium .	$CaCl_2$	$= CaCl_2$
Bromide of calcium .	$CaBr_2$	$= CaBr_2$
Iodide of calcium .	CaI_2	$= CaI_2$
Fluoride of calcium .	$CaFl_2$	$= CaFl_2$
Nitrate of lime . .	N_2O_5,CaO	$= N_2Ca\Theta_6$
Hypochlorite of lime .	Cl_2O,CaO	$= Cl_2Ca\Theta_2$
Chlorate of lime . .	Cl_2O_5,CaO	$= Cl_2Ca\Theta_6$
Sulphate of lime . .	SO_3,CaO	$= SCa\Theta_4$
Sulphite of lime . .	SO_2,CaO	$= SCa\Theta_3$
Carbonate of lime .	CO_2,CaO	$= CCa\Theta_3$
Acetate of lime . .	$C_4H_6O_3,CaO$	$= C_4H_6Ca\Theta_4$
Valerate of lime . .	$C_{10}H_{18}O_3,CaO$	$= C_{10}H_{18}Ca\Theta_4$
Benzoate of lime . .	$C_{14}H_{10}O_3,CaO$	$= C_{14}H_{10}Ca\Theta_4$
Lactate of lime . .	$C_6H_{10}O_5,CaO$	$= C_6H_{10}Ca\Theta_6$
Oxalate of lime . .	C_2O_3,CaO	$= C_2Ca\Theta_4$
Tartrate of lime† .	$C_4H_4O_5,CaO$	$= C_4H_4Ca\Theta_6$

It is evident that we shall observe the same coincidence in the formula of the numerous compounds that correspond to the preceding, and which contain, instead of calcium, other diatomic metals. Concerning other compounds we will also quote the following formulæ :—

	Formulæ of Berzelius.	New Formulæ.
Water	H_2O	$= H_2\Theta$
Peroxide of hydrogen . .	H_2O_2	$= H_2\Theta_2$
Sulphuretted hydrogen . .	H_2S	$= H_2S$

* *Vide* Cannizzaro "*Sunto di un corso di filosofia chimica,*" page 48.

† With regard to the oxalate and the tartrate, the coincidence of formulæ is accidental, and arises from the circumstance that Berzelius looked upon oxalic and tartaric acids as monobasic.

	Formulæ of Berzelius.	New Formulæ.
Bisulphide of hydrogen .	. H_2S_2	$= H_2\bar{S}_2$
Sulphurous acid . . .	. SO_2	$= \bar{S}\Theta_2$
Anhydrous sulphuric acid	. SO_3	$= \bar{S}\Theta_3$
Hydrated sulphuric acid	. SO_3,H_2O	$= \bar{S}H_2\Theta_4$
Anhydrous nitric acid .	. N_2O_5	$= N_2\Theta_5$
Nitrous acid	. N_2O_3	$= N_2\Theta_3$
Protoxide of nitrogen .	. N_2O	$= N_2\Theta$
Peroxide of barium .	. BaO_2	$= \bar{Ba}\Theta_2$
" of manganese .	. MnO_2	$= Mn\Theta_2$
" of lead . . .	. PbO_2	$= \bar{Pb}\Theta_2$
" of platinum .	. PtO_2	$= \bar{Pt}\Theta_2$
" of tin . . .	. SnO_2	$= \bar{Sn}\Theta_2$
Red oxide of manganese	. Mn_3O_4	$= Mn_3\Theta_4$
Minium	. Pb_3O_4	$= \bar{Pb}_3\Theta_4$
Sesquioxide of iron .	. Fe_2O_3	$= \bar{Fe}_2\Theta_3$
Alumina	. Al_2O_3	$= \bar{Al}_2O_3$
Platinous chloride . .	. $PtCl_2$	$= \bar{Pt}Cl_2$
Platinic chloride . . .	. $PtCl_4$	$= \bar{Pt}Cl_4$
Stannous chloride . .	. $SnCl_2$	$= \bar{Sn}Cl_2$
Stannic chloride . . .	. $SnCl_4$	$= \bar{Sn}Cl_4$
Ferric chloride . . .	. Fe_2Cl_6	$= \bar{Fe}_2Cl_6$
Aluminic chloride . .	. Al_2Cl_6	$= \bar{Al}_2Cl_6$
Sulphate of alumina .	. $3SO_3,Al_2O_3$	$= \bar{S}_3\bar{Al}_2\Theta_{12}$
Ferric sulphate . . .	. $3SO_3,Fe_2O_3$	$= \bar{S}_3\bar{Fe}_2\Theta_{12}$

It has been seen that we have barred the letters or symbols which represent elements whose *atoms* are double their equivalents. Berzelius formerly barred the letters which represented the *equivalents* of certain bodies, formed, according to him, of 2 atoms (double atoms). Our barred letters differ, then, from those of Berzelius, inasmuch as they represent atoms which we suppose indivisible. In other respects the bar is a purely conventional sign, but a convenient one, since it enables us to distinguish at the first glance the new notation from the equivalent notation. In adopting it, in this moment of transition, and, it must be said, of confusion, that embarrassment is avoided, which might arise in the mind of the reader by the use of formulæ to which he is not accustomed.

PART II.

THEORY OF TYPES AND ATOMICITY

SECTION I.

Theory of Types.

THE idea of types arises from the fact of substitutions. After having discovered trichloracetic acid (1840) M. Dumas first expressed the opinion that when chlorine is substituted atom for atom for hydrogen in an organic compound, the new chlorinated body and the hydrogenated body from whence it is derived belong to the same type. He has applied the same view to those bodies in which bromine, oxygen, &c., have replaced hydrogen.

The primitive hydrogenated substance, and also the bodies formed by substitution, belong to the same *chemical type*, when the fundamental properties are preserved after the change undergone in the composition. It is the same with acetic acid and with trichloracetic acid, which are both powerful monobasic acids, and which split up in a similar manner under the influence of alkalies, one giving off marsh gas, and the other chloroform.

The primitive substance, and the bodies derived from it by substitution, belong to the same *mechanical type*, when the fundamental properties are modified by the effect of the substitution, the number of elementary atoms having nevertheless remained the same.

Such are the fundamental principles of the theory of types of M. Dumas. We must add that the idea of mechanical types belongs to M. Regnault.

In its first form this theory united in the same group a given organic compound and the bodies derived from it by direct substitution of one element by another. Later M. Dumas added to the groups thus formed the nitrogenated compounds resulting from the substitution of nitrous vapour ($NO_4 = N\Theta_2$) for hydrogen. And this is a most important development; for it has led the way to the existing ideas concerning the substitution of compound radicals, mineral or organic, for elements.

But another and perhaps more striking point sprang from the new doctrine. It is the way in which M. Dumas viewed chemical combinations. Dualism represented them as formed from two elements, themselves simple or compound. M. Dumas conceived them as forming a whole, the different parts of which are connected together. Comparing them to a planetary system, he admitted that the atoms are maintained there by affinity. Let one atom be removed, if it is replaced by a different atom to the first, the system remains intact. This replacement can even be effected by a compound atom without the general constitution being modified.

Who does not see that these ideas are the basis of our present theories, and particularly that they form the starting-point of what Gerhardt afterwards called the *unitary system*?

But to return to the chemical types. It is the peculiarity of true ideas to prove themselves fruitful. This latter bore in it the germs of an immense development.

In its early form it was not capable of any great generalisation. It admitted as many types as primitive combinations, and between these types it established no common connexion.

But it has now taken a new form; it has referred all organic and inorganic compounds to a small number of types, chosen so as to represent different forms of combination; a profound idea which is in harmony with one of the fundamental properties of matter; the combining capacity of the elements, or atomicity. Such is the work of the followers of M. Dumas. We will give that portion established by each of them.

Laurent, first, compared certain oxides to water. Hydrate of potassa, said he, is water in which an atom of hydrogen is replaced by potassium. The same view has been applied to the anhydrous oxides. The following formulæ express these ideas:—

$$H_2O \quad K_2O \quad (KH)O \quad (NaH)O \quad Ag_2O.$$

There the new types begin.

In 1849 I discovered the compound ammonias. In the first communication made on this subject,* I remarked that these bodies may be looked upon as simple ethers in which the equivalent of oxygen would be replaced by an equivalent of amidogen, or *as ammonias in which an equivalent of hydrogen is replaced by methylium C_2H_3, or by ethylium C_4H_5.*

I expressed the relations existing between these bodies and ammonia by the following formulæ:—

NH_3 Ammonia.	NH_2,H Hydramide.
NH_5C_2 Methyl-ammonia.	NH_2,C_2H_3. Methyl-amide.
NH_7C_4 Ethyl-ammonia.	NH_2,C_4H_5. Ethyl-amide.

This last view represents the idea of types. Some

* *Comptes Rendus*, xxviii., p. 224, February, 1849.

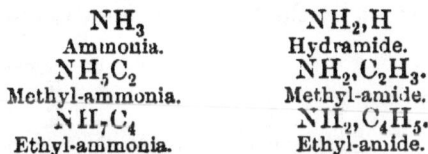

months later Dr. Hofmann gave it the preference in the interpretation of his fine discovery of diethylamine and triethylamine.* These bodies, said he, are ammonias in which two or three equivalents of hydrogen have been replaced by two or three ethylic groups—

$$N\left\{\begin{matrix} H \\ H \\ H \end{matrix}\right. \qquad N\left\{\begin{matrix} \text{Ȼ}_2H_5 \\ H \\ H \end{matrix}\right. \qquad N\left\{\begin{matrix} \text{Ȼ}_2H_5 \\ \text{Ȼ}_2H_5 \\ H \end{matrix}\right. \qquad N\left\{\begin{matrix} \text{Ȼ}_2H_5 \\ \text{Ȼ}_2H_5 \\ \text{Ȼ}_2H_5 \end{matrix}\right.$$

Ammonia. Ethylamine. Diethylamine. Triethylamine.

Besides, the idea of regarding ammonia as the combination type of the ammoniacal compounds was introduced of itself by a comparison of their properties. Whatever it might be, the ammoniacal type was established; but it was then only an isolated idea, it was not yet a doctrine. This latter began with the experiments of Dr. Williamson on etherification, and his brilliant discovery of mixed ethers.†

This eminent chemist has given a satisfactory demonstration of this point; if the molecule of alcohol contains one ethylic group, that of ether contains two; if we represent the first by the formula—

$$\text{Ȼ}_2H_5.H.\text{Ɵ},$$

the second contains

$$(\text{Ȼ}_2H_5)_2\text{Ɵ}.$$

He has compared both compounds not only with water but with the hydrates and oxides of inorganic chemistry. Water has become the type of all these bodies differing from each other so much by their properties, but analogous in their molecular structure. He has made these analogies apparent by the following notation :—

TYPE.	HYDRATES.	OXIDES.
$\left.\begin{matrix} H \\ H \end{matrix}\right\}\text{Ɵ}$	$\left.\begin{matrix} K \\ H \end{matrix}\right\}\text{Ɵ}$	$\left.\begin{matrix} K \\ K \end{matrix}\right\}\text{Ɵ}$
	Hydrate of potassium.	Oxide of potassium.

* *Comptes Rendus*, xxx., p. 147.

† Among the first promoters of the idea of types I must also mention Mr. Sterry Hunt.

Type.	Hydrates.	Oxides.
$\left.\begin{matrix}H\\H\end{matrix}\right\}\Theta$	$\left.\begin{matrix}Na\\H\end{matrix}\right\}\Theta$ Hydrate of sodium.	$\left.\begin{matrix}Ag\\Ag\end{matrix}\right\}\Theta$ Oxide of silver.
	$\left.\begin{matrix}\bar{C}H_3\\H\end{matrix}\right\}\Theta$ Hydrate of methyl.	$\left.\begin{matrix}\bar{C}H_3\\\bar{C}H_3\end{matrix}\right\}\Theta$ Oxide of methyl.
	$\left.\begin{matrix}\bar{C}_2H_5\\H\end{matrix}\right\}\Theta$ Hydrate of ethyl.	$\left.\begin{matrix}\bar{C}_2H_5\\\bar{C}_2H_5\end{matrix}\right\}\Theta$ Oxide of ethyl.
		$\left.\begin{matrix}\bar{C}_2H_5\\\bar{C}H_3\end{matrix}\right\}\Theta$ Oxide of methyl and ethyl.

This theory establishes between alcohol and ether, relations of the same nature as those which exist between the acids and their compound ethers. These latter were compared to salts. Thus, acids, salts, and compound ethers were looked upon as combinations of the same order, and placed under the type of water.

Type.	Acids.	Salts.	Compound Ethers.
$\left.\begin{matrix}H\\H\end{matrix}\right\}\Theta$	$\left.\begin{matrix}N\Theta_2\\H\end{matrix}\right\}\Theta$ Nitric acid.	$\left.\begin{matrix}N\Theta_2\\K\end{matrix}\right\}\Theta$ Nitrate of potash.	$\left.\begin{matrix}N\Theta_2\\\bar{C}_2H_5\end{matrix}\right\}\Theta$ Nitrate of ethyl.
	$\left.\begin{matrix}\bar{C}_2H_5\Theta\\H\end{matrix}\right\}\Theta$ Acetic acid.	$\left.\begin{matrix}\bar{C}_2H_5\Theta\\Na\end{matrix}\right\}\Theta$ Acetate of soda.	$\left.\begin{matrix}\bar{C}_2H_5\Theta\\\bar{C}_2H_5\end{matrix}\right\}\Theta$ Acetate of ethyl.

Gerhardt adopted this view and generalised it. The hydrogen and hydrochloric acid types were added to the types of water and ammonia, which were themselves enlarged.

Under the hydrogen type Gerhardt placed the metals, the organic radicals, the aldehydes, and the acetones.

Type.	Simple Bodies.	Organic Radicals.	Alderhydes and Derivations.
$\left.\begin{matrix}H\\H\end{matrix}\right\}$ Hydrogen.	$\left.\begin{matrix}Cl\\Cl\end{matrix}\right\}$ Chlorine.	$\left.\begin{matrix}Cy\\Cy\end{matrix}\right\}$ Cyanogen.	$\left.\begin{matrix}\bar{C}_2H_3\Theta\\H\end{matrix}\right\}$ Hydride of acetyl (aldehyde).
	$\left.\begin{matrix}Br\\Br\end{matrix}\right\}$ Bromine	$\left.\begin{matrix}\bar{C}H_3\\\bar{C}H_3\end{matrix}\right\}$ Methyl.	$\left.\begin{matrix}\bar{C}_2H_3\Theta\\\bar{C}H_3\end{matrix}\right\}$ Methylide of acetyl (acetone).

TYPE.	SIMPLE BODIES.	ORGANIC RADICALS.	ALDEHYDES AND DERIVATIONS.
$\left.\begin{matrix}H\\H\end{matrix}\right\}$	$\left.\begin{matrix}K\\K\end{matrix}\right\}$ Potassium.	$\left.\begin{matrix}\text{Ꞓ}H_3\\H\end{matrix}\right\}$ Hydride of methyl.	$\left.\begin{matrix}\text{Ꞓ}_7H_5\text{Ɵ}\\H\end{matrix}\right\}$ Hydride of benzoyl.
	$\left.\begin{matrix}Ag\\Ag\end{matrix}\right\}$ Silver	$\left.\begin{matrix}\text{Ꞓ}_2H_5\\\text{Ꞓ}_2H_5\end{matrix}\right\}$ Ethyl.	$\left.\begin{matrix}\text{Ꞓ}_7H_5\text{Ɵ}\\\text{Ꞓ}_6H_5\end{matrix}\right\}$ Phenylide of benzoyl.

Under the type of hydrochloric acid, which is only, in reality, a subdivision of the preceding, he united the organic and inorganic chlorides, bromides, iodides, &c.

$\left.\begin{matrix}H\\Cl\end{matrix}\right\}$ Hydrochloric acid.	$\left.\begin{matrix}I\\Cl\end{matrix}\right\}$ Protochloride of iodine.	$\left.\begin{matrix}\text{Ꞓ}H_3\\Cl\end{matrix}\right\}$ Chloride of methyl.	$\left.\begin{matrix}\text{Ꞓ}_2H_3\text{Ɵ}\\Cl\end{matrix}\right\}$ Chloride of acetyl.
	$\left.\begin{matrix}K\\Cl\end{matrix}\right\}$ Chloride of potassium.	$\left.\begin{matrix}\text{Ꞓ}_2H_5\\Cl\end{matrix}\right\}$ Chloride of ethyl..	$\left.\begin{matrix}\text{Ꞓ}_4H_7\text{Ɵ}\\Cl\end{matrix}\right\}$ Chlorine of butyryl.
	$\left.\begin{matrix}Hg\\Cl\end{matrix}\right\}$ Chloride of Mercury.	$\left.\begin{matrix}Cy\\Cl\end{matrix}\right\}$ Chloride of cyanogen.	$\left.\begin{matrix}\text{Ꞓ}_7H_5\text{Ɵ}\\Cl\end{matrix}\right\}$ Chloride of benzoyl.

His beautiful discovery of anhydrous acids gave him an opportunity of enlarging the type of water. He had formerly maintained that anhydrous monobasic acids did not exist, and, singularly enough, he discovered them himself. And yet his first assertion was not altogether unfounded; he had said that the molecule of acetic acid did not contain the elements necessary for forming a molecule of water by simple dehydration, and in that he was right; but he had not foreseen that *two* molecules of acetic acid would unite to form a molecule of water and a molecule of anhydrous acid, and that the latter would contain the remainder of two molecules of hydrated acid:—

$$2\left[\left.\begin{matrix}\text{Ꞓ}_2H_3\text{Ɵ}\\H\end{matrix}\right\}\text{Ɵ}\right]=\left.\begin{matrix}\text{Ꞓ}_2H_3\text{Ɵ}\\\text{Ꞓ}_2H_3\text{Ɵ}\end{matrix}\right\}\text{Ɵ}+\left.\begin{matrix}H\\H\end{matrix}\right\}\text{Ɵ}$$

Acetic acid. Anhydrous acetic acid.

This point has been established by abundant proof. Far from being an obstacle, it has become a confirmation of the theory, and the very clear reactions of chloride of acetyle have afforded a satisfactory proof of the fact that the hydrogen of water can be replaced by an organic group.

$$\left.\begin{matrix} H \\ H \end{matrix}\right\} \Theta + \left.\begin{matrix} C_2H_3\Theta \\ Cl \end{matrix}\right\} = \left.\begin{matrix} C_2H_3\Theta \\ H \end{matrix}\right\} \Theta + \left.\begin{matrix} H \\ Cl \end{matrix}\right\}$$

Water. Chloride of acetyl. Acetic acid. Hydrochloric acid.

$$\left.\begin{matrix} C_2H_3\Theta \\ Na \end{matrix}\right\} \Theta + \left.\begin{matrix} C_2H_3\Theta \\ Cl \end{matrix}\right\} = \left.\begin{matrix} C_2H_3\Theta \\ C_2H_3\Theta \end{matrix}\right\} \Theta + \left.\begin{matrix} Na \\ Cl \end{matrix}\right\}$$

Acetate of soda. Chloride of acetyl. Anhydrous acetic acid. Chloride of sodium.

In the first reaction, the chlorine of the chloride of acetyle takes an atom of hydrogen from the water and supplies the acetyle in its place. In the second, the sodium of the acetate, which represents the second atom of hydrogen of the water is similarly replaced by the acetyl. By the effect of this double substitution acetic acid is first formed, then anhydrous acetic acid, and these two bodies are thus united to water by a direct experiment.

Here the idea of a water type appears no more as a mere speculation; a cause for it is found in the most natural interpretation of facts, which may almost be said to insist upon it.

It is also obvious, by the preceding example, why Gerhardt has named his types, *types of double decomposition*. He admitted that, when molecules conflict together, an exchange always takes place between the atoms. This exchange is double decomposition—in fact, a sort of reaction by far the most frequent, but not the only one, as Gerhardt would have inferred it was.

Here is another example, selected from among a thousand, which may express this thought:—

$$\left.\begin{matrix} C_2H_3 \\ Cl\Theta \end{matrix}\right\} + \left.\begin{matrix} H \\ H \\ H \end{matrix}\right\} N = \left.\begin{matrix} C_2H_3\Theta \\ H \\ H \end{matrix}\right\} N + HCl$$

Chloride of acetyl. Ammonia. Acetamide.

The analogous reactions to the last have made him refer to the type of ammonia, not only the compound ammonia and the organic alkalies, but also the amides. The amides, said he, only differ from the alkaloids by the oxygenated nature of their radical: ethylamine and acetamide are combinations of the same order, and the remarkable differences of their properties are owing to the influence of the oxygen which has entered into the radical.

$$\left.\begin{matrix}H\\H\\H\end{matrix}\right\}N \qquad \left.\begin{matrix}C_2H_5\\H\\H\end{matrix}\right\}N \qquad \left.\begin{matrix}C_2H_3O\\H\\H\end{matrix}\right\}N$$

Type. Ethylamine. Acetamide.

This influence is so great that the introduction of oxygenated radicals into the molecule of ammonia can, in certain cases, give it the character of an acid.

Thus the properties of compound bodies are in some sort a function of the nature and grouping of the elementary atoms which they contain. If, on the one hand, bodies containing the same elements can differ in molecular arrangement, on the other hand, bodies offering the same atomic grouping may differ according to the nature of the elements.

In both cases the differences of their properties must be stated, and we must not be surprised in consequence to meet in the same type with bodies very dissimilar in character and chemical qualities. Thus, starting from water, which is neutral, we can form energetic acids or powerful bases. It is only necessary in the one case to replace hydrogen by an oxygenated radical; in the other by a strongly electro-positive element—as potassium. Such a thought has determined the arrangement of the following table,* in which Gerhardt has given an early view of his theory of types:—

* This table, which first appeared in an English journal, was reprinted by Gerhardt in his memoir on the anhydrous organic acids.—*Annales de Chimie et de Physique*, 3rd series, xxxvii., p. 339.

	Left, or positive extremity.	Intermediate terms.	Right, or negative extremity.
Water type . $\left.\begin{matrix}H\\H\end{matrix}\right\}O$	$\left.\begin{matrix}C_2H_5\\H\end{matrix}\right\}O$ Alcohol	. . .	$\left.\begin{matrix}C_2H_3O\\H\end{matrix}\right\}O$ Acetic acid
	$\left.\begin{matrix}C_2H_5\\C_2H_5\end{matrix}\right\}O$ Ether	. . .	$\left.\begin{matrix}C_2H_3O\\C_2H_3O\end{matrix}\right\}O$ Anhydrous acetic acid
	$\left.\begin{matrix}C\,H_3\\C_2H_5\end{matrix}\right\}O$ Ethylmethylic ether	. . .	$\left.\begin{matrix}C_2H_3O\\C_7H_5O\end{matrix}\right\}O$ Acetate of benzoyle
	. . . . .	$\left.\begin{matrix}C_2H_3O\\C_2H_5\end{matrix}\right\}O$ Acetic ether.	. . . . .
Hydrogen type $\left.\begin{matrix}H\\H\end{matrix}\right\}$	$\left.\begin{matrix}C_2H_5\\H\end{matrix}\right\}$ Hydride of ethyl	. . .	$\left.\begin{matrix}C_2H_3O\\H\end{matrix}\right\}$ Aldehyde
	$\left.\begin{matrix}C_2H_5\\C_2H_5\end{matrix}\right\}$ Ethyl	. . .	$\left.\begin{matrix}C_2H_3O\\C_2H_3O\end{matrix}\right\}$ Acetyle
	. . . . .	$\left.\begin{matrix}C\,H_3\\C_2H_3O\end{matrix}\right\}$ Acetone.	. . . . .
Hydrochloric acid type . $\left.\begin{matrix}H\\Cl\end{matrix}\right\}$.	$\left.\begin{matrix}C_2H_5\\Cl\end{matrix}\right\}$ Hydrochloric ether	. . .	$\left.\begin{matrix}C_2H_3O\\Cl\end{matrix}\right\}$ Chloride of acetyle
Ammonia type $\left.\begin{matrix}H\\H\\H\end{matrix}\right\}N$	$\left.\begin{matrix}C_2H_5\\H\\H\end{matrix}\right\}N$ Ethylamine	. . .	$\left.\begin{matrix}C_2H_3O\\H\\H\end{matrix}\right\}N$ Acetamide
	$\left.\begin{matrix}C_2H_5\\C_2H_5\\H\end{matrix}\right\}N$ Diethylamine	. . .	. . . . .
	$\left.\begin{matrix}C_2H_5\\C_2H_5\\C_2H_5\end{matrix}\right\}N$ Triethylamine	. . .	. . . . .

Condensed Types.—It will be seen that this theory embraced a very large number of compounds, but was far from including them all. It was, in fact, impossible to compare the molecule of the polybasic acids to a single molecule of water; and Dr. Williamson* was the first to make known the convenience of adopting types resulting from the condensation of several molecules of water. Thus, he referred sulphuric acid to the double type,—

$$\left.\begin{matrix} H_2 \\ H_2 \end{matrix}\right\} \Theta_2 \quad \text{or} \quad \left\{\begin{matrix} \left.\begin{matrix} H \\ H \end{matrix}\right\} \Theta \\ \left.\begin{matrix} H \\ H \end{matrix}\right\} \Theta \end{matrix}\right.$$

writing the formula of this acid

$$\left.\begin{matrix} S\Theta_2 \\ H_2 \end{matrix}\right\} \Theta_2 \quad \text{or} \quad \left.\begin{matrix} H \\ S\Theta_2 \\ H \end{matrix}\right\} \Theta_2$$

The two molecules of water are bound together by the bibasic radical sulphuryle (SO_2), which takes the place of two atoms of hydrogen. This is an important development of the theory of types. It is the origin of the theory of condensed types and of polyatomic radicals. Such radicals have the power of replacing the hydrogen of several molecules of water, so as to encroach on each of them and bind the remainders closely together. This property has been illustrated in a most evident manner by my experiments on the formation of glycol. I showed that two molecules of acetate of silver are bound together by the diatomic radical ethylene, when iodide of ethylene reacts on acetate of silver.

$$\begin{matrix} \left.\begin{matrix} C_2H_3\Theta \\ Ag \end{matrix}\right\} \Theta \\ \left.\begin{matrix} Ag \\ C_2H_3\Theta \end{matrix}\right\} \Theta \end{matrix} + C_2H_4I_2 = \left.\begin{matrix} C_2H_3\Theta \\ (C_2H_4) \\ C_2H_3\Theta \end{matrix}\right\} \Theta_2 + 2AgI.$$

Two molecules of acetate of silver.	Iodide of ethylene.	Diacetic glycol.

* *Quarterly Journal of the Chemical Society*, vol. iv., page 353. *Ibid*, vol vii., page 182.

In glycol the same radical unites the remains of two molecules of water ($2H_2\Theta - H_2$) by replacing in each of them one atom of hydrogen.

$$\left.\begin{matrix} H \\ H_2 \\ H \end{matrix}\right\} \begin{matrix} \Theta \\ \\ \Theta \end{matrix} \qquad \left.\begin{matrix} H \\ (\Theta_2H_4) \\ H \end{matrix}\right\} \begin{matrix} \Theta \\ \\ \Theta \end{matrix}$$

Glycol.

I had already applied this view to glycerine. Interpreting in a manner then new the fine results obtained by M. Berthelot in the synthesis of the neutral fatty bodies, I had stated that glycerine could be looked upon as being derived from a water type thrice condensed. The remains of three molecules of water ($3H_2\Theta - H_3$) are there united by the triatomic radical glyceryle $(\Theta_3H_5)'''$.

$$\left.\begin{matrix} H_3 \\ H_3 \end{matrix}\right\} \Theta_3 \qquad \left.\begin{matrix} (\Theta_3H_5)''' \\ H_3 \end{matrix}\right\} \Theta_3$$

Glycerine.

Glycerine was compared to ferric hydrate and aluminic hydrate, which were then regarded as triatomic. Dr. Odling had represented their composition by the formulæ

$$\left.\begin{matrix} Fe''' \\ H_3 \end{matrix}\right\} \Theta_3 \text{ and } \left.\begin{matrix} Al''' \\ H_3 \end{matrix}\right\} \Theta_3$$

and had thus admitted the triatomicity of iron and aluminium.

Thus the most diverse organic and inorganic compounds were referred to the doubly and trebly condensed water type, the polybasic acids by Dr. Williamson and by M. Gerhardt, the polyacid bases by Dr. Odling, and the polyatomic alcohols by myself.

We must add that M. Cannizzaro was the first to consider (in 1858) certain metals as diatomic, and this has permitted us to connect with the diatomic alcohols a great number of the hydrates of inorganic chemistry.

TYPE.	HYDRATED INORGANIC BASES.	ALCOHOLS.	INORGANIC ACIDS.	ORGANIC ACIDS.
$\left.\begin{matrix}H_2\\H_2\end{matrix}\right\}\Theta_2$	$\left.\begin{matrix}(\mathrm{Ca})''\\H_2\end{matrix}\right\}\Theta_2$ Hydrate of lime.	$\left.\begin{matrix}(C_2H_4)''\\H_2\end{matrix}\right\}\Theta_2$ Glycol.	$\left.\begin{matrix}(C\Theta)''\\H_2\end{matrix}\right\}\Theta_2$ Carbonic acid (hypothetical hydrate).	$\left.\begin{matrix}(C_2H_2\Theta)''\\H_2\end{matrix}\right\}\Theta_2$ Glycolic acid.
	$\left.\begin{matrix}(\mathrm{Ba})''\\H_2\end{matrix}\right\}\Theta_2$ Hydrate of baryta.	$\left.\begin{matrix}(C_3H_6)''\\H_2\end{matrix}\right\}\Theta_2$ Propylglycol.	$\left.\begin{matrix}(S\Theta)''\\H_2\end{matrix}\right\}\Theta_2$ Sulphurous acid.	$\left.\begin{matrix}(C_2\Theta_2)''\\H_2\end{matrix}\right\}\Theta_2$ Oxalic acid.
	$\left.\begin{matrix}(\mathrm{Cu}'')\\H_2\end{matrix}\right\}\Theta_2$ Hydrate of copper.	$\left.\begin{matrix}(C_5H_{10})''\\H_2\end{matrix}\right\}\Theta_2$ Amylglycol.	$\left.\begin{matrix}(S\Theta_2)''\\H_2\end{matrix}\right\}\Theta_2$ Sulphuric acid.	$\left.\begin{matrix}(C_4H_4\Theta_2)''\\H_2\end{matrix}\right\}\Theta_2$ Succinic acid.
$\left.\begin{matrix}H_3\\H_3\end{matrix}\right\}\Theta_3$	$\left.\begin{matrix}(\mathrm{Sb})'''\\H_3\end{matrix}\right\}\Theta_3$ Hydrate of antimony.	$\left.\begin{matrix}(C_3H_5)'''\\H_3\end{matrix}\right\}\Theta_3$ Glycerine.	$\left.\begin{matrix}P'''\\H_3\end{matrix}\right\}\Theta_3$ Phosphorous acid.	$\left.\begin{matrix}(C_3H_3\Theta)'''\\H_3\end{matrix}\right\}\Theta_3$ Glyceric acid.
	$\left.\begin{matrix}(\mathrm{Bi})'''\\H_3\end{matrix}\right\}\Theta_3$ Hydrate of bismuth.	$\left.\begin{matrix}(C_5H_9)'''\\H_3\end{matrix}\right\}\Theta_3$ Amylglycerine.	$\left.\begin{matrix}(P\Theta)'''\\H_3\end{matrix}\right\}\Theta_3$ Phosphoric acid.	

Still more condensed types have been admitted; but at present we will confine ourselves to indicating the precedents which explain the principal of them.

As a polyatomic radical can unite several molecules of water, so also it can unite into one bundle several molecules of hydrogen or ammonia. The following examples show that a number of compounds can be referred to the hydrogen and ammonia types, more or less condensed:—

TYPE.	TYPE.	TYPE.	TYPE.
$\left.\begin{matrix}H_2\\H_2\end{matrix}\right\}$ or $\left\{\begin{matrix}Cl_2\\H_2\end{matrix}\right.$	$\left.\begin{matrix}H_3\\H_3\end{matrix}\right\}$ or $\left\{\begin{matrix}Cl_3\\H_3\end{matrix}\right.$	$\left.\begin{matrix}H_2\\H_2\\H_2\end{matrix}\right\}N_2$	$\left.\begin{matrix}H_3\\H_3\\H_3\end{matrix}\right\}N_3$
$\left.\begin{matrix}(S\Theta_2)''\\Cl_2\end{matrix}\right\}$ Chloride of sulphuryle.	$\left.\begin{matrix}(P\Theta)'''\\Cl_3\end{matrix}\right\}$ Chloride of phosphoryle.	$\left.\begin{matrix}(C\Theta)''\\H_2\\H_2\end{matrix}\right\}N_2$ Urea.	$\left.\begin{matrix}Cy_3\\H_3\\H_3\end{matrix}\right\}N_3$ Melamine.
$\left.\begin{matrix}(C\Theta)''\\Cl_2\end{matrix}\right\}$ Chloride of carbonyle. (phosgene gas).	$\left.\begin{matrix}\mathrm{Bo}'''\\Cl_3\end{matrix}\right\}$ Chloride of boron.	$\left.\begin{matrix}(C_2\Theta_2)''\\H_2\\H_2\end{matrix}\right\}N_2$ Oxamide.	$\left.\begin{matrix}(C\Theta)''\\(C\Theta)''\\H_3\end{matrix}\right\}N_3$ Biuret.

YPE.	TYPE.	TYPE.	TYPE.
$\left.\begin{matrix} Ca'' \\ Cl_2 \end{matrix}\right\}$	$\left.\begin{matrix} Bi''' \\ Cl_3 \end{matrix}\right\}$	$\left.\begin{matrix} (C_2H_4)'' \\ H_2 \\ H_2 \end{matrix}\right\} N_2$	$\left.\begin{matrix} (C_2H_4)'' \\ (C_2H_4)'' \\ H_3 \end{matrix}\right\} N_3$
Chloride of alcium.	Chloride of bismuth.	Ethylene-diamine.	Diethylene-triamine.
$\left.\begin{matrix} (C_2H_4)'' \\ Cl_2 \end{matrix}\right\}$	$\left.\begin{matrix} (C_3H_5)''' \\ Cl_3 \end{matrix}\right\}$	$\left.\begin{matrix} (C_6H_4)'' \\ H_2 \\ H_2 \end{matrix}\right\} N_2$	$\left.\begin{matrix} (C_6H_3)'' \\ H_3 \\ H_3 \end{matrix}\right\} N_3$
Chloride of ethylene.	Trichloride of allyle.	Phenylene-diamine.	Picramine.

It is seen that all these combinations, which are referred to condensed types, contain either an element or a polyatomic radical. Several molecules are thus united in a more complex one, because, in each of them, an atom is removed, and the space thus formed is filled by a single element or by a single indivisible group. It is necessary to understand well this action of the radicals or polyatomic elements, and it may be represented by the following notation :—

$$\begin{matrix} ClH \\ ClH \end{matrix} \qquad \left.\begin{matrix} Cl \\ Cl \end{matrix}\right\} Ca'' \qquad \left.\begin{matrix} Cl \\ Cl \end{matrix}\right\} (C_2H_4)'' \qquad \left.\begin{matrix} Cl \\ Cl \end{matrix}\right\} (SO_2)''$$

Chloride of calcium. Chloride of ethylene. Chloride of sulphuryle.

$$\begin{matrix} HHHN \\ HHHN \end{matrix} \qquad (CO)'' \left\{\begin{matrix} HHN \\ HHN \end{matrix}\right. \qquad (C_2H_4)'' \left\}\begin{matrix} HHN \\ HHN \end{matrix}\right.$$

Urea. Ethylene-diamine.

Mixed Types.—It may be similarly understood that an element or a polyatomic radical may connect together several molecules of different natures. Thus a diatomic element or radical can unite a molecule of hydrochloric acid to a molecule of water, replacing in each of them a molecule of hydrogen. By the same means a molecule of water can be joined to a molecule of ammonia. Three molecules, two of hydrochloric acid and one of water, or two of water and one of hydrochloric acid, can be connected by a triatomic radical or by two diatomic radicals. A few examples will suffice to explain the meaning of these mixed types, which were introduced into the science by Dr. Odling :—

Type	Type.	Type.	Type.
$\left.\begin{matrix}H\\H\end{matrix}\right\}\Theta$ HCl	$\left.\begin{matrix}H\\H\end{matrix}\right\}\Theta$ $\left.\begin{matrix}H\\H\\H\end{matrix}\right\}N$	$\left.\begin{matrix}H\\H\end{matrix}\right\}\Theta$ HCl $\left.\begin{matrix}H\\H\end{matrix}\right\}\Theta$	HCl HCl $\left.\begin{matrix}H\\H\end{matrix}\right\}\Theta$
$\left.\begin{matrix}H\\(C_2H_4)''\end{matrix}\right\}\begin{matrix}\Theta\\Cl\end{matrix}$ Hydrochloric glycol.	$\left.\begin{matrix}H\\(C_2\Theta_2)''\end{matrix}\right\}\Theta$ $\left.\begin{matrix}H\\H\end{matrix}\right\}N$ Oxamic acid.	$\left.\begin{matrix}H\\(C_3H_5)'''\\H\end{matrix}\right\}\begin{matrix}\Theta\\Cl\\\Theta\end{matrix}$ Monochlorhydrine.	$\left.\begin{matrix}(C_3H_5)'''\\H\end{matrix}\right\}\begin{matrix}Cl_2\\\Theta\end{matrix}$ Dichlorhydrine.
$\left.\begin{matrix}H\\(S\Theta_2)''\end{matrix}\right\}\begin{matrix}\Theta\\Cl\end{matrix}$ Chlorosulphuric acid of Dr. Williamson.	$\left.\begin{matrix}(C_2H_5)'\end{matrix}\right\}\Theta$ $(C_2\Theta_2)''$ $\left.\begin{matrix}H\\H\end{matrix}\right\}N$ Oxamethane.	$\left.\begin{matrix}H\\(C_3H_5)'''\\(C_2H_3\Theta)'\end{matrix}\right\}\begin{matrix}\Theta\\Cl\\\Theta\end{matrix}$ Monochloracetine.	$\left.\begin{matrix}(C_2H_4)''\\(C_2H_4)''\end{matrix}\right\}\begin{matrix}Cl_2\\\Theta\end{matrix}$ Dichlorhydrine diethylenic.
$\left.\begin{matrix}(C_3H_5)'''\end{matrix}\right\}\begin{matrix}\Theta\\Cl\end{matrix}$ Epichlorhydrine of M. Berthelot.	$\left.\begin{matrix}(C_2H_5)'\end{matrix}\right\}\Theta$ $(C\Theta)''$ $\left.\begin{matrix}H\\H\end{matrix}\right\}N$ Urethane.	$\left.\begin{matrix}H\\(C_2H_4)''\\(C_2H_4)''\end{matrix}\right\}\begin{matrix}\Theta\\Cl\\\Theta\end{matrix}$ Diethylenic monochlorhydrine.	$\left.\begin{matrix}(C_3H_5)'''\\(C_2H_3\Theta)'\end{matrix}\right\}\begin{matrix}Cl_2\\\Theta\end{matrix}$ Dichloracetine.

The preceding examples will give a condensed, but, I think, sufficient idea of the theory which was first suggested by Dr. Williamson, and of which M. Gerhardt has been the chief promoter. But the work of M. Gerhardt has been extended. Dr. Odling and M. Kekulé have added some important developments, and I think I may be allowed to state that my experiments on glycol and the interpretation I have given of the valuable researches of M. Berthelot on glycerine, have given a solid basis to the theory of condensed types, making evident the action of the polyatomic radicals in complex molecules. My experiments and researches had reference to the water type. Dr. Hofmann, in his classical investigations of the polyamines, has extended them in the most skilful and complete manner to the ammonia type. Thus, the theory has grown with the riches of science itself. New facts, far from being a hindrance, have given it increased force. And if these discoveries have in a manner formed the completion of the theory, has not the latter in its turn originated experiments, corrected views, established relationships, supplied deficiencies? In organic chemistry it has brought into the interpretation of reactions a clearness and simplicity before unknown. Let us refer back to the time when Gerhardt, in his earlier method, rejected all the rational formulæ which had nevertheless been so happily introduced into the science by the classic labours of MM. Dumas and Boullay on ethers, and of MM. Liebig and Wöhler on the benzoyle compounds. In conformity with the unitary idea, compound bodies were represented by a single expression, their crude formulæ. Formulæ of this kind expressed only the atomic composition and the size of the molecule. They neither represented the mode of generation nor the ties of relationship. They gave no account of the properties, and only an insufficient one of the reactions. When I adopted for the principal derivatives of acetic acid the formulæ,

$\left.\begin{matrix} C_2H_3\Theta \\ H \end{matrix}\right\} \Theta$	$\left.\begin{matrix} C_2H_3\Theta \\ K \end{matrix}\right\} \Theta$	$\left.\begin{matrix} C_2H_3\Theta \\ C_2H_5 \end{matrix}\right\} \Theta$	$\left.\begin{matrix} C_2H_3\Theta \\ C_2H_3\Theta \end{matrix}\right\} \Theta$
Acetic acid.	Acetate of potassium.	Acetic ether.	Anhydrous acetic acid.
$\left.\begin{matrix} C_2H_3\Theta \\ H \end{matrix}\right\} S$	$\left.\begin{matrix} C_2H_3\Theta \\ CH_3 \end{matrix}\right\}$	$\left.\begin{matrix} C_2H_3\Theta \\ Cl \end{matrix}\right\}$	$\left.\begin{matrix} C_2H_3\Theta \\ H \\ H \end{matrix}\right\} N$
Thiacetic acid.	Acetone.	Chloride of acetyle.	Acetamide.

I first observed that they all contained a common element: the acetyle radical $C_2H_3\Theta$. This is the connexion which unites all these bodies; it discloses relationships between them as close as those which are shown in the copper compounds by the existence of the copper radical.

The formula

$$\left.\begin{matrix} C_2H_3\Theta \\ H \end{matrix}\right\} \Theta$$

in which one atom of the hydrogen is not confounded with the three others, reminds me next of this fact, that of the four atoms of hydrogen in the acetic acid, one only is easily replaced by metals or organic groups; that acetic acid is monobasic, that it forms only one ether, one chloride, and one amide; only one ether because only one atom of hydrogen is capable of being replaced by an alcoholic group; only one chloride, because only one group HΘ is capable of being replaced by chlorine, &c.

If we take a bibasic acid—succinic acid, for example—the formula

$$\left.\begin{matrix}\Theta_4H_4\Theta_2\\H_2\end{matrix}\right\}\Theta_2$$

shows us that this acid contains two equivalents of hydrogen capable of being replaced by a metal or organic group; that it is bibasic—that it can form two ethers, two chlorides, and two amides: two ethers because each of the two equivalents of hydrogen can be replaced by an alcoholic group; two chlorides—

$$\left.\begin{matrix}\Theta_4H_4\Theta_2\\H\end{matrix}\right\}\begin{matrix}\Theta\\Cl\end{matrix} \text{ and } \Theta_4H_4\Theta_2Cl_2$$

because each of the two groups HΘ can be replaced by an atom of chlorine; lastly, two amides, because each of these two groups can be replaced by a group NH_2.

If we next pass to a compound of a higher order—glycerine, for example, the formula

$$\left.\begin{matrix}(\Theta_3H_5)'''\\H_3\end{matrix}\right\}\Theta_3$$

shows us immediately the triatomic nature of this combination; it reminds us that three atoms of its hydrogen may each be replaced by a radical of acid, that the three groups (or typical residues) HΘ which it contains may be replaced by chlorine, bromine, or by groups of NH_2, and that three series of combinations may occur in consequence of these substitutions.

What can be more convincing, or more simple, than the way in which the theory explains all these exchanges? What clearness it gives to the generating equations which we have already mentioned in the preceding pages, and which we might multiply indefinitely! But for what purpose, since the question is evident almost *à priori?* The theory of types takes its origin from a sounder interpretation of an immense number of reactions which it regards as double decompositions. It is their symbolic representation. It is quite natural, then, that it should account in a satisfactory manner for these same properties which M. Kekulé has called typical,* and which have reference to the very exchanges under discussion.

In place of all this, what do we see in the original formulæ? Nothing but the relative size of the molecules.

What do the formulæ

$$C_2H_4\Theta_2 \text{ and } C_4H_8\Theta_2$$

tell us concerning the relationship between acetic acid and acetic ether, and how would the second allow us to distinguish between acetic ether and the isomeric methylpropionic ether, propylformic ether, and butyric acid? These formulæ are absolutely useless for this object, and to avoid such confusion we must return to the generating equations

$$\underset{\text{Alcohol.}}{C_2H_6\Theta} + \underset{\text{Acetic acid.}}{C_2H_4\Theta_2} = \underset{\text{Acetic ether.}}{C_4H_8\Theta_2} + H_2\Theta$$

Gerhardt did so at the time that he defended the unitary system in the strict sense of the word. But it was an evasion, an inconvenient and even insufficient expedient, for the formulæ and the typical equations which Gerhardt afterwards employed are more explicit than the generating equations in question.

The following are the formulæ :—

$$\underset{\text{Acetic acid.}}{\left.\begin{matrix} C_2H_3\Theta \\ H \end{matrix}\right\}\Theta}, \quad \underset{\text{Acetate of ethyl.}}{\left.\begin{matrix} C_2H_3\Theta \\ C_2H_5 \end{matrix}\right\}\Theta}, \quad \underset{\text{Propionate of methyl.}}{\left.\begin{matrix} C_3H_5\Theta \\ CH_3 \end{matrix}\right\}\Theta}.$$

* *Lehrbuch der Organischen Chemie*, t. i., p. 124.

$$\left.\begin{array}{c} CHO \\ C_3H_7 \end{array}\right\} \Theta, \qquad \left.\begin{array}{c} C_4H_7\Theta \\ H \end{array}\right\} \Theta.$$

Formiate of propyl.   Butyric acid.

Here is one of the typical equations,—

$$\left.\begin{array}{c} C_2H_3\Theta \\ H \end{array}\right\} \Theta + \left.\begin{array}{c} C_2H_5 \\ H \end{array}\right\} \Theta = \left.\begin{array}{c} H \\ H \end{array}\right\} \Theta + \left.\begin{array}{c} C_2H_3\Theta \\ C_2H_5 \end{array}\right\} \Theta$$

Acetic acid.   Alcohol.   Acetic ether.

Is it possible to express in a clearer and more simple manner this fact,—that the reaction of acetic acid on alcohol consists of an exchange of elements, and that the formation of acetic ether is necessarily connected with that of water? Certainly the typical equation gives account of the essential conditions, and, in a manner, of the mechanism of the reaction. There is a singular difference of opinion among some chemists on this subject. Among the detractors of the typical notation, some affirm that it says too much, others regret that it does not say enough. Admitting, say the former, these exchanges of simple bodies for groups in the systems which it considers as typical, the theory implies hypotheses on the molecular grouping. It does not confine itself to representing facts, it goes beyond them.

It is true, say the others, that it perfectly interprets certain reactions, but it is powerless to express them all. For after all, these molecular changes, these double decompositions which it depicts so well, are not the only reactions; there are molecular additions and subtractions; and when it becomes necessary to account for those more or less profound changes, which attack not only the external scaffolding, but the very substance of the molecule, the typical formulæ afford very slight, if any, assistance.

The following considerations will reduce these objections to their proper value.

SECTION II

Application of the Theory of Types.

THE molecules of compound bodies consist of an aggregation of atoms, which occupy a definite position in space. It is impossible to represent this arrangement by a formula or a plane figure, and the typical formulæ have no such pretension.* But experience and reason teach us that in a molecular system the atoms do not exercise the same attractions upon each other. According to their nature, their number, and their position, some are united closer to each other than they are to their neighbouring atoms. When therefore, the equilibrium being disturbed, the molecule splits in certain directions, there may be found among the fragments groups where the stronger attractions are predominant. We call them compound radicals, and we represent them as separate and distinct members in the typical formulæ. Are we to say, then, that this graphic disposition indicates the real position of the atoms, that these members thus separated represent actual groups, occupying the places assigned to them in the formula? By no means. They recall the fact that certain aggregations of atoms are capable of resisting shocks which break up the rest of the molecule; or, if you like, they mark certain directions in which the molecule can separate. In a word, this artificial arrangement of the formula only gives those instructions respecting the real constitution of the molecule which we could gather from the reactions themselves.

When I compare the composition of ethylamine with

* Kekulé, Lehrbuch, t. i., page 158.

that of ammonia, I observe that the former contains C_2H_4 more than the latter. That is the fact. When I say that ethylamine is ammonia in which 1 atom of hydrogen is replaced by the ethyl group, I, in truth, pass the limit which separates fact from hypothesis; but my hypothesis is only the interpretation of experiment, and the typical formula

$$\left.\begin{matrix} C_2H_5 \\ H \\ H \end{matrix}\right\} N$$

shows the constitution of ethylamine only to the same extent that the reaction of bromide of ethyl with ammonia itself, discloses.

$$\left.\begin{matrix} H \\ H \\ H \end{matrix}\right\} N + C_2H_5Br = HBr + \left.\begin{matrix} C_2H_5 \\ H \\ H \end{matrix}\right\} N$$

It tells me that in this complex molecule 5 atoms of hydrogen are more closely united to the carbon than the two others; and in this it leads me into no error, for we know that the two atoms of typical hydrogen may easily be replaced by another group (Hofmann), whilst it is not the same with the other atoms of hydrogen.

It may be seen, then, that this formula is only the expression of certain facts. It does not go beyond them; it only recalls the conclusions that we may draw from experiment, if not on the exact position of all the atoms, at least on the mutual relations, and the functions of some of them.

Can such a formula express all the facts? Evidently not. When I write acetic acid

$$\left.\begin{matrix} C_2H_3O \\ H \end{matrix}\right\} O$$

I recall its formation by chloride of acetyle and water, or by the action of oxygen on aldehyde; but I do not foresee the possibility of forming acetate of sodium with carbonic acid and sodium methyl (Wanklyn),*

* *Annales de Chimie et de Physique*, 3rd series, t. lvii., p. 358.

$$CO \cdot O \quad + \quad \left.\begin{matrix} CH_3 \\ Na \end{matrix}\right\} \quad = \quad \left.\begin{matrix} CO \cdot CH_3 \\ Na \end{matrix}\right\} O$$

Carbonic acid. Sodium methyl. Acetate of sodium.

or the action of soda on cyanide of methyl (Dumas, Malaguti, and Le Blanc). I neither give account of the electrolytic decomposition of acetate of soda nor of the formation of acetone. All these reactions disclose a certain grouping of the atoms in the acetyle radical, which is not indicated by the term C_2H_3O, which is represented as a whole in the typical formula

$$\left.\begin{matrix} C_2H_3O \\ H \end{matrix}\right\} O$$

But in the case of acetic acid nothing is easier than to make the formula agree with the facts just mentioned. To do so it is only necessary to decompose the radical into two groups—CH_3 and CO—and to write this formula

$$\left.\begin{matrix} CO \cdot CH_3 \\ H \end{matrix}\right\} O$$

In truth, it is now less simple, but it represents a greater number of facts. This methyl group which is shown there, existed in the cyanide of methyl, in the sodium methyl, and it passes into acetone

$$\left.\begin{matrix} CO \cdot CH_3 \\ CH_3 \end{matrix}\right\}$$

We must remark that the molecule of acetic acid only contained two atoms of carbon, and that the groups CO and CH_3 each contain one. This formula then can hardly be further decomposed. It is on that account that, without ceasing to be simple, it explains so well all the reactions. By means of similar processes we can perfect the typical formulæ, by decomposing the terms expressing the radicals into a certain number of factors. Thus nothing prevents us from representing the bodies homologous with acetic acid by the formulæ

$$\left.\begin{matrix} CO \cdot C_2H_5 \\ H \end{matrix}\right\} O, \quad \left.\begin{matrix} CO \cdot C_3H_7 \\ H \end{matrix}\right\} O, \quad \left.\begin{matrix} CO \cdot C_4H_9 \\ H \end{matrix}\right\} O,$$

Propionic acid. Butyric acid, &c. Valeric acid, &c.

nor from giving analogous formulæ to the acetones derived from these acids. It is unnecessary to insist on this point, which is generally admitted. But we must not forget that such changes introduced into the typical formulæ must represent facts, without ever going beyond them, for fear of becoming arbitrary; in the next place that in these decompositions of formulæ there is a limit which must be respected for fear of taking from the typical notation its principal advantage, that of simplicity. It seems to me that some chemists have been unable to avoid this latter danger, and that in their desire to be complete and profound on the subject, they have submitted to become obscure. How could it be otherwise, since they attempted to decompose the formulæ of complex bodies? In such a proceeding, supposing every error were avoided, we should certainly not escape the embarrassment of a complicated, if not confused, notation. I insist upon this consideration, and I will strengthen it by an example which offers a particular interest. I formerly represented the composition of lactic acid by the formula

$$\left.\begin{matrix}(\Theta_3H_4\Theta)'' \\ H_2\end{matrix}\right\} \Theta_2$$

to show that this acid is derived from propylglycol,

$$\left.\begin{matrix}(\Theta_3H_6)'' \\ H_2\end{matrix}\right\} \Theta_2$$

that it is diatomic, and capable of forming a dichloride, $\Theta_3H_4\Theta \cdot Cl_2$, and an anhydride $\Theta_3H_4\Theta \cdot \Theta$. This formula then, represents a certain number of the reactions of this acid. It is far from representing them all. In fact, in the same way that dicyanhydric glycol, or dicyanide of ethylene divide under the influence of caustic potash into ammonia and succinic acid,* so monocyanhydric glycol by the action of alkalies gives lactic acid.†

* Maxwell Simpson, *Annales de Chimie et de Physique*, 3rd series, vol. lxi., p. 224.

† Wislicenus, *Annalen der Chemie und Pharmacie*, vol. cxxviii., p. 9.

Quite lately Mr. A. R. Catton has obtained lactic acid by passing a current of carbonic acid into alcohol in which he at the same time dissolved sodium.*

The formula

$$\left.\begin{matrix}C_3H_4\Theta\\ H_2\end{matrix}\right\}\Theta_2$$

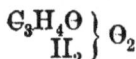

does not account in a satisfactory manner for these new cases of the formation of lactic acid; for it does not show that the radical $C_3H_4\Theta$ is composed, according to every appearance, of two terms, as the two preceding experiments indicate. But it is both easy and allowable to give satisfaction on this point by introducing into the formula of lactic acid a change analogous to that made in acetic acid. The formula

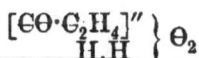

$$\left.\begin{matrix}[C\Theta\cdot C_2H_4]''\\ H,H\end{matrix}\right\}\Theta_2$$

expresses in a satisfactory manner these new reactions.

I have often insisted on the different functions which, in lactic acid, are fulfilled by the two atoms of hydrogen which we look upon as typical, and which I have separated in the preceding formula. Mr. Perkin,† has very cleverly expressed this idea, by saying that lactic acid is at once acid and alcohol. M. Wislicenus‡ has recently

---

$$\left.\begin{matrix}C_2H_4\\ H\end{matrix}\right\}\begin{matrix}CN\\ \Theta\end{matrix} + 2H_2\Theta \qquad \left.\begin{matrix}\left.\begin{matrix}C\Theta\cdot C_2H_4\\ H\end{matrix}\right\}\Theta\\ H\end{matrix}\right\}\Theta + NH_3$$

Monocyanhydric glycol. Lactic acid.

the lactic acid thus formed is identical with the paralactic acid extracted from meat. The synthesis of ordinary lactic acid has since been accomplished by M. Strecker by means of alanine obtained by the action of cyanhydric acid on aldehyde. M. Wislicenus has arrived at the same result by starting from aldehyde.

* $$\left.\begin{matrix}C_2H_5\\ Na\end{matrix}\right\}\Theta + C\Theta\cdot\Theta = C\Theta + \left.\begin{matrix}C_2H_4\\ Na,H\end{matrix}\right\}\Theta_2$$

Ethylate of sodium. Carbonic acid. Lactate of sodium.

† CHEMICAL NEWS, 1861, p. 82.

‡ *Annalen der Chemie und Pharmacie*, vol. cxxv., p. 41, and vol cxxviii., p. 1.

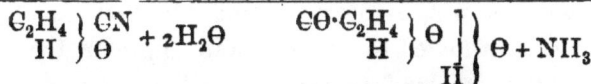

even tried to translate it into the notation, by writing the formula in question—

$$\left.\begin{matrix}(\mathrm{C}\Theta)'' \\ \left.\begin{matrix}(\mathrm{C}_2\mathrm{H}_4)'' \\ \mathrm{H}\end{matrix}\right\}\Theta \\ \mathrm{H}\end{matrix}\right\}\Theta$$

The two atoms of hydrogen here occupy perfectly distinct positions; one forms part of the group

$$\left.\begin{matrix}\mathrm{C}_2\mathrm{H}_4 \\ \mathrm{H}\end{matrix}\right\}\Theta$$

and cannot be replaced by an electro-positive metal; the other, the basic hydrogen, is outside the group.

By introducing into the formula of lactic acid the group, or typical residue, as he calls it,

$$\left.\begin{matrix}\mathrm{C}_2\mathrm{H}_4 \\ \mathrm{H}\end{matrix}\right\}\Theta$$

M. Wislicenus explains the experiment of the decomposition of monocyanhydric glycol.* He founds his formula upon a fact; he is in the right. But I question if this formula expresses as clearly as the more simple one the relationship of lactic acid to propoglycol, or the formation of chloride of lactyle and of the polylactic compounds, and whether the inconvenience caused by a complicated form is compensated by the advantages the formula offers in the interpretation of other reactions. We may be allowed to doubt it, and to prefer for ordinary use the simpler formulæ

$$\left.\begin{matrix}(\mathrm{C}\Theta\cdot\mathrm{C}_2\mathrm{H}_4)'' \\ \mathrm{H}\cdot\mathrm{H}\end{matrix}\right\}\Theta_2 \text{ and } \left.\begin{matrix}\mathrm{C}_3\mathrm{H}_4\Theta \\ \mathrm{H}\cdot\mathrm{H}\end{matrix}\right\}\Theta_2$$

in which the two typical residues $\mathrm{H}\Theta$ are placed together.

I think it should not be forgotten that the theory of types and the notation springing from it are marvellous instruments of explanation and classification, and that the services they have rendered to science arise

* See note † in page 94.

greatly from the simplicity of the idea and the clearness of the form. These advantages have caused it to be adopted by the authors of the most valuable works on organic chemistry that have appeared within the last few years—viz., by Weltzein in his remarkable "Systematic Table of the Organic Combinations," * by Limpricht,† in his excellent "Treatise," and above all by Kekulé in his admirable "Treatise on Organic Chemistry."‡ "But," it will be asked, "is this the only signification of the theory of types? Is it only a convenient expedient to explain reactions? Is it not subordinate to some general principle which is the cause of its existence?" These are important questions and require serious examination.

An eminent chemist some years ago made an attack upon the theory of types, which was more serious than might at first sight have appeared.§

"How can we admit," said M. Kolbe, "that nature could so restrict herself as to form all organic and inorganic combinations in the mould of four substances, chosen at hazard,—hydrogen, hydrochloric acid, water, and ammonia, and to produce nothing but variations on these four themes?"

"Further, what natural connexion is there between the majority of organic compounds, and water, hydrogen, or hydrochloric acid?"

According to Kolbe, these typical relationships are artificial and arbitrary, and he agrees to consider the

* "Systematische Zusammenstellung der organischen Verbindungen." By C. Weltzien. Brunswick. 1860.

† "Lehrbuch der organischen Chemie." By H. Limpricht. Brunswick. 1860.

‡ "Lehrbuch der organischen Chemie oder Chemie der Cohlenstoff Verbindungen." By Dr. Aug. Kekulé. Vol. i. Erlangen. 1859.

§ See chiefly Kolbe, "Ueber den natürlichen Zusammenhang der organischen mit den unorganischen Verbindungen," etc.—*Annalen der Chemie und Pharmacie*, vol. cxiii., p. 293.

organic combinations—that is to say, the combinations of carbon, as being derived from carbonic acid, which is the first source of them.

These objections are not without weight. I have replied to them * by showing that the types of hydrogen, water, and ammonia are not chosen at hazard, but represent three forms of combination, between which the theory can establish a connexion. We may in a manner reduce these three types to one, and refer them to hydrogen more or less condensed. Thus, water appears as hydrogen doubly condensed, in which the diatomic atom oxygen has taken the place of H_2. Ammonia appears as hydrogen condensed three times, in which the triatomic element nitrogen has taken the place of H_3. This idea is expressed by the following formulæ:—

H H	H Cl	Hydrochloric acid.
H_2H_2	$H_2\Theta''$	Water.
H_3H_3	H_3N'''	Ammonia.
H_4H_4	$H_4\text{C}^{\text{iv.}}$	Marsh gas.
H_5H_5	$Cl_5P^{\text{v.}}$	Perchloride of phosphorus.
H_6H_6	$Cl_6(Al_2)^{\text{vi.}}$	Chloride of aluminium.

Thus, whilst chlorine only possesses the power of replacing one atom of hydrogen, oxygen can replace two, nitrogen three, &c., and these differences in the power of substitution are represented in the preceding formulæ by the accents ′ ″ ‴, and the Roman figures iv., v., vi.†

But oxygen, which can replace two atoms of hydrogen, can also combine with two atoms of hydrogen; its power of combination is equal to its power of substitution, and

* *Répertoire de Chimie Pure*, vol. ii., p. 354, and *Répertoire de Chimie Pure*, vol. iii., p. 418.

† Since 1855 I have sought to point out and define the fundamental principle of the theory of types by showing that the tie which unites them consists in the different powers of substitution possessed by hydrogen, chlorine, oxygen, nitrogen, and phosphorus. I represented *tribasic* phosphorus by the formula P=ps (three small atoms triatomic).—*Annales de Chimie et de Physique*, 3rd series, vol. xliv., p. 305.

is double that of chlorine; it is diatomic. Similarly, nitrogen, which replaces three atoms of hydrogen, can also combine with three atoms of hydrogen; its combining power is triple that of chlorine; it is triatomic. We may then say, by giving another and a clearer form to the idea above expressed, that a water type exists, because there exists a diatomic element, oxygen; and that we are justified in admitting an ammonia type, because there exists a triatomic element, nitrogen.*

Thus the theory of types is subordinate to a fundamental principle which in a manner governs it, and upon which it depends. The types are not chosen at hazard, since they represent forms of combination determined by a fundamental property of the elements; their power of substitution, their combining power, their atomicity. It is evident that we might multiply them by following this train of ideas, and carry the number of fundamental types from three to five, as the table on the next page shows.

Nothing would prevent us, moreover, from admitting types resulting from the condensation of the preceding, and to combine them to represent compounds of a higher order. Two atoms of aluminium, by joining or combining with each other, acquire a power of combination = 6. Hence the condensed type Al_2Cl6.

* Kekulé, "Lehrbuch," vol. i., p. 114. A. Wurtz, "Nouvelles Observations sur la Theorie des Types."—*Répertoire de Chimie Pure*, vol. iii., p. 419.

HH' Hydrogen.	$H_2\Theta''$ Water.	H_3N''' Ammonia.
HCl' Hydrochloric acid.	H_2S'' Sulphuretted hydrogen	H_3P''' Phosphuretted hydrogen.
HBr' Hydrobromic acid.	H_2Se'' Selenluretted hydrogen	H_3As''' Arseniuretted hydrogen.
$K'Cl$ Chloride of potassium.	$HK\Theta''$ Hydrate of potassium.	Et_3N''' Triethylamine.
$Ag'Cl$ Chloride of silver.	$Ag_2\Theta''$ Oxide of silver.	Et_3P''' Triethyl-phosphine.
HEt' Hydride of ethyl.	$HEt\Theta''$ Hydrate of ethyl.	Cl_3As''' Chloride of arsenic.
$EtEt'$ Ethyl.	$Et_2\Theta''$ Oxide of ethyl.	Cl_3Sb''' Chloride of antimony.
$Et'Cl$ Chloride of ethyl.	Et_2S'' Sulphide of ethyl.	Cl_3Bo''' Chloride of boron.
	$\Theta a''\Theta''$ Oxide of calcium.	Cl_3Bi''' Chloride of bismuth.
	$(\Theta_2H_4)''\Theta''$ Oxide of ethylene.	Cl_3V''' Chloride of vanadium.
		$Cl_3(\Theta_3H_5)'''$ Trichloride of allyle.

$H_4\text{Ꞓ}$ iv. Marsh gas.	Cl_5P v. Perchloride of phosphorus.	Cl_6Al_2 vi. Chloride of aluminium.
$Cl_4\text{Ꞓ}^{iv}$ Perchloride of carbon.	ClH_4N^{v} Hydrochlorate of ammonia.	$\text{Ɵ}_3Al_2^{vi}$ Oxide of aluminium.
$\text{Ɵ}''_2\text{Ꞓ}^{iv}$ Carbonic acid.	IH_4P^{v} Hydriodide of phosphuretted hydrogen.	$Cl_6Fe_2^{vi}$ Chloride of iron.
$\text{S̶}''_2\text{Ꞓ}^{iv}$ Sulphide of carbon.	$Et_3P\text{S̶}^{v}$ Sulphide of triethyl phosphine.	$\text{Ɵ}_3Fe_2^{vi}$ Oxide of iron.
$Cl_4\text{S̶i}^{iv}$ Chloride of silicium.	Cl_5Sb^{v} Perchloride of antimony.	$Cl_6(\text{Ꞓ}_6H_3)^{vi}$ Trichlorated trichloride of benzine.
$\text{Ɵ}_2\text{S̶i}^{iv}$ Silicic acid.	$I_2Et_3Sb^{v}$ Di-iodide of triethylstibine.	$Cl_6\text{Ꞓ}_2^{vi}$ Sesquichloride of carbon.
$Et_4\text{S̶i}^{iv}$ Silicium-ethyl.	$ClEt_4As^{v}$ Chloride of tetrethylarsine	$H_6\text{Ꞓ}_2^{vi}$ Hydride of ethyl.
$Cl_4\text{S̶n}^{iv}$ Perchloride of tin.	$Cl_2Et_3As^{v}$ Dichloride of triethylarsine.	$\text{Ɵ}''H_4\text{Ꞓ}_2^{vi}$ Aldehyde.
Et_4Sn^{iv} Stannethyl.	$Cl_3Et_2As^{v}$ Trichloride of diethylarsine.	
Cl_4Ti^{iv} Chloride of titanium.	Cl_4EtAs^{v} Tetrachloride of monethylarsine.	
$Cl_4\text{Z̶r}^{iv}$ Chloride of zirconium.		
$Br_4\begin{bmatrix}\text{Ꞓ}_3H_3\\ \text{Ꞓ}_3H_5\end{bmatrix}^{iv}$ Tetrabromide of allyle.		

The organic combinations might all be derived from the type $\text{Ꞓ}H_4$.*

* We should also have the following formulæ:—

$$\text{Ꞓ}\left\{\begin{matrix}H\\H\\H\\H\end{matrix}\right. \quad \text{Ꞓ}\left\{\begin{matrix}H\\H\\H\\Cl\end{matrix}\right. \quad \text{Ꞓ}\left\{\begin{matrix}H\\Cl\\Cl\\Cl\end{matrix}\right. \quad \text{Ꞓ}\left\{\begin{matrix}H\\H\\H\\(H\Theta)'\end{matrix}\right.$$

Marsh gas. Chloride of methyl. Chloroform. Hydrate of methyl.

$$\text{Ꞓ}\left\{\begin{matrix}H\\H\\H\\(\text{Ꞓ}H_3.\Theta)'\end{matrix}\right. \quad \text{Ꞓ}\left\{\begin{matrix}H\\\Theta''\\(H\Theta)'\end{matrix}\right. \quad \text{Ꞓ}\left\{\begin{matrix}N'''\\H\end{matrix}\right. \quad \text{Ꞓ}\left\{\begin{matrix}N'''\\(H\Theta)'\end{matrix}\right. \text{\&c}$$

Oxide of methyl. Formic acid. Hydrocyanic acid. Cyanic acid.

$$\text{Ꞓ}\left\{\begin{matrix}(\text{Ꞓ}H_3)'\\H\\H\\H\end{matrix}\right. \quad \text{Ꞓ}\left\{\begin{matrix}(\text{Ꞓ}H_3)'\\H\\H\\Cl\end{matrix}\right. \quad \text{Ꞓ}\left\{\begin{matrix}(\text{Ꞓ}H_3)'\\\Theta\\H\end{matrix}\right. \quad \text{Ꞓ}\left\{\begin{matrix}(\text{Ꞓ}H_3)'\\H\\H\\(H\Theta)'\end{matrix}\right.$$

Hydride of ethyl. Chloride of ethyl. Aldehyd. Hydrate of ethyl.

$$\text{Ꞓ}\left\{\begin{matrix}\text{Ꞓ}H_3\\H\\H\\(\text{Ꞓ}_2H_5.\Theta)'\end{matrix}\right. \quad \text{Ꞓ}\left\{\begin{matrix}\text{Ꞓ}H_3\\\Theta''\\(H\Theta)'\end{matrix}\right. \quad \text{Ꞓ}\left\{\begin{matrix}(H\Theta)'\\H\\(\text{Ꞓ}H_2)'\\(H\Theta)'\end{matrix}\right. \quad C\left\{\begin{matrix}(H\Theta)'\\H\\(\text{Ꞓ}H\Theta)'\text{ \&c.}\\(H\Theta)'\text{ \&c.}\end{matrix}\right.$$

Oxyde of ethyl. Acetic acid. Glycol. Glycolic acid.

For the formulæ of the higher series it would be sufficient to replace the group $(\text{Ꞓ}H_3)$ by the more complicated alcoholic groups; and nothing prevents us from decomposing the latter, and from writing ethyl—

$$\begin{bmatrix}\text{Ꞓ}H_2\\\text{Ꞓ}H_3\end{bmatrix} = \text{Ꞓ}_2H_6 - H, \text{\&c.}$$

The preceding compounds are saturated; they are derived from the saturated type $\text{Ꞓ}H_4$. As for those that are not so, they may be referred to the type of carbonic oxide $\text{Ꞓ}\Theta$, which is equal to $\text{Ꞓ}H_2$.

$$\text{Ꞓ}\Theta \text{ or } \text{Ꞓ}\left\{\begin{matrix}H\\H\end{matrix}\right. \quad \text{Ꞓ}\left\{\begin{matrix}(CH)'\\H\end{matrix}\right. \quad C\left\{\begin{matrix}(\text{Ꞓ}H_3)'\\H\end{matrix}\right.$$

Type. Acetylene. Ethylene.†

$$\text{Ꞓ}\left\{\begin{matrix}(\text{Ꞓ}_2H_3)'\\H\end{matrix}\right. \quad \text{Ꞓ}\left\{\begin{matrix}(\text{Ꞓ}_2H_5)'\\H\end{matrix}\right.$$

Allylene. Propylene.

But it seems to me that such formulæ do not offer any advantages, at least for explanation, over the generally-used typical formulæ. They are less simple, and, after all, they differ less than might be thought. A distinguished chemist, M. Debus, has just proposed for acetic acid the formula given in this system. I may be allowed to remark that the two formulæ

$$\left.\begin{matrix}\text{Ꞓ}\Theta,\text{Ꞓ}H_3\\H\end{matrix}\right\}\Theta \text{ and } \text{Ꞓ}\left\{\begin{matrix}\text{Ꞓ}H_3\\\Theta\\H\Theta\end{matrix}\right.$$

do not differ essentially from each other; the group $H\Theta$, which is shown there (as in those which M. Kolbe employs), only represents

† Formula of Kolbe.

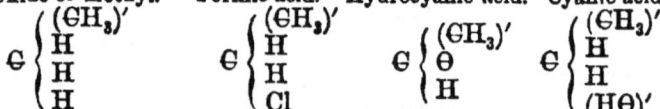

But it must be remarked that this type might be referred to the doubly condensed water type.*

As for the carbonic acid type, as adopted by M. Kolbe, it is confounded with the water type.†

And it is evident that the water type, $H_2\Theta$, has this advantage over the type $(\text{C}\Theta)'\Theta''$, that it permits the introduction of a single monatomic group in place of an atom of hydrogen: H_2 is divisible, $(\text{C}\Theta)''$ is not.

However this may be, what we have sought to establish seems to be proved—viz., that the principle of the atomicity of the elements forms a natural connection between the types.

In the following pages we shall seek to define this principle, and show its importance in reference to the general theories of chemistry.

---

the typical residue $H_2\Theta - H$. The group, $\text{C}H_3$, exists in both; and the second atom of carbon is in direct connection with the atom of oxygen. Thus, whether acetic acid be referred to the type water or to the type $\text{C}H_4$, almost the same groups are admitted in it; and how could it be otherwise, since both formulæ are founded on the interpretation of the reactions of acetic acid.

* $\left.\begin{matrix}H_2\\H_2\end{matrix}\right\}\Theta_2$ $\left.\begin{matrix}H_2\\H_2\end{matrix}\right\}\text{C}$ $\left.\begin{matrix}\Theta''\\\Theta''\end{matrix}\right\}\text{C}$; C^{iv}. equals Θ_4 Θ_2 equal H_2

† $[\text{C}_2\Theta_2]\Theta_2$ or $\text{C}\Theta''.\Theta$ equal $H_2\Theta''$.

SECTION III.

Atomicity of Radicals.

THE principle of atomicity was established in the science slowly and by degrees. The germ of it is contained in the law of multiple proportions, and above all in the following laws of Gay-Lussac concerning the volumetric relations which regulate the combinations of the gaseous bodies:—

1 volume of chlorine combines with 1 volume of hydrogen.

1 volume of oxygen combines with 2 volumes of hydrogen.

1 volume of nitrogen combines with 3 volumes of hydrogen.

The combining capacity of the three bodies for hydrogen is, therefore, essentially different. Chemists were less struck with the importance of this deduction, because the law of multiple proportions taught them also that the combining power of one element for another is exerted by degrees. How could they have given the attention it deserved to the fact of the triatomicity of the nitrogen in ammonia, when they knew that 1 volume of nitrogen combined also with half a volume of oxygen, which equals 1 volume of hydrogen?

Besides, the idea of the atomicity or equivalency of atoms could only attain development when the notion of the atom was clearly separated from that of the equivalent; and we know what confusion there has long existed on this point. But, when this distinction was established, it was seen at once that the simple or compound radicals were not all equivalent to each other, and did not possess the same power of substitution or combination. In his article on thiacetic acid, Kekulé mentioned the *bibasic nature of sulphur*.[*]

Developing the idea of Dr. Williamson on the substitution value of the group $S\Theta_2$, in sulphuric acid,

$$\left.\begin{array}{c} S\Theta_2 \\ H_2 \end{array}\right\} \Theta_2$$

where it replaces 2 atoms of hydrogen, Dr. Odling[†] applied this view to other compound radicals, and, which is of considerable importance, to a certain number of elements. He remarked that, whilst potassium displaces only 1 atom of the hydrogen of water, and, consequently, has a substitution value only equal to that of hydrogen, bismuth, for example, possesses a substitution value equal to that of 3 atoms of hydrogen. He put this view in a very clear form by representing the composition of potassa and oxide of bismuth by the formulæ

$$\left.\begin{array}{c} K' \\ H' \end{array}\right\} O'' \quad \text{and} \quad \left.\begin{array}{c} Bi''' \\ Bi''' \end{array}\right\} 3O''$$

in which the accents show precisely this substitution value,—now called atomicity.

I have called attention myself to the differences which exist between the combining powers of the elements, in an article on the organic radicals, where I speak of nitrogen and phosphorus as " tribasic radicals."[‡]

This was the origin of the theory of the atomicity of the elements. But this theory acquired a real importance only when the notion of polyatomic radicals was admitted into organic chemistry. I believe I was the first to introduce it, and my deductions were based, in the first place, on M. Berthelot's works on glycerine, and then on my own researches upon the glycols. It

* *Annalen der Chemie und Pharmacie*, vol. xc., p. 310. July, 1865.

† "On the Constitution of Acids and Salts."—*Quarterly Journal of the Chemical Society*, vol. vii., p. 1, January. 1855.

‡ *Annales de Chimie et de Physique*, 3rd series, vol. xliv., p. 360.

will be advisable, then, to show the logical connection and successive development of all these ideas; to define, in the first place, what is meant by this expression, now so often used, of polyatomic radicals; and to explain how the notion of radical compounds, in general, is derived from that of the saturation of bodies.

Saturation.—A considerable number of carbides of hydrogen are known. Now, experience teaches us that in none of these bodies does the proportion of this element exceed that indicated by the general formula

$$C_nH_{2n+2}.$$

Thus, the carbides richest in hydrogen that are known are the following:—

CH_4	Hydride of	methyl.
C_2H_6	"	ethyl.
C_3H_8	"	propyl.
C_4H_{10}	"	butyl.
C_5H_{12}	"	amyl.
C_6H_{14}	"	hexyl.
C_7H_{16}	"	heptyl.
C_8H_{18}	"	octyl.
C_9H_{20}	"	nonyl.
$C_{10}H_{22}$	"	decyl.

These carbides of hydrogen are called saturated, because they cannot enter into direct combination with any other element. Taken as a whole, they are quite indifferent; they can only be modified by substitution.

Let us take the hydride of propyl C_3H_8. Bromine can only react on this body on condition of taking away some of its hydrogen;

$$C_3H_8 + Br_2 = C_3H_7Br + HBr.$$

In this first reaction the hydrocarbon C_3H_8 acts as an hydride; the group C_3H_7 has passed intact from the primitive carbide of hydrogen into the brominated compound C_3H_7Br. The latter is saturated like the former; the sum of the atoms of hydrogen and bromine is equal to 8. It acts like the bromide of a radical C_3H_7, and we see that this radical is derived from the saturated carbide C_3H_8 by subtracting 1 atom of hydrogen. This being removed, the remainder, $C_3H_7 = C_3H_8 - H$, is no longer saturated. It acts as a monatomic radical; it can replace 1 atom of hydrogen; it can also combine with 1 atom of hydrogen, or with the equivalent of 1 atom of hydrogen—for example, with 1 atom of chlorine, of bromine, of iodine, of cyanogen, of amidogen, of propyl, &c. Its saturation is then complete. The following compounds in which it enters are all saturated:—

$(C_3H_7)'Cl$	Chloride of propyl.
$(C_3H_7)'Br$	Bromide of propyl.
$(C_3H_7)'I$	Iodide of propyl.
$(C_3H_7)'(HO)'$	Propylic alcohol.
$(C_3H_7)'Cy$	Cyanide of propyl.
$(C_3H_7)'(H_2N)'$	Propylamine.
$(C_3H_7)'(C_3H_7)'$	Free propyl.

The carbide C_3H_6, propylene, differs from the saturated carbide C_3H_8 by containing 2 atoms less hydrogen. To complete its saturation it is then necessary for it to combine with the equivalent of 2 atoms of hydrogen. We know, in fact, that it can combine directly with 2 atoms of chlorine or bromine;

$(C_3H_6)''$	Propylene.
$(C_3H_6)''Cl_2$	Chloride of propylene.
$(C_3H_6)''Br_2$	Bromide of propylene.

It has then a combining power equal to 2 atoms of hydrogen, and it can replace 2 atoms of hydrogen. This is expressed by saying that it acts as a diatomic radical.

In the following compounds it takes the place of 2 atoms of hydrogen;

$(C_3H_6)''(H\Theta)_2$ Propylglycol.*
$(C_3H_6)''(NH_2)_2$ Propylene-diamine.

Now, supposing the saturated carbide C_3H_8 to lose 3 atoms of hydrogen, then, to complete its saturation, it must combine with the equivalent of 3 atoms of hydrogen; it must be able to replace 3 atoms of hydrogen; and in a word, to function as a triatomic radical. It acts thus in the following compounds:—

$(C_3H_5)'''Cl_3$	Trichlorhydrine.
$(C_3H_5)'''Br_3$	Tribromhydrine.
$(C_3H_5)'''(H\Theta)'Cl_2$	Dichlorhydrine.
$(C_3H_5)'''(H\Theta_2)'Cl$	Monochlorhydrine.
$(C_3H_5)'''3(H\Theta)'$	Glycerine.

In short, the atomicity of a hydrocarbon radical depends upon its state of saturation. For each atom of hydrogen that is removed from the saturated hydrocarbon, the residue or remainder, which acts as a radical, advances a step in atomicity.†

* This formula differs nothing from the typical formula

$$\left.\begin{matrix}(C_3H_6)''\\ H_2\end{matrix}\right\}\Theta_2$$

This latter would express that propylene is substituted for two atoms of hydrogen. The other formula would rather imply the analagous idea that propylene has a combining power =2. In fact, each of the groups $H\Theta$ equals 1 atom of hydrogen, since they require H to form water. The residue $(H\Theta)' = H_2\Theta - H$ acts as a monoatomic radical. With regard to this, it may be useful to add that this residue in no way represents oxygenated water, as certain chemists declare. The latter is $H_2\Theta_2 = (H\Theta)'(H\Theta')$, and contains the remainder of *two* molecules of water which have lost two atoms of hydrogen $H_4\Theta_2 - H_2$.

† I think I was the first to express the idea that the atomicity of a hydrocarbon radical depends upon the amount of hydrogen that this radical has lost. The following is a remark I made in April, 1855,

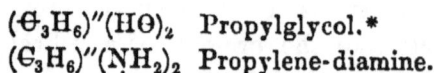

C_3H_8 Saturated hydrocarbon.

$C_3H_8 - H = (C_3H_7)'$ Monatomic radical propyl.

$C_3H_8 - H_2 = (C_3H_6)''$ Diatomic radical propylene.

$C_3H_8 - H_3 = (C_3H_5)'''$ Triatomic radical glyceryle.

These considerations are of great importance, and it is advisable to define them clearly and to generalise them.

Hydrogen combines, as we know, with 1 atom of chlorine, 1 atom of bromine, &c. It is a monatomic element; it has a combining power represented by 1 ; it represents a unit of combination or affinity. Every time, then, that we remove from any combination whatever, that is saturated, 1 atom of hydrogen, or a monatomic element like hydrogen, or a group equivalent to 1 atom of hydrogen, we lessen by one unit the sum of the affinities which reside in all the elements of this combination, and which are there satisfied. The residue or remainder then acts like a monatomic radical. And again, if we remove from any saturated compound 2 atoms of hydrogen, or chlorine, &c., the remainder will act as a diatomic radical.

Here are some examples : —

$$H_2\Theta - H = (H\Theta)'.$$
$$H_3N - H = (H_2N)'.$$
Amidogen.
$$NH\Theta_3 - (H\Theta)' = (N\Theta_2)'.$$
Nitric acid.   Hyponitride.

(*Annales de Chemie et de Physique*, 3rd series, vol. xliii., p. 492), in a note in which, for the first time, the radical C_3H_5 was considered as triatomic:—"If we express the constitution of propylic alcohol by the formula

$$\left.\begin{array}{c} C_6H_7 \\ H \end{array}\right\} O_2,$$

in which the radical C_6H_7 rep'aces 1 equivalent of hydrogen, we see then that the group $C_6H_5 = C_6H_7 - H_2$ can replace 3 equivalents of hydrogen, and thus form the junction between 3 molecules of water."

$C_2H_3ClO_2 - Cl$ Chloracetic acid.	=	$(C_2H_3O_2)'$. Oxacetyle.
$C_2H_4O_2 - (HO)'$ Acetic acid.	=	$(C_2H_3O)'$. Acetyle.
$C_2H_4Br_2 - Br$	=	$(C_2H_4Br)'$. Bromethyle.
$C_2H_6O_2 - (HO)'$ Glycol.	=	$(C_2H_5O)'$. Oxethyle.
$(CO)Cl_2 - Cl_2$ Chloride of carbonyle.	=	$(CO)''$. Carbonyle (Carbonic oxide).
$C_2H_2O_4 - 2(HO)'$ Oxalic acid.	=	$(C_2O_2)''$. Oxalyle.
$C_4H_6O_4 - 2(HO)'$ Succinic acid.	=	$(C_4H_4O_2)''$. Succinyle.
$C_4H_6O_4 - H_2$ Succinic acid.	=	$(C_4H_4O_4)''$. Fumaric and malic acids.
$C_5H_8O_4 - H_2$ Pyro-tartaric acid.	=	$(C_5H_6O_4)''$. Citraconic acid and isomeric forms.
$C_2H_6O - H_2$ Alcohol.	=	$(C_2H_4O)''$. Aldehyde.

Reciprocally, the atomicity of a residue or of a radical will diminish a step by each addition of an atom of hydrogen, or, in general, of an element or group representing a unit of combination.

$$(CO)'' + H = (COH)'$$
$$(C_2H_4)'' + H = (C_2H_5)'$$
$$(C_2H_4)'' + Br = (C_2H_4Br)'$$
$$(C_2H_4)'' + (HO)' = (C_2H_5O)'$$
$$(C_2H_5)' + O'' = (C_2H_5O)'$$
$$(C_3H_5)''' + O'' = (C_3H_5O)'$$
$$(C_2H_2)^{iv} + Br_2 = (C_2H_2Br_2)''.$$

It will be useful to define the functions that these so-formed remainders or residues can fulfil, either as groups possessing a certain substitution value, or as radicals properly so-called, capable of entering into direct combination. These considerations will give us an opportunity, not only of entering further into the notion of the atomicity of the radicals, but also of defining the meaning, at present rather vague, of the word radical.

We must first observe that none of the monatomic remainders or radicals, hydrocarbons or otherwise, that we have hitherto considered, exist in a free state; the same remark applies to the triatomic radicals, and in general to the (carburetted) organic radicals of uneven atomicity. The radicals which are of even atomicity, on the contrary, such as ethylene and its homologous compounds, and carbonyle, can exist in a free state and enter into direct combination with the elements. This is a consequence of the atomicity of the elements, as we shall prove further on. For the time being we will merely state the fact; the monatomic radicals, as such, do not exist in a free state. To become free they must combine, in a manner, with themselves; their molecule being double, like that of the monatomic elements themselves. Thus, if we remove H from $ϴ_2H_6$, we have a residue $(ϴ_2H_5)'$ whose value of combination and substitution = 1, and which therefore can replace one atom of the hydrogen in water; but, directly it is set free, this group combines with itself to form free ethyl—

$$ϴ_2H_5 + ϴ_2H_5 = ϴ_4H_{10},$$

a saturated combination. Similarly, if from water

$$\left.\begin{matrix} H \\ H \end{matrix}\right\} Θ$$

we remove H, the remainder, $(HΘ)'$, possesses a substitution value = 1. In oxygenated water, $H_2Θ_2$, this residue or remainder is contained twice; it is in a manner combined with itself—

$$H_2Θ_2 = \left\{\begin{matrix} (HΘ)' \\ (HΘ)'. \end{matrix}\right.$$

The group $(HΘ)'$ equals a unit of combination; so it is

represented in the preceding table in the same way as hydrogen, chlorine, bromine, &c.

The oxacetyle remainder,

$$(C_2H_3O_2)' = C_2H_3ClO_2 - Cl,$$

which represents chloracetic acid minus chlorine, acts as a monatomic radical; it enters as such into the formula—

$$\left.\begin{matrix} (C_2H_3O_2)' \\ H \\ H \end{matrix}\right\} N$$

which expresses the composition of glycocol. By producing this body under the influence of ammonia, according to the beautiful reaction discovered by M. Cahours, the chloracetic acid acts, in reality, like the chloride of the monatomic radical oxyacetyle:

$$\underset{\text{Chloracetic acid.}}{[C_2H_3O_2]'Cl} + \left.\begin{matrix} H \\ H \\ H \end{matrix}\right\} N = HCl + \underset{\text{Glycocol.}}{\left.\begin{matrix} [C_2H_3O_2]' \\ H \\ H \end{matrix}\right\} N}$$

It acts in the same way when it is transformed, under the influence of potash, into glycolic acid, according to MM. R. Hoffmann and Kekulé:

$$\underset{\text{Chloracetic acid.}}{[C_2H_3O_2]'Cl} + \left.\begin{matrix} H \\ K \end{matrix}\right\} O = HCl. + \underset{\text{Glycolate of potassium.}}{\left.\begin{matrix} [C_2H_3O_2]' \\ K \end{matrix}\right\} O}$$

Fumaric and malic acids* differ from succinic acid by containing two atoms less hydrogen, and if the latter acid be saturated, as everything seems to prove, the other two can only arrive at a state of saturation by combining with two elements, or with two groups representing two units of combination. Thus, according to the beautiful researches of M. Kekulé, they can absorb directly either two atoms of hydrogen to form succinic

* See list on page 110.

acid, or three atoms of bromine to form dibromosuccinic acid. As M. Kekulé has shown, there is between fumaric acid and dibromosuccinic acid exactly the same relation as between ethylene and bromide of ethylene.*

$(C_4H_4O_4)'' + Br_2$	$=$	$C_4H_4O_4Br_2$
Fumaric acid.		Dibromosuccinic acid.
$(C_2H_4)'' + Br_2$	$=$	$C_2H_4Br_2$
Ethylene.		Dibromide of ethylene.

Ethylene and fumaric acid combine directly with bromine to become saturated; they each act the part of a radical in this reaction.

The same remarks apply to citraconic, itaconic, and mesaconic acids, which differ from pyrotartaric acid by two atoms of hydrogen, and which can combine directly with two atoms of bromide.†

We might extend these considerations to a great number of other compounds that are not saturated. Let it suffice to show by some examples that a number of reactions, to all appearance the most diverse, have in reality a great likeness, when considered from the general point of view we have just explained, and which establishes a correlation between the atomicity of the radicals and their state of saturation:

$C_2H_4 + H_2$	$=$	C_2H_6 (Berthelot)
$C_2H_4 + Br_2$	$=$	$C_2H_4Br_2$
$Zn + Br_2$	$=$	$ZnBr_2$
$C_2H_4 + HBr$	$=$	C_2H_5Br (Berthelot)
$NH_3 + HBr$	$=$	NH_4Br
$PCl_3 + Cl_2$	$=$	PCl_5
$C_2H_4O + H_2$ Aldehyde.	$=$	C_2H_6O (A. Wurtz) Alcohol.
$C_6H_{10} + H_2I_2$ Allyle.	$=$	$C_6H_{12}I_2$ (A. Wurtz) Dihydriodate of allyle.

* *Annales de Chimie et de Physique*, 3rd series, vol. lxiii., p. 371.

† Kekulé, *Annales de Chimie et de Physique*, 3rd series, vol. xlv. p. 117.

$$\underset{\text{Acrolein.}}{C_3H_4O} + H_4 = \underset{\text{Propylic Alcohol.}}{C_3H_8O} \text{ (Linnemann)}$$

$$\underset{\text{Hydrocyanic acid.}}{C_2NH} + H_4 = \underset{\text{Methyl-amine.}}{C_2NH_5} \text{ (Mendius)}$$

We may say that all bodies which have the property of uniting directly with 1 molecule of hydrogen, chlorine, bromine, hydrobromic acid, &c., act as diatomic radicals, in the same manner as olefiant gas or zinc.

All these radicals are of even atomicity, and exist in a free state. Those of uneven atomicity cannot exist as such in a free state. They are residues which can enter into combination, and which then possess a substitution value in accordance with their state of saturation. Such are ethyl and its homologous compounds, allyle and its homologous compounds, glyceryle, &c. As soon as they are set free they double their molecule, and combine, as it were, with themselves.

$$\left.\begin{matrix}(C_3H_5)' \\ (C_3H_5)'\end{matrix}\right\} = C_6H_{10}$$

Free allyl.

A very important remark occurs with regard to these latter radicals; some of them are at once monatomic and triatomic. This requires some explanation.

Propylene, C_3H_6, is not saturated, but it can exist in a free state. If, then, we take from it 1 atom of hydrogen, it will require 1 unit of combination to return to the state in which it existed as propylene. In this manner, the remainder, $C_3H_6 - H = C_3H_5$, can act as a monatomic radical. But if, instead of comparing it with propylene, which is in a state of incomplete saturation or unstable equilibrium as it were, we compare it with hydride of propyl C_3H_8, which is the saturated compound of the group, we see that it differs from it by 3 atoms of hydrogen; it can then act also as a triatomic radical. The same remarks apply to the homologous compounds of allyle, as will be seen from the following examples :—

CH	(C_2H_3)	C_3H_5
Formene.	Aldehydene.	Allyle.

$(CH)'''Cl_3$	$(C_2H_3)'Cl$	$(C_2H_3)'''Cl_3$	$(C_3H_5)'Br$	$(C_3H_5)'''Br_3$
Chloroform.	Chloride of aldehydene (chlorated ethylene).	Trichloride of aldehydene (chlorated chloride of ethylene).	Bromide of allyle.	Tribromide of allyle.

$$\left.\begin{array}{c}CH)''' \\ C_2H_5)_3\end{array}\right\}\Theta_3 \quad \left.\begin{array}{c}(C_2H_3)' \\ H\end{array}\right\}\Theta \quad \left.\begin{array}{c}(C_2H_3)''' \\ H_3\end{array}\right\}\Theta_3 \quad \left.\begin{array}{c}(C_3H_5)' \\ H\end{array}\right\}\Theta \quad \left.\begin{array}{c}(C_3H_5)''' \\ H_3\end{array}\right\}\Theta_3$$

Ethylate of formene.	Hydrate of aldehydene (acetyleuic alcohol).	Ethylic glycerine (unknown).	Allylic alcohol.	Glycerine.

Other radicals are at once diatomic and tetratomic ; thus the acetylene of M. Berthelot, and its homologous compounds, appear to combine sometimes with 2, and sometimes with 4 atoms of bromine (Reboul). This may be readily understood, for the carbide C_2H_2 is diatomic with regard to ethylene C_2H_4 ; it is tetratomic with regard to hydride of ethyl C_2H_6. It can then, to arrive at the state of saturation, pass through two stages, as it were. The first brings it to the family of ethylene, the second to that of hydride of ethyl.

SECTION IV.

Atomicity of the Elements.

The notion of saturation has given a theoretical basis to the considerations relating to the atomicity of the radicals. It has become the starting point of a still more important theory: that of the atomicity of the elements.

M. Kekulé, in an important article published in 1858,* first proved that carbon ought to be looked upon as a tetratomic element, for, said he, when we consider the simplest saturated compounds of carbon we see that the smallest quantity of carbon that can enter into a compound—that is to say, 1 atom of carbon—requires invariably 4 atoms of a monatomic element or 2 atoms of a diatomic element; in a word, that the elements combined with 1 atom of carbon represent 4 units of chemical force. It is thus in the following combinations.

$\overset{IV}{C}H_4$	Marsh gas.
CCl_4	Perchloride of carbon.
CH_3Cl	Chloride of methyl.
CH_2Cl_2	Chlorated chloride of methyl.
$CHCl_3$	Chloroform.
CO''_2	Carbonic acid.
$CC''lO_2$	Chloride of carbonyl.
CS''_2	Carbonic sulphide.

But if we take series containing several atoms of carbon, we must admit, according to M. Kekulé, that the latter are themselves united by a portion of the

* Ueber die Constitution und die Metamorphosen der Chemischen Verbindungen und über die chemische Natur des Kohlenstoffs. *Annalen der Chemie und Pharmacie*, vol. cvi., p. 136.

force existing in them. Thus, in all the saturated combinations which contain 2 atoms of carbon, 1 atom of carbon is combined directly with another atom of carbon and exchanges with it a unit of chemical force, in such a way that of the 8 units of chemical force which reside in 2 atoms of carbon, 2 units are satisfied by the combination of carbon with carbon, and there remain only 6 which are, so to say, disposable. On this account 2 atoms of carbon can never take more than 6 atoms of a monatomic element, therefore the body C_2H_6 constitutes the hydrocarbide limit of the series of combinations of carbon and hydrogen which contain 2 atoms of carbon. M. Kekulé represents this partial saturation of carbon by carbon by a diagram* similar to the following:—

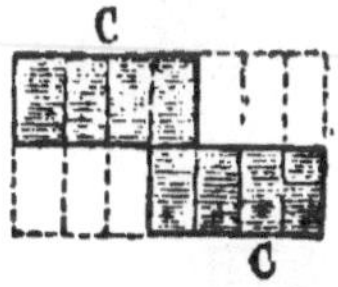

It will be seen that the two atoms of carbon are so placed that one overlaps the other. The two atoms are there made to touch for a quarter of their lengths, in order to indicate that they exchange a quarter of their affinities.

The six atoms of hydrogen arrange themselves round this framework of carbon so as to occupy the six vacant places, and are bounded by the dotted lines of the preceding figure—

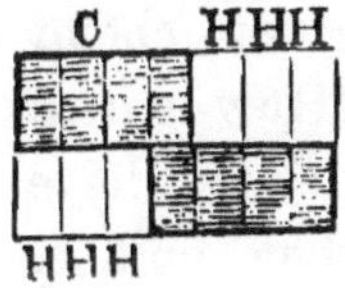

* It is as well to point out that this figure and those following do not represent in any manner either the form or the position of the atoms. They simply indicate their mutual relationships, and to a certain extent the points of junction of the affinities. Each compartment represents a unit of chemical force or affinity.

As we advance in the series each atom of carbon unites itself in some way to another atom of carbon, and with these atoms is also increased the number of spaces where the atoms of hydrogen can joint on in their turn, since the affinities of the carbon have there remained free.

Thus, as all the atoms of carbon touch, and each loses an affinity by its contact (its combination) with each of its neighbours (except the two last, which only lose one, since they only have one neighbour), it is evident that the greatest number of atoms of hydrogen which can join on to this chain of atoms of carbon will be twice the sum of the latter, plus two. This explains the formation of the saturated series $ЄnH_{2n+2}$. If necessary, we can convince ourselves that it must be so by continuing the construction of the figure given above, which, it must be understood, represents neither the form of the atoms nor that of the molecule.

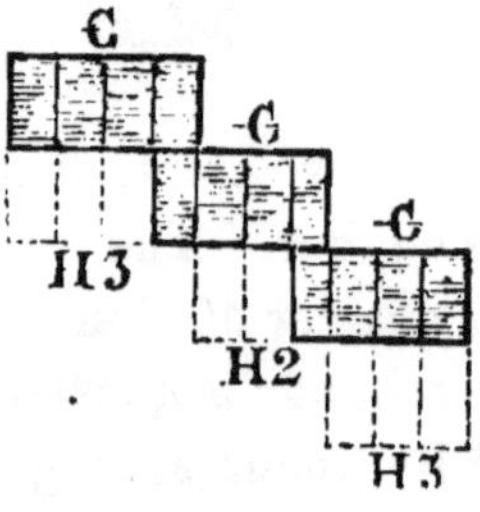

The idea of the combination of carbon with carbon is as natural and legitimate as that of the combination of hydrogen with hydrogen or of oxygen with oxygen (page 54). A most important chemical fact testifies in favour of this idea. How is it that marsh gas has not a single polymere? It cannot have any. For how could several atoms of carbon hold together when all the affinities of each of them were satisfied by hydrogen? By adding H_2 to $Є_2H_6$ we do not make $Є_2H_8$; we must necessarily make two molecules of $ЄH_4$, which cannot unite because in each of them all the affinities are satisfied. Thus it is that the series in which tetratomic carbon is entirely saturated by hydrogen is only represented by one term—marsh gas—and that in the carbides of hydrogen, which contain several atoms of carbon, the ratio of one to four between the number of these atoms and those of hydrogen is never reached. We know, in fact, that the carbides richest in hydrogen are,

$$n\text{C}H_4 - H_{(2n-2)}$$

which means that in a carbide containing *n* atoms of carbon, $2n-2$ affinities or units of combination are employed to connect the atoms of carbon with each other.

But the carbides of hydrogen are not always saturated, and when this is the case, we might imagine that one or more atoms of carbon would manifest the combining power that this element exerts in oxide of carbon.*

This deserves some consideration.

Oxide of carbon contains a single atom of carbon, and a single atom of oxygen; carbon there acts as a diatomic element, for it is combined with one atom of a diatomic element.

Suppose now that 2 atoms of diatomic carbon exchange 2 affinities, 2 others remain free and can unite with 2 atoms of hydrogen. We may thus represent the constitution of acetylene C_2H_2.

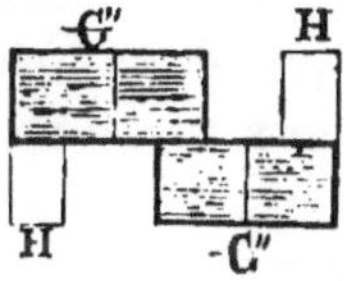

But we know that oxide of carbon can combine directly with oxygen and with chlorine; diatomic carbon passes then to the state of tetratomic carbon. Its affinities were, so to say, lying dormant; they awake, and we see

* The idea that carbon can act sometimes as a tetratomic and sometimes as a diatomic element was first suggested by M. Couper.—*Annales de Chimie et de Physique*, 3rd series, vol. liii., p. 459.

them completely satisfied in carbonic acid and in chloride of carbonyle (chloroxycarbonic gas). This being allowed, it seems natural to suppose that carbon, which is diatomic in oxide of carbon and tetratomic in carbonic acid, may enter into organic combinations, as, for example, in many carbides of hydrogen, sometimes as a diatomic and sometimes as a tetratomic element. This latter case is shown in the saturated carbides of the series G_nH_{2n+2}. But in certain carbonated hydrogens less rich in hydrogen, one or more atoms of carbon exist in the state of a diatomic element whilst the other atoms are tetratomic. This is why these non-saturated carbides can enter into direct combination with chlorine, bromine, or even hydrogen; the diatomic carbon which they contain tends to become tetratomic carbon, as in the case of oxide of carbon becoming oxychloride. Let us take one example to define this idea. In olefiant gas we must have one atom of diatomic carbon and 1 atom of tetratomic carbon. These 2 atoms being united, the first combines with 1 atom of hydrogen and the second with 3.

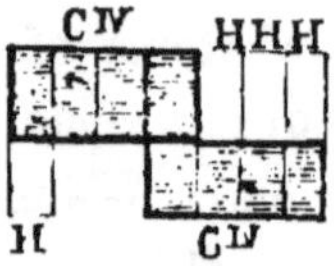

But when chlorine intervenes, the affinities of the diatomic carbon are excited, and the two atoms of chlorine unite with the non-saturated element.

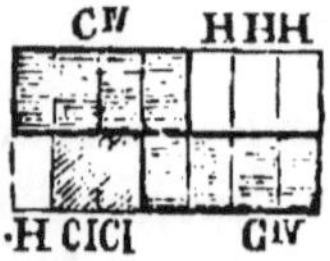

Another case may occur. There are carbides of hydrogen, such as naphthaline $\text{G}_{10}H_8$ which are very far from a state of saturation, and which yet show no great tendency to arrive at it. It is doubtless on account of several atoms of tetratomic carbon being joined together so as to exchange *two* affinities. Thus, in the following system the intermediate atom of carbon is entirely saturated by the affinities of the other 2 atoms of carbon—

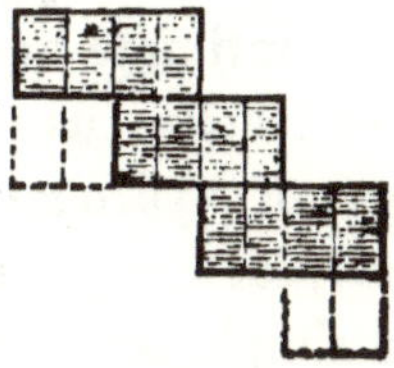

The latter each preserve two affinities free.

I do not wish to pursue further these developments, and I think the preceding instances will suffice to show the importance of the theory we are expounding — namely, the atomicity of the elements. This theory alone permits of attempting and of answering in a satisfactory manner this great question. How do the organic molecules hold together, and why is it that the elective affinity, which the atoms of carbon, hydrogen, and oxygen exercise upon each other, does not exhaust itself in the most simple compounds? Why can so great a number of atoms accumulate in the complex molecules of organic nature, and in general in all complex compounds, whatever be the elements contained?

The answer is this—All these molecules are cemented, so to say, by polyatomic elements which possess the property of uniting them together so as to partially neutralise their power of combination, without completely destroying it, for this power is multiple. Such is the action of carbon in organic compounds; but this action is not confined exclusively to carbon; it belongs also to oxygen and nitrogen, which, like it, are polyatomic elements. They also can serve to unite the various parts of the molecule, and it must not be thought that in an organic compound all the elements, with the exception of carbon, are united directly to the latter, as in the case of the hydrocarbons. Let us take some examples—

Alcohol, or hydrate of ethyl, contains C_2H_6O. Now, we know that the carbide C_2H_6 is already saturated; we at once infer that the 6 atoms of hydrogen are not all in direct connexion, and in intimate union with the 2 atoms of carbon. Experience teaches us, on the other hand, that one of the 6 atoms of hydrogen is easily replaced either by a simple body, such as potassium, or by a group of atoms acting like a simple body, whilst this is not the case with the other 5 atoms of hydrogen.

This would seem to show that these latter are united directly to the carbon, and that the sixth unit of combination necessary to complete the saturation of C_2 is supplied by the oxygen. But the latter being diatomic, has one affinity remaining which is saturated by the sixth atom of hydrogen. Thus the indivisible atom of oxygen here serves as a connexion between the incompletely saturated group C_2H_5 and the sixth atom of hydrogen. Such is the true meaning of the typical formula

$$\left.\begin{matrix} C_2H_5 \\ H \end{matrix}\right\} O \text{ or } (C_2H_5)OH.$$

And we see that this formula, which is based upon the interpretation of the reactions of alcohol, shows better than any other the mutual relations of the elements. The same remarks apply to ethylamine: the non-saturated group (C_2H_5) exchanges one affinity with triatomic nitrogen, the latter preserving two which are saturated by 2 atoms of hydrogen, and serving thus to unite the latter with the ethyl group.

$$\left.\begin{matrix} C_2H_5 \\ H \\ H \end{matrix}\right\} N''' = (C_2H_5)N \left\{\begin{matrix} H \\ H \\ H \end{matrix}\right.$$

It is well known that in ethyl itself the atoms are joined together by tetratomic carbon.

In glycol, as we have above observed, the remains of 2 molecules of water are joined together by the diatomic radical ethylene. But whence has this radical the power, if not from the tetratomic carbon it contains? We find there Θ_2 united to H_4; two units of combination are then wanting. In glycol one is furnished by 1 atom of oxygen, the second by the other atom of oxygen, and the 2 atoms of hydrogen which remain are seized by either atom of oxygen. Thus the 2 atoms of the latter element which are both retained by the hydrocarbonated nucleus, serve to unite the latter to the two remaining atoms of hydrogen. We may express these relations by representing glycol by the following formula :—

$$\begin{array}{c} H \\ \Theta \\ \text{Θ}H_2 \\ \text{Θ}H_2 \\ \Theta \\ H \end{array}$$

But is it not plain that this formula is only a typical formula slightly lengthened, and that the two poles of this group of atoms are none other than the two typical remainders HΘ, proceeding from 2 molecules of water, 2 atoms of whose hydrogen have been replaced by the diatomic radical ethylene?

$$\left.\begin{array}{c} H \\ H \end{array}\right\} \Theta \qquad\qquad \left.\begin{array}{c} H \\ \text{Θ}_2H_4 \end{array}\right\} \Theta$$
$$\left.\begin{array}{c} H \\ H \end{array}\right\} \Theta \qquad\qquad \left.\begin{array}{c} \\ H \end{array}\right\} \Theta$$

The same remark applies to the formula of glycolic acid, $\text{Θ}_2H_4\Theta_3$—one of the products of the oxidation of glycol. Whether we seek to express the relations existing between the atoms by the formula

$$\begin{array}{c} H \\ \Theta \\ C\Theta \\ CH_2 \\ \Theta \\ H \end{array}$$

or whether we adopt the typical formula*

$$\left.\begin{array}{r} H \\ C_2H_2\Theta \\ H \end{array}\right\} \begin{array}{l} \Theta \\ \Theta \end{array}$$

deduced from the reactions of glycolic acid, in both cases we see the typical remainders $H\Theta'$ united by a group of atoms which we regard as a radical.

The glycolic group

$$\left\{\begin{array}{l} C\Theta \\ CH_2 \text{ or } C_2H_2\Theta, \end{array}\right.$$

which is shown in the formula of glycolic acid, and which results from the oxidation of the ethylene group

$$\left\{\begin{array}{l} CH_2 \\ CH_2 \end{array}\right.$$

contains 1 atom of oxygen whose two affinities are saturated by the carbon. From this point of view this atom of oxygen differs from the two others which are partly saturated by the hydrogen. The typical formula perfectly expresses this difference, since it places the first atom of oxygen in the radical, and the two others without. It is an important fact that M. Hermann Kopp†

* I gave these formulæ in a note inserted in the *Annales de Chimie et de Physique*, 3rd series, vol. lxvii., p. 108, January, 1863.

† *Annalen der Chemie und Pharmacie*, vol. c., p. 19. *Annales de Chimie et de Physique*, 3rd series, vol. xli., p. 468. The specific or atomic volume is the volume occupied by quantities of matter corresponding to the atomic weights. It is obtained by dividing the atomic weights by the densities. By comparing the specific volumes of homologous combinations, M. H. Kopp perceived that, for each increase of CH_2, the specific volume of the molecule increased on an average by 22. He found, in the second place, that two combinations, one of which con-

has proved that this difference in the position of the atoms of oxygen corresponds to a difference in their specific volume, the specific volume of oxygen situated inside the radical being 12·2, and that of oxygen situated

tains nC more and nH_2 less than the other, possess the same specific volume, so that C can replace 2H without producing any change in the specific volume. From this he concluded that the specific volume of C was equal to that of H_2, and was able to deduce this volume from this known specific volume (22) of ΘH_2. He thus found for the specific volume of Θ the value $\frac{22}{2} = 11$, and for that of H the value $\frac{22}{4} = 5{\cdot}5$. He then determined the specific volume of the oxygen contained in a radical by comparing the specific volume of an acetone or an aldehyde, for example, with that of the corresponding hydro carbide. Thus, by subtracting from the specific volume of the acetone—

$$\left.\begin{matrix}\Theta_2H_3\Theta \\ \Theta H_3\end{matrix}\right\} = \Theta_3H_6\Theta(77{\cdot}3-77{\cdot}6)$$

that of the carbide—

$$\Theta_3H_6(66),$$

he found for the specific volume of Θ the number 11·3–11·6. By subtracting from the specific volume of the aldehyde—

$$\left.\begin{matrix}\Theta_2H_3O \\ H\end{matrix}\right\} = \Theta_2H_4\Theta(56{\cdot}0-56{\cdot}9)$$

that of

$$\Theta_2H_4(44),$$

he found for the specific volume of Θ the numbers 12·0–12·9. H therefore took the mean, the number 12·2, for the specific volume of the oxygen contained in a radical. To find the specific volume of typical oxygen, he subtracted from the specific volume of water (calculated for the boiling point) the specific volume of $H_2 = 2 \times 5{\cdot}5$. He thus found the specific volume 7·8 for the oxygen Θ situated outside the radical—that is to say, forming part of a typical residue $H\Theta$. These numbers being thus determined, he could calculate the specific volume of a combination $\Theta_aH_b(\Theta_c)\Theta_d$* by means of the formula—

$$a.11 + b.5{\cdot}5 + c.12{\cdot}2 + d.7{\cdot}8.$$

In the formula $\Theta_aH_b(\Theta)_c\Theta_d$, (Θ) denotes the oxygen contained in the radical, and Θ that contained outside the radical. The values thus calculated *à priori* coincide satisfactorily with those given by experiment, a fact which verifies the theory, and particularly the supposition that oxygen has a different specific volume when it forms part of a radical—that is to say, when it is entirely united to the carbon, to what it has when placed outside.

* *Comptes Rendus*, vol. lvii., page 283.

outside the radical being 7·8. Thus the typical formulæ have received a double confirmation. On the one hand they are supported by the considerations on the specific volumes of the liquid bodies; on the other hand by the theory of atomicity. The latter has revealed the important property of the polyatomic elements of serving to unite different portions of the molecule, a property which is shown in a great number of typical formulæ. The following are very significant in this respect:—

$\left.\begin{matrix}Cl\\H\end{matrix}\right\rangle\Theta$	$\left.\begin{matrix}K\\H\end{matrix}\right\rangle\Theta$	$\left.\begin{matrix}C_2H_5\\C_2H_5\end{matrix}\right\rangle\Theta$	$\left.\begin{matrix}C_2H_3\Theta\\C_2H_3\Theta\end{matrix}\right\rangle\Theta$	$\left.\begin{matrix}C_2H_5\\C_2H_5\\C_2H_5\end{matrix}\right\rangle N$
Hypochlorous acid.	Hydrate or potassium.	Oxide of ethyl.	Anhydrous acetic acid.	Triethylamine.

But the theory of atomicity has allowed us to make a further step in advance, for it gives account of the manner in which the atoms hold together the radicals themselves. The latter are represented in the typical notation as compact groups; it is now possible to resolve them, so to say, into their elements. That is the object and meaning of the formulæ we have given above (pages 123 and 124), in which the symbols are, as it were, distributed. Are we, then, to say that formulæ so lengthened out should be employed in preference to the clear and simple typical formulæ? I am far from thinking so, for under the pretext of wishing to represent everything by such a formula, we run the risk of becoming embarrassed by an obscure or arbitrary representation. I will show this by a single example.

We attempted further back to give an account of the respective relationships of the atoms in glycol. This attempt was successful since it referred to a simple compound. But take a slightly more complicated compound diethylenic alcohol $C_4H_{10}\Theta_3$. We know by its mode of formation, and by its reactions that this body contains

2 ethylene radicals. They are joined to 2 atoms of hydrogen and to 2 atoms of oxygen. The considerations relating to atomicity allow us to represent in the following manner the relations of these different elements to each other :—

$$\begin{matrix} H \\ \Theta \\ \mathrm{C}_2H_4 \\ \mathrm{C}_2H_4 \\ \Theta \\ \Theta \\ H \end{matrix}$$

The 2 ethylene groups which, for the sake of simplicity, we have not thought right to decompose, exchange one affinity. There remains, then, another in each group to be disposed of; it is satisfied on either side by an affinity of each of the atoms of oxygen which are connected with the ethylene. The other affinity of these latter serves to unite on the one side with the hydrogen, on the other with another atom of oxygen, which in its turn unites with the hydrogen.

But we might also suppose that the two ethylene groups are joined together by 1 atom of oxygen. If this were the case, the molecular arrangement of the diethylenic alcohol would be expressed by the following formula :—

$$\begin{matrix} H \\ \Theta \\ \mathrm{C}_2H_4 \\ \Theta \\ \mathrm{C}_2H_4 \\ \Theta \\ H \end{matrix}$$

This corresponds to the typical formula :—

$$\left.\begin{matrix} \left[\left.\begin{matrix} \mathrm{C}_2H_4 \\ \mathrm{C}H \end{matrix}\right\} \Theta \right]'' \\ H_2 \end{matrix}\right\} O_2$$

The more simple formula

$$\left.\begin{matrix}(C_2H_4)\\(C_2H_4)\\H_2\end{matrix}\right\}O_3$$

which I have hitherto adopted, merely indicates in a general manner that the 3 atoms of oxygen serve to unite 2 ethylene radicals and 2 atoms of hydrogen. But what are the precise relations of these 3 atoms of oxygen with the other constituent elements? Are the atoms of ethylene joined together directly, or through the medium of an atom of oxygen? It is impossible to solve these questions *à priori.*

The second of the formulæ of constitution given above, perhaps better accounts for the fact that in diethylenic alcohol the 2 ethylene radicals do not form a single radical (C_4H_8).*

But, on the other hand, we see that it may be so, merely by supposing that the 2 ethylene radicals are directly contiguous, as we have above allowed. In fact, if it is true that the combining power of a group or of a radical depends on the atomicity of its elements—if it is true that such a group possesses the property of uniting with other elements only because it contains one or more imperfectly saturated element, experience teaches us, on the other hand, that the elements thus attached are often retained by an affinity less strong than that which joins together the elements of the group itself. The effect, then, is as if the whole group were to act according to the resultant of all the affinities residing in it. Doubtless the ethylene radical can unite with chlorine and bromine only because it contains an imperfectly saturated atom of carbon. But I consider it probable that under these circumstances it acts not so

* When hydriodic acid is made to act upon diethylenic alcohol, the ethylene radicals are separated again, and iodide of ethylene is formed.

much by this atom of carbon as like an entire group, for we know that carbon possesses only a slight affinity for bromine or chlorine. Certainly it possesses a greater affinity for hydrogen than for these two elements, and though ethylene does not combine directly with hydrogen as it does with chlorine, yet this is doubtless due to the fact that the hydrogen of the ethylene group contributes its share in attracting the chlorine. It is, then, the whole group that is active, and that acts by the resultant of all the affinities of its elementary atoms.*

Thus we may imagine one group united to another group without being confounded with it.

It results, then, from this discussion that when it is necessary to represent the molecular constitution of certain complicated combinations by starting from the data relative to the atomicity of the elements, we can often construct different and equally satisfactory formulæ; and we should run the risk of being arbitrary by selecting exclusively one of them without justifying such a choice by reasons derived from experience. Thus, then, while I recognise in it a new method, I think it should only be used with prudence. Here, as in all else, abuse does not exclude use, and these formulæ of constitution or of

* This idea appears to me important, for it serves to explain a certain number of cases of isomerism. It enables me especially to account for that which I have discovered between the alcohols, properly so called, and the hydrates of the carburetted hydrogens. In amylic alcohol

$$\left.\begin{matrix}Ꞓ_5H_{11}\\ H\end{matrix}\right\} Θ$$

the eleven atoms of hydrogen are in direct connexion with the carbon. We may suppose that in the hydrate of amylene

$$\left.\begin{matrix}[(Ꞓ_5H_{10})''H]'\\ H\end{matrix}\right\} Θ$$

the eleventh atom of hydrogen in the radical is less strongly held than the corresponding atom of the amyl group $Ꞓ_5H_{11}$, and in that case this eleventh atom of hydrogen would be in connexion with the whole amylene group, whose atomicity would thus be reduced by a unit.

structure, as M. Boutlerow calls them, by which we seek to express the relations existing between atoms and groups in chemical compounds, are destined to render great service in explanation of the facts of isomerism.*

But there is another consequence of the theory of the atomicity of the elements, and especially of the atomicity of carbon. We have long known, and Laurent and Gerhardt have dwelt much on these facts, that in organic compounds the number of atoms of hydrogen is always even, and that, further, the sum of the atoms of nitrogen, hydrogen, chlorine, &c., is always an even number.

How could it be otherwise, since the other elements of organic combinations, carbon and oxygen, are of even atomicity? Either can combine only with an even number of atoms of hydrogen, and if nitrogen is also present, as it is of uneven atomicity, evidently an uneven number of atoms of hydrogen, chlorine, or other monatomic elements must unite with nitrogen or with the other triatomic elements so as to saturate the elements of even atomicity.

In that which precedes we have considered the atomicity of the principal elements of organic compounds, especially that of carbon. But it is evident that the reasoning we have pursued would apply to the other chemical elements, metalloids, and metals. Among the works which have helped to generalise these ideas on the atomicity of the elements, we will mention those of

* To pursue this point would lead us beyond the plan we have laid down for this work. On this subject should be consulted an important article published by M. Kekulé under the title "Considérations sur quelques cas d'isomérie," (*Annales de Chimie et de Physique*, 3rd series, vol. lxvi., page 482); the remarks I have published on the "Isomerism of the Hydrocarbons," (*Comptes Rendus*, vol. lvi., p. 354); an article by M. Boutlerow, entitled "Sur l'explication de divers cas d'isomerie, (*Bulletin de la Société Chimique*, vol. vi. page 100); and an article by M. Erlenmeyer, headed "Hypothèses sur l'isomérie Chimique, et sur la Constitution Chimique (*Zeitschrift für Chemie und Pharmacie*, vol. vii., p. 1).

Dr. Frankland, on the organo-metallic radicals, and the researches of MM. Baeyer and Cahours on the same subject.

In his fourth article on the organo-metallic compounds, whose important discovery is owing to him, Dr. Frankland* first compared iodide of stannethyl† $(SnC_4H_5)I$, and stannodiethyl with diniodide of tin:

$$Sn\left\{\begin{matrix}I\\I\end{matrix}\right. \qquad Sn\left\{\begin{matrix}C_4H_5\\I\end{matrix}\right. \qquad Sn\left\{\begin{matrix}C_4H_5\\C_4H_5\end{matrix}\right.$$

Diniodide of tin. Iodide of stannethyl. Stannodiethyl.

He observed that stannethyl, Sn (C_4H_5), like iodide of tin SnI, combines with iodine in the same way as the latter to pass to the type of stannic iodide (saturated compound). To this type belongs also stannodiethyl, which is incapable of combining with an electro-negative element without first losing at least one equivalent of ethyl.

M. Cahours has generalised these conclusions, and given them a clearer form, by insisting upon the fact that all compounds containing tin and alcoholic radicals arrive at a state of stable molecular equilibrium—that is to say, at the state of saturation — only when 2 equivalents of their tin (Sn = 59) are combined with 4 equivalents of a radical or of a monobasic element, so as to make the general formula of all these combinations

$$Sn_2X_4.$$

Here are some examples:—

Sn_2Cl_4 = 4 vols. Chloride of tin.§
Sn_2Et_4 = 4 vols. Perethylide of tin.
Sn_2Me_4 = 4 vols. Permethylide of tin.
$Sn_2Et_2Me_2$ = 4 vols. Diethyl-dimethylide of tin.
Sn_2Me_3Et = 4 vols. Trimethyl-ethylide of tin.

* *Proceedings of the Royal Society*, vol. ix., page 672, March, 1859, *Répertoire de Chemie Pure*, vol. i., page 416.

† C = 6. Sn = 59.

‡ *Annales de Chimie et de Physique*, 3rd series, vol. lxii., p. 257. 1861.

§ HO = 2 vols.

Sn_2MeEt_3 = 4 vols. Methyl-triethylide of tin.
Sn_2Et_3Cl = 4 vols. Chloride of triethylide of tin (chloride of sesquistannethyl).
Sn_2Et_3I = 4 vols. Iodide of triethylide of tin.
$Sn_2Me_2I_2$ = 4 vols. Diiodide of dimethylide of tin.

The smallest quantity of tin that exists in these volatile compounds of tin being represented by $Sn_2 = 118$, we may look upon this quantity as representing the weight of one atom of tin. Hence the general formula of all these saturated compounds of tin becomes

$$\text{S̶n}X_4.$$

Tin itself, *in its saturated compounds*, plays the part of a tetratomic element.

I say "in its saturated compounds," for in those which are not saturated, in the chloride S̶nCl_2, for example, it plays a different part. This point is very important, and I will illustrate it by another example from the same class of compounds. It follows from the works of M. Baeyer* that the methylated compounds of arsenic, when they are saturated, belong to the type

$$AsX_5.$$

The following are known:—

$AsMe_4Cl$ Chloride of tetramethylarsonium.
$AsMe_3Cl_2$ Dichloride of trimethylarsonium.
$AsMe_2Cl_3$ Trichloride of dimethylarsonium.
$AsMe\ Cl_4$ Tetrachloride of monomethylarsonium.

The compound $AsCl_5$, which would correspond to the perchloride of phosphorus PCl_5, has not as yet been obtained. In the other compounds which form part of this saturated series, the arsenic acts as a pentatomic element. But, independent of this series, there exists another in which it enters as a triatomic element.

* *Annalen der Chemie und Pharmacie*, vol. cvii., p. 257. 1858.

$AsMe_3$ Arsentrimethyl.
$AsMe_2Cl$ Monochloride of arsendimethyl.
$AsMeCl_2$ Dichloride of arsenmonomethyl.
$AsCl_3$ Trichloride of arsenic.

The compounds belonging to this second series are not saturated. In contact with chlorine the three first absorb 2 of its atoms, and are converted into the compounds of the saturated series AsX_5. But it is none the less true that in arsentrimethyl or in trichloride of arsenic the arsenic only exhibits a combining power represented by 3 units, just as the nitrogen in ammonia only exhibits a combining power represented by 3. And it is also to be remarked that with respect to chlorine the combining capacity of arsenic is exhausted in the trichloride, as with respect to hydrogen it is exhausted in arseniuretted hydrogen. We may conclude from these facts that the atomicity of an element can change with the combinations into which it enters. And this proposition is sufficiently important for us to seek to establish it by other examples. We have already considered carbon as diatomic in oxide of carbon and as tetratomic in carbonic acid, because it manifests* a combining power equal to two units in the former, and to four units in the latter.

Nitrogen seems to us diatomic in binoxide of nitrogen, triatomic in ammonia, pentatomic in sal-ammoniac—

$$N''\Theta''$$
$$N'''H_3$$
$$N^{v}(H_4Cl)$$

Phosphorus is triatomic in phosphuretted hydrogen and in protochloride of phosphorus, pentatomic in the perchloride.

$$P'''H_3$$
$$P^{v}Cl_5$$

* I say "manifests," not possesses.

Iodine is monoatomic in monochloride of iodine, triatomic in perchloride.

$$ICl$$
$$I'''Cl_3$$

Lead is diatomic in the dichloride, tetratomic in the tetrethylide or in the tetramethylide.

$$Pb''Cl_2$$
$$Pb^{iv}Et_4$$
$$Pb^{iv}Me_4$$

We also know by the law of multiple proportions that the combining capacity of the elements is satisfied by degrees, until it arrives at a maximum which it does not exceed. This maximum combining capacity represents, according to some authors, the atomicity; it is invariable for each element, for it is shown by the limit of saturation. But for me the word atomicity has a more extended meaning, which I will define. I will endeavour to specify the part which each element plays in any given combination to give to it its actual combining power, and not that which it might assume in another compound. Can we say, absolutely, that nitrogen is a triatomic element? Then we do not account for its position in sal-ammoniac, where the sum of the elements combined with it represents 5 units of chemical force. Can we say the tin is tetratomic because it can combine with 4 atoms of chlorine? Then we do not consider its value of combination or substitution in the stannous compounds, where it represents only 2 units of combination ($SnCl_2$ = stannous chloride). Shall we say, as a final instance, that iron is hexatomic or tetratromic or triatomic?*

We do not consider its part in the ferrous compounds where it equals 2 atoms of hydrogen or chlorine

($FeCl_2$ = ferrous chloride).

* $FeCl_3$ = Ferric chloride.

The true meaning that we attribute to the word atomicity will now be apparent. This word expresses less the *virtual* and *absolute* combining capacity of an element or group, than the *actual* combining capacity which it possesses in a given compound, and which may vary in other compounds.*

And on this head I will point out that the word *capacity* of combination does not seem to me the correct term; for it implies the idea of a latent force. I will then define atomicity considered in the elements as *the equivalence of the atoms*—that is to say, *their value of combination or of substitution*. This value may change for one and the same element, according to the combinations into which it enters. Nitrogen can unite with 3 atoms of hydrogen, it can replace 3 atoms of hydrogen in a great number of organic compounds, but it can also combine with 4 atoms of hydrogen + 1 atom of chlorine. It is then at once triatomic and pentatomic, according to

* It is evident that there are here two ideas, each of which is important, and which must not be confused. The maximum combining power of an element, that which it possesses in reality, and which it exerts in its saturated compounds, must be distinguished from the combining value or value of substitution which it shows in a given compound. The first is measured by the sum of the units of chemical force that exist in the element, the second by the sum of the units of chemical force that it shows in a compound saturated or non-saturated. The maximum combining power is invariable; the value of substitution may change. If we call the former *atomic power* or *atomicity* we must find a term corresponding to the latter, as the German word *Æquivalentigkeit* corresponds to *Atomigkeit*. I do not undertake to find a word to express this idea of "equivalent power of the atoms" which shall at the same time be French, and I do not care to make one which should not. In face of this difficulty I thought proper to apply the word atomicity to this wider idea, as ancient as the atomic theory—namely, this capacity of variable combination of one body with another which is exhausted by degrees, as is shown by the law of Dalton. The absolute or maximum atomicity, which some persons call atomicity, appears thus as a particular instance of the power of combination exerted by bodies; it is the complete manifestation of it. It is likewise plain that this is merely a question of words; the ideas are clearly separate from each other.

the combinations into which it enters. Similarly, iodine can unite with 1 atom of hydrogen, or replace 1 atom of hydrogen (Θ_2H_6 and Θ_2H_5I), but it can also combine with 3 atoms of chlorine and replace 3 atoms of hydrogen.*

It seems to me useless to insist upon this point; I simply wish to point out in conclusion that the elements act, in this respect, like groups or compound radicals themselves. We know, in fact, that the group Θ_3H_5 is sometimes monoatomic and sometimes triatomic. All admit that it is so. If, then, the atomicity of groups, which depends upon that of the elements may vary, we must also admit that the latter may likewise vary.

Measure of the Atomicity.—Nothing is more simple than to determine the atomicity of an element when it is in combination with another element known to be monatomic—such as hydrogen or chlorine. The atomicity of this element in a given compound is expressed by the sum of the monatomic elements which are combined with it. It is evident, likewise, that the compound groups which equal one monatomic element may similarly give the measure of the atomicity. It is thus with the alcoholic radicals ethyl (Et), methyl (Me), which have already served to fix the atomicity of tin and arsenic.

Again, it is sufficient to glance at the table on pages 100 and 101 to understand how the atomicity of an

* M. Schützenberger has described (*Comptes Rendus*, vol. liv., page 1026) a combination containing

$$\left.\begin{matrix}(\Theta_2H_3\Theta)_3 \\ I'''\end{matrix}\right\} \Theta_3$$

in which the triatomic iodine of the chloride Cl_3I, by replacing 3 atoms of the hydrogen of 3 molecules of acetic acid

$$3\left[\left.\begin{matrix}\Theta_2H_3\Theta \\ H\end{matrix}\right\} \Theta\right]$$

joins together the remainders of these 3 molecules.

element is determined by the number of monatomic elements with which it can combine.

Similarly the measure of the atomicity is free from difficulty in the case of the combination of a simple body with a *single* polyatomic element. In oxide of carbon, carbon only displays 2 affinities, since it is joined to a *single* atom of diatomic oxygen. We express this by saying that it is diatomic in oxide of carbon. But when several atoms of oxygen Θ or of another polyatomic element enter into combination with another simple body, it may not be correct to express the atomicity of the latter by the sum of the affinities residing in the atoms of oxygen. In fact, two cases may here be met with. Either all the affinities of the oxygen are saturated by those of the other element; and thus it is with carbonic, silicic, phosphoric, boracic, stannic acids, &c.

$$\Theta^{iv}\Theta''_2 \qquad \left.\begin{matrix}P^v\\P^v\end{matrix}\right\}\Theta''_5$$

$$Si^{iv}\Theta''_2$$

$$Sn^{iv}\Theta''_2 \qquad \left.\begin{matrix}Bo'''\\Bo'''\end{matrix}\right\}\Theta''_3$$

Or else the atoms of oxygen partially saturate each other, forming, so to say, a chain at the extremities of which other elements join on. Can we say that chlorine is heptatomic in anhydrous perchloric acid?

$$\left.\begin{matrix}Cl\\Cl\end{matrix}\right\}\Theta_7,$$

That it is tetratomic in hydrated perchloric acid?

$$\left.\begin{matrix}Cl\\H\end{matrix}\right\}\Theta_4.$$

By no means. In these compounds the atoms of oxygen join on to each other, each losing one affinity by its union with each of its neighbours, so that the last alone preserve one affinity free, which is satisfied either by the hydrogen or by the chlorine.

$$\overset{\prime}{Cl}\text{-}\overset{\prime\prime}{\Theta}\text{-}\overset{\prime\prime}{\Theta}\text{-}\overset{\prime\prime}{\Theta}\text{-}\overset{\prime\prime}{\Theta}\text{-}\overset{\prime\prime}{\Theta}\text{-}\overset{\prime\prime}{\Theta}\text{-}\overset{\prime\prime}{\Theta}\text{-}\overset{\prime}{Cl}$$

Anhydrous perchloric acid.

These remarks also apply to the metals; the atomicity of the latter is not always measured by the sum of the affinities existing in the polyatomic elements combined with them. Thus, in the peroxides which contain 2 atoms of oxygen, the metals should not necessarily be considered as tetratomic; they may be diatomic, for the 2 atoms of oxygen joined together only leave free 2 affinities, which are satisfied by the diatomic metal. We may suppose that in these compounds the atoms are symmetrically arranged round a centre.

The instability even of these peroxides, the facility with which they lose an atom of oxygen, the manner in which they behave with hydrochloric acid, are all characteristic traits which distinguish them from other oxides containing, like them, 2 atoms of oxygen, but in which all the affinities of the oxygen are saturated by a tetratomic metal. On this account stannic acid evidently belongs to a different type to peroxide of manganese, and these differences are perfectly expressed by the formulæ

$$(Mn\Theta)''\Theta \qquad Sn\Theta_2.$$

Similarly we should not say that manganese is necessarily hexatomic in manganic acid,

$$Mn\Theta_3,$$

or that iron is necessarily tetratomic in pyrites,

$$FeS_2.$$

Iron *may* be tetratomic in pyrites, but this is not certain; for the tetrachloride

$$FeCl_4$$

corresponding to pyrites has not yet been discovered, and the faculty which iron possesses of combining with 2 atoms of sulphur does not give a certain measure of the combining power which it displays in pyrites, since the two atoms of sulphur may be joined together. Each of them thus losing an unit of chemical force, we may imagine that the group

$$[\bar{\mathrm{S}}'', \bar{\mathrm{S}}'']''$$

might saturate

$$\bar{\mathrm{F}}\mathrm{e}''$$

in pyrites, or else that the group

$$[\bar{\mathrm{F}}\mathrm{e}'', \bar{\mathrm{S}}'']''$$

might combine with $\bar{\mathrm{S}}''$.

These examples, which might easily be multiplied, are such as to show that the atomicity which a simple body possesses in certain compounds is only measured exactly by the number of monatomic elements or groups which are combined with a single atom of this simple body.

In this way there would be no doubt about the atomicity of iron in the ferric compounds, since we know, by the classic experiments of MM. Deville and Troost, that two volumes of this chloride contain six volumes of chlorine. Therefore, one molecule of ferric chloride contains six atoms of chlorine, and the smallest quantity of iron that exists in the ferric chloride, and, generally, in any ferric compound is represented by 112. Iron, then, seems to be hexatomic in the ferric compounds, or rather, ferricum seems to be hexatomic. This conclusion, which results from the density of the vapour of ferric chloride, is strengthened by considerations arising from the chemical constitution of certain ferric compounds, and the beautiful researches of M. Scheurer-Kestner have, on this point, led to very significant results.*

* *Comptes Rendus*, vol. liii., p. 653.

Among other compounds, this chemist described some acetonitrates of iron belonging to the type—

$$\begin{matrix} H_6 \\ H_6 \end{matrix}\Theta_6$$

and in which, H_6 being replaced by ferricum, a single atom of hydrogen is replaced by nitrous gas, an evident proof that the molecules of these compounds cannot present a complication less than that expressed by the following formulæ :—

$$\left.\begin{matrix} H_6 \\ H_6 \end{matrix}\right\}\Theta_6 \qquad \left.\begin{matrix} \mathrm{Ffe}^{vi} \\ H_6 \end{matrix}\right\}\Theta_6$$

Type. Normal ferric hydrate.

$$\left.\begin{matrix} \mathrm{Ffe}^{vi} \\ 4(C_2H_3\Theta)' \\ (N\Theta_2)' \\ H \end{matrix}\right\}\Theta_6 + 4H_2\Theta \qquad \left.\begin{matrix} \mathrm{Ffe}^{vi} \\ 3(C_2H_3\Theta)' \\ (N\Theta_2)' \\ H_2 \end{matrix}\right\}\Theta_6 + 2H_2\Theta.$$

Tetracetonitrate of iron. Triacetonitrate of iron.

The sign Ffe represents in these formulæ 112 of iron, or, if preferred, an atom of ferricum, an atom of ferrosum (= 56) being represented by the symbol—

$$\mathrm{Fe}.$$

Ferricum, then, is formed by the union of two atoms of ferrosum, and in the preceding formulæ we may replace the sign—

$$\mathrm{Fe}^{vi} \text{ by the sign } \mathrm{Fe}^{vi}{}_2.$$

But here there is a difficulty. How can two atoms of diatomic ferrosum form, by uniting, a hexatomic couple

$$\mathrm{Fe}_2\,?$$

M. Friedel has removed this difficulty in a very ingenious manner, by considering each of these atoms, not as diatomic, but as tetratomic.* It may be admitted that iron is tetrátomic† in pyrites‡—

$$\mathrm{Fe}S_2.$$

* *Bulletin de la Société Chimique*, vol. v. p. 202.

† With the reservations expressed (p. 139), since the tetrachloride, $FeCl_4$, is not known.

‡ See also an article by M. Erlenmeyer, *Zeitschrift fur Chemie und Pharmacie*, vol. v., p. 87 and 129.

If, then, we suppose that two atoms of tetratomic iron unite by exchanging an affinity, this couple Fe_2, which has thus lost two affinities, should be hexatomic. It is in this case with iron as with carbon in the compounds containing C_2, and this ferric chloride may be compared to the perchloride of carbon—

$$Fe^{vi}{}_2Cl_6 \qquad\qquad C^{vi}{}_2Cl_6.$$
Ferric chloride.   Chloride of carbon.

As long as these two atoms of iron remain united, they preserve their combining power, which is equal to six units. They preserve it in all the ferric compounds, and, when they are again separated, the ferric combination is thereby destroyed, as an organic combination containing 2 atoms of carbon is destroyed when these 2 atoms are separated from each other. The couple

$$Fe_2$$

is ferricum. It is a true double atom, which acts as a radical in the ferric compounds. It is plain that this idea is fundamentally the same as that above given, and expressed by the symbol Ffe. There is only a difference in the form, in the notation, but this is not unimportant, because, being based upon analogies furnished by organic chemistry,* it accounts for the hexatomicity of ferricum.†

It must, however, be admitted that this idea, when applied to aluminium, becomes slightly arbitrary, since

---

* Here is one of these analogies ; the allyle group C_3H_5 is monatomic and triatomic. When two triatomic allyle groups unite, we obtain a tetratomic group. Free allyle combines with 4 atoms of bromine,

$$\left.\begin{array}{c}(C_3H_5)''' \\ Br_3\end{array}\right\} \qquad \left[\begin{array}{c}C_3H_5 \\ C_3H_5\end{array}\right] \qquad \left[\begin{array}{c}C_3H_5 \\ C_3H_5\end{array}\right]Br_4$$
Tribromide of allyle.   Allyle.   Tetrabromide of diallyle.

† There are several ways of regarding the radical of the ferric combinations. Gerhardt admitted 2 equivalents for iron, represented by 28 and $\dfrac{2 \times 28}{3}$. He represented these two equivalents by the signs Fe and fe, and the corresponding oxides by the formulæ $Fe_2\Theta$ and $fe_2\Theta$. This idea is perfectly correct, and applicable to the construction of equivalent formulæ.

we are forced to admit in the aluminic compounds, which are isomorphous with the ferric compounds, the couple $Al^{vi}_2 = 54$, which would be formed of 2 atoms of tetratomic aluminium. Now we know of no compound of aluminium corresponding either to pyrites or to the ferrous compounds; but since this is merely a question of notation, we may disregard it. The fundamental part is ascertained. The quantity of iron that exists in a molecule of any ferric compound is never less than 112; the quantity of aluminium that exists in any aluminic compound is never less than 54. These quantities equal 6 atoms of hydrogen. The densities of the vapour of the chlorides of iron and aluminium are conclusive on this point, and in no case ought iron or aluminium to be considered as triatomic.

If this were so, the chlorides of these metals should contain 3 atoms of chlorine, and we should have—

$$FeCl_3 = 2 \text{ volumes.}$$
$$AlCl_3 = 2 \text{ volumes.}$$

While we know that these formulæ ought to be doubled.

But if we examine the quantity of iron which exists in a molecule of a ferric compound, we find that this quantity is equal to 112, and we can now admit one of two things—either this matter represents a particular aggregation of the matter of iron, *one* hexatomic atom; or else it represents *two* atoms of tetratomic iron. In this second hypothesis iron possesses in all its combinations only one atomic weight $= 56$, which coincides with that deduced from the specific heat. But the substitution value of the atom of iron may change; it is sometimes diatomic and sometimes tetratomic, and we can name as ferricum a couple of two atoms of tetratomic iron. Such a couple acts as a hexatomic radical. I have adopted this hypothesis, which seems the simplest. I will, however, mention one very remarkable fact, which seems to prove that such couples sometimes act as true atoms. H. Rose has proved that the combinations of hyponiobium which contain 2 atoms of niobium, Nb^{vi}_2, cannot be directly transformed into combinations of niobium, which circumstance has led him to admit that these two sorts of compounds contain two radicals which differ from each other in their allotropic state.

These considerations may be applied to *cuprosum* and to *mercurosum*. In the cuprous and mercurous salts two atoms of diatomic copper or mercury are joined together. As each of them loses an affinity by uniting with its neighbour, it follows that the couples—

$$Cu_2 \quad Hg_2$$

are diatomic. The cuprous and mercurous chlorides are then represented by the formulæ—

$$Cu_2Cl_2 \text{ and } Hg_2Cl_2.$$

In truth the latter would seem to be invalidated by the density of the vapour of calomel, which is only half the theoretical density deduced from the formula Hg_2Cl_2. But we may reasonably suppose that this is a case of dissociation; for we know how readily the mercurous compounds resolve themselves into mercury and mercuric compounds.*

It must be added that the formula Cu_2S of cuprous sulphide harmonises with the well known fact of the isomorphism of this sulphide with sulphide of silver—

$$Ag_2S.$$

Such are the considerations which we would offer upon the atomicity of the elements. It is a theory of yesterday, whose consequences are daily being developed. And yet the fundamental idea on which this theory is based is as ancient as the atomic theory itself; it is the law of multiple proportions. It rests upon this fact, that the combining power of one element for another is exhausted by degrees until it reaches a maximum which it does not exceed.

But it is far from this scarcely defined idea to the general theory of saturation, so important on account of

* The density of the vapour of calomel = 8·35. It leads to the formula—

$$HgCl.$$

The density of the vapour calculated according to the formula—

$$Hg_2Cl_2 = 16{\cdot}308.$$

the consequences which flow from it concerning the molecular constitution of bodies. We must also remark that the old statement of the law of multiple proportions did not always give the true molecular formulæ. I will give an instance of this in conclusion.

Let us take the best known example, and represent, according to Berzelius, the composition of the compounds of oxygen and nitrogen. We have the following series:—

N_2O = 2 vol. protoxide of nitrogen
N_2O_2 = 4 vol. binoxide of nitrogen
N_2O_3 = ,, nitrous acid
N_2O_4 = ,, hyponitric acid
N_2O_5 = ,, nitric acid.

These formulæ show well that the combining power or the affinity of the nitrogen for the oxygen is exhausted by degrees. But they do not represent quantities which are comparable; they give inexact ideas about the relative sizes of the molecules. The true molecular formulæ of the compounds of oxygen and nitrogen are the following, which are referred to the same volume:—

$N_2\Theta$ = 2 vol. protoxide of nitrogen
$N\,\Theta$ = ,, binoxide of nitrogen
$N_2\Theta_3$ = ,, nitrous acid
$N\,\Theta_2$ = ,, hyponitric acid
$N_2\Theta_5$ = ,, anhydrous nitric acid.

In this series the molecular complication of the different compounds is in accordance with their density. The protoxide, denser than the binoxide, shows a greater molecular complication. And this fact harmonises with other physical properties of the two gases. The former is condensable, the latter is permanent; which circumstance it would be difficult to explain if the binoxide were a gas of greater molecular complication than the protoxide.

PART III.

CONNEXION BETWEEN ORGANIC AND INORGANIC CHEMISTRY.

SECTION I.

Atomicity as a means of Classification.

THE reasoning which we have applied to atomicity establishes a solid relationship between organic and inorganic chemistry. Struck with the fact that the atoms of carbon, hydrogen, and oxygen could be heaped up in organic compounds so as to form very complex molecules, chemists were of opinion that this peculiarity impressed a special stamp upon the combinations of carbon. But it is not so, and it is easy to show that the property in question is displayed in other polyatomic elements. This accounts for the complication of the combinations of silicium, which may be compared, on this point, to the combinations of carbon. Why, then, is the chemistry of silicium so different from that of carbon? It arises from these two circumstances—that, on the one hand, silicium forms with oxygen a fixed compound; and, on the other hand, that its affinity for hydrogen seems to be exhausted in a single combination, which cannot exist in presence of air, since it is spontaneously inflammable.

Without carbides of hydrogen there would be no organic chemistry; and if there existed silicides of hydrogen corresponding to the carbides, it is clear that the bodies derived from these silicides might be very numerous. But it is none the less true that the natural silicates often show great molecular complication, and may be compared, in this respect, to the organic compounds of carbon. And the reason of such a molecular complication is contained, as we will show, in the polyatomic nature of silicium and of certain of the metals which are united with this element in the silicates. Our investigations upon atomicity establish, between compounds otherwise very unlike in nature and properties, connexions in constitution or molecular structure which it is desirable to point out. They allow of convenient grouping together, and furnish, both for inorganic and organic chemistry, elements of classification that it would in future be impossible to neglect. Our task shall be further to develope these points.

A celebrated chemist has said*:—"Organic chemistry is the chemistry of the compound radicals." We know now that such radicals do not belong exclusively to organic combinations; but, as regards their power of combination, we know that they act as elements. We have then the right to compare, with respect to their atomicity, the radicals of organic chemistry, not only to the compound radicals but also to the simple elements of inorganic chemistry. As in organic chemistry we find monatomic, diatomic, triatomic radicals, &c., so also in inorganic chemistry we find radicals and elements of different atomicity, and it is evident that inorganic and organic combinations containing radicals or elements of the same atomicity should present a certain analogy of structure, which might show itself by a certain analogy

* Liebig, "*Traité de Chimie Organique*," vol. i., p. 1.

in their reactions. For simple as well as for compound bodies their atomicity is the principal means of classification. The natural families of metalloids established by M. Dumas* are groups of simple bodies of equal atomicity:—

Mon-atomic.	Diatomic.	Triatomic.	Tetratomic.	Triatomic and pentatomic.
Fluorine.	Oxygen.	Boron.	Carbon.	Nitrogen.
Chlorine.	Sulphur.		Silicium.	Phosphorus.
Bromine.	Selenium.			Arsenic.
Iodine.	Tellurium.			Antimony.

Similar groups might be formed among the metals, and such classifications are much better founded than the artificial relationships established between the metals by their degree of affinity for oxygen.

It must be allowed that, in a large number of cases, the classification formerly adopted by Thenard breaks the natural connexions established between the metals by the general composition of their combinations. It is thus, for example, with silver, which is monatomic, and which should be placed along with the alkaline metals.

The following is this very natural group of monatomic metals:—

Hydrogen.

Rubidium.
Cæsium.
Potassium.
Sodium.
Lithium.
Silver.

Thallium.

Lead should be classed with the diatomic metals barium, strontium, calcium. To this group would be

* Dumas, "*Traité de Chimie appliquée aux Arts,*" vol. i., p. lxxvii. 1828.

joined the diatomic metals isomorphous with the magnesian series, magnesium, manganese, iron, zinc, &c. The tetratomic metals form a very natural group. It is convenient to place them after silicium. We have thus the following family:—

Carbon.
Silicium.

Zirconium.
Titanium.
Tin.
Tantalum.

Niobium.

But it must be added that in this attempt at classification, as in all attempts of this character, difficulties are encountered arising from the circumstance that among the metals, even more than among the metalloids, each element bears the impress of a strongly marked individuality. It shows certain points of contact with its neighbours with regard to some combinations, but seldom a complete analogy in every combination. Thus thallium, which in some points resembles the alkaline metals, differs from them in the property it possesses of forming a sesquichloride and a terchloride. Iron, which, when considered in the ferrous combinations, resembles manganese and zinc, should be classed with aluminium when it is considered in the ferric combinations. Copper, which shows a point of contact with the magnesian series in the cupric combinations, also, to a certain point, resembles mercury. The general composition of the cuprous and mercurous, cupric and mercuric oxides and chlorides is the same.

If from simple we pass to compound bodies, we shall see that the notion of atomicity allows us to establish very curious, and often very unexpected, relationships between certain inorganic and organic compounds.

SECTION II.

Oxides, Hydrates, and Salts, Inorganic and Organic.

Let us first take the oxides and the hydrates. We know that Berzelius likened the oxidised bodies of organic chemistry to the inorganic oxides and acids. He looked upon acetic acid as the teroxide of an acetyle radical (C_4H_6 in his notation), and compared it to sulphuric acid.

$(C_4H_6).O_3$ Acetic acid.
$S.O_3$ Sulphuric acid.

Comparing ether to oxide of potassium, he called it oxide of ethyl, and this name has remained to it, for the comparison was very reasonable. It has, in fact, been found that ether can enter into direct combination with the acids. Dr. Wetherill, in 1848, obtained sulphate of ethyl (sulphatic ether) by directly combining oxide of ethyl with anhydrous sulphuric acid. Afterwards M. Berthelot prepared other compound ethers by combining ether directly with the acids.

Thus oxide of etbyl and its homologues were found to resemble oxides not merely by the symbolic representation of their composition, but also by a certain analogy of properties. But it must be owned that this analogy was not of a very striking nature, the affinities of oxide of ethyl being very far from equalling those of the mineral oxides. This is not the case with the oxide of ethylene, whose reactions are much more energetic, and which is able to enter into direct combination, not only with the acids, but also with water and ammonia, like certain metallic oxides. Oxide of ethylene

$$(C_2H_4)''\Theta$$

contains the diatomic radical ethylene, and we can compare it to the oxides formed by the diatomic metals. We are thus led to establish the following parallel between the oxides of inorganic and those of organic chemistry :—

Monatomic oxides.	Diatomic oxides.	Triatomic oxides.	Tetratomic oxides.
$\left.\begin{matrix}K\\K\end{matrix}\right\}\Theta$ Oxide of potassium.	$Ca''\Theta$ Oxide of calcium.	$\left.\begin{matrix}Sb'''\\Sb'''\end{matrix}\right\}\Theta_3$ Oxide of antimony.	$Zr^{iv}\Theta_2$ Oxide of zirconium.
$\left.\begin{matrix}Na\\Na\end{matrix}\right\}\Theta$ Oxide of sodium.	$Zn''\Theta$ Oxide of zinc.	$\left.\begin{matrix}Bi'''\\Bi'''\end{matrix}\right\}\Theta_3$ Oxide of bismuth.	$Sn^{iv}\Theta_2$ Stannic acid.
$\left.\begin{matrix}Ag\\Ag\end{matrix}\right\}\Theta$ Oxide of silver.	$Cu''\Theta$ Oxide of copper.	——	$Ti^{iv}\Theta_2$ Titanic acid.
——	——	$\left.\begin{matrix}(C_3H_5)'''\\(C_3H_5)'''\end{matrix}\right\}\Theta_3$ Oxide of glyceryle.	$Nb^{iv}\Theta_2$ Niobic acid.
$\left.\begin{matrix}(CH_3)'\\(CH_3)'\end{matrix}\right\}\Theta$ Oxide of methyl.	$(C_2H_4)''\Theta$ Oxide of ethylene.		$Ta^{iv}O_2$ Tantalic acid.
$\left.\begin{matrix}(C_2H_5)'\\(C_2H_5)'\end{matrix}\right\}\Theta$ Oxide of ethyl.	$(C_3H_6)''\Theta$ Oxide of propylene.		
$\left.\begin{matrix}(C_3H_5)'\\(C_3H_5)'\end{matrix}\right\}\Theta$ Oxide of allyl.	$(C_5H_{10})''\Theta$ Oxide of amylene.		

Thus, as we have above remarked, oxide of ethylene combines directly with water to form glycol or hydrate of oxide of ethylene. This reaction is similar to the direct hydration of lime, and leads us to compare glycol to hydrated lime.

$$(C_2H_4)''\Theta + H_2\Theta = \left.\begin{matrix}(C_2H_4)''\\H_2\end{matrix}\right\}\Theta_2$$

Oxide of ethylene. Hydrate of ethylene.

$$Ca\Theta + H_2\Theta = \left.\begin{matrix}Ca''\\H_2\end{matrix}\right\}\Theta_2$$

Oxide of calcium. Hydrate of calcium.

Alcohol itself has long been compared to hydrate of

potassium, although no one has yet succeeded in obtaining it by directly combining the elements of water with oxide of ethyl. But the resemblance in question is founded on the analogy of the reactions which acids exercise both upon hydrate of potassium and upon alcohol or hydrate of ethyl. Here are some examples of these reactions:—

$$\left.\begin{matrix}K\\H\end{matrix}\right\}\Theta + \left.\begin{matrix}N\Theta_2\\H\end{matrix}\right\}\Theta = \left.\begin{matrix}H\\H\end{matrix}\right\}\Theta + \left.\begin{matrix}N\Theta_2\\K\end{matrix}\right\}\Theta$$

Hydrate of potassium. Nitric acid. Nitrate of potassium.

$$\left.\begin{matrix}C_2H_5\\H\end{matrix}\right\}\Theta + \left.\begin{matrix}N\Theta_2\\H\end{matrix}\right\}\Theta = \left.\begin{matrix}H\\H\end{matrix}\right\}\Theta + \left.\begin{matrix}N\Theta_2\\C_2H_5\end{matrix}\right\}\Theta$$

Hydrate of ethyl. Nitric acid. Nitrate of ethyl.

$$\left.\begin{matrix}K\\H\end{matrix}\right\}\Theta + \left.\begin{matrix}H\\Cl\end{matrix}\right\} = \left.\begin{matrix}H\\H\end{matrix}\right\}\Theta + \left.\begin{matrix}K\\Cl\end{matrix}\right\}$$

Hydrate of potassium. Hydrochloric acid. Chloride of potassium.

$$\left.\begin{matrix}C_2H_5\\H\end{matrix}\right\}\Theta + \left.\begin{matrix}H\\Cl\end{matrix}\right\} = \left.\begin{matrix}H\\H\end{matrix}\right\}\Theta + \left.\begin{matrix}C_2H_5\\Cl\end{matrix}\right\}$$

Hydrate of ethyl. Hydrochloric acid. Chloride of ethyl.

The same relations exist between the inorganic and the organic hydrates which contain polyatomic radicals. We may therefore establish the following parallel:—

Monatomic hydrates.	Diatomic hydrates.	Triatomic hydrates.
$\left.\begin{matrix}K'\\H\end{matrix}\right\}\Theta$	$\left.\begin{matrix}Mg''\\H_2\end{matrix}\right\}\Theta_2$	$\left.\begin{matrix}Bi'''\\H_3\end{matrix}\right\}\Theta_3$
Hydrate of potassium.	Hydrate of magnesium (brucite).	Hydrate of bismuth.
$\left.\begin{matrix}(C_2H_5)'\\H\end{matrix}\right\}\Theta$	$\left.\begin{matrix}(C_2H_4)''\\H_2\end{matrix}\right\}\Theta_2$	$\left.\begin{matrix}(C_3H_5)'''\\H_3\end{matrix}\right\}\Theta_3$
Hydrate of ethyl.	Hydrate of ethylene (glycol).	Hydrate of glyceryl (glycerine).

Tetratomic hydrates.	Hexatomic hydrates.
$\left.\begin{matrix}Sn^{iv}\\H_4\end{matrix}\right\}\Theta_4$	$\left.\begin{matrix}[Fe_2]^{vi}\\H_6\end{matrix}\right\}\Theta_6$
Stannic hydrate.	Ferric hydrate.
$\left.\begin{matrix}(C_4H_6)^{iv}\\H_4\end{matrix}\right\}\Theta_4$	$\left.\begin{matrix}[C_6H_8]^{vi}\\H_6\end{matrix}\right\}\Theta_6$
Erythrite.	Mannite.

Ethers may be compared to salts. This is evident from their mode of formation, as shown by the preceding equations. It is also proved by certain of their reactions. Thus the action of potash upon ethers may be compared to the action of potash upon salts. When ethers composed of alcohol, glycol, or glycerine are treated with potash, the corresponding hydrates are set free, as hydrate of copper is set free when potash acts upon a salt of copper. And further, MM. Friedel and Crafts have recently proved that an alcohol, when heated with an ether of another alcohol, sets free a certain quantity of the latter, as potash sets free hydrate of copper in a solution of the sulphate. I do not think it advisable to insist upon those analogies which are not evident and recognised by all chemists. I merely wish to compare some ethers of glycol to certain salts.

We may form ethers of glycol by combining directly oxide of ethylene with acids. Thus, by the action of acetic acid upon oxide of ethylene, we may easily obtain two ethers, which are formed by virtue of the following reactions:—

$$C_2H_4\Theta + \left.\begin{matrix}C_2H_3\Theta\\ H\end{matrix}\right\}\Theta = \left.\begin{matrix}C_2H_4\\ C_2H_3\Theta\\ H\end{matrix}\right\}\Theta_2$$

Oxide of ethylene. Acetic acid. Monacetic glycol.

$$C_2H_4\Theta + 2\left[\left.\begin{matrix}C_2H_3\Theta\\ H\end{matrix}\right\}\Theta\right] = \left.\begin{matrix}C_2H_4\\ 2(C_2H_3\Theta)\end{matrix}\right\}\Theta_2 + H_2\Theta.$$

Oxide of ethylene. Acetic acid. Diacetic glycol.

These reactions correspond in all points to those of acetic acid upon oxide of lead or oxide of copper—

$$Pb\Theta + \left.\begin{matrix}C_2H_3\Theta\\ H\end{matrix}\right\}\Theta = \left.\begin{matrix}Pb\\ C_2H_3\Theta\\ H\end{matrix}\right\}\Theta_2.$$

Oxide of lead. Acetic acid. Bibasic acetate of lead.

$$Pb\Theta + 2\left[\left.\begin{matrix}C_2H_3\Theta\\ H\end{matrix}\right\}\Theta\right] = \left.\begin{matrix}2(C_2H_3\Theta)\\ Pb\end{matrix}\right\}\Theta_2 + H_2\Theta$$

Oxide of lead. Acetic acid. Neutral acetate of lead.

Certain basic nitrates have a similar composition—

$$\left.\begin{matrix} Pb'' \\ N\Theta_2 \\ H \end{matrix}\right\} \Theta_2$$

Basic nitrate of lead of M. Pelouze.

$$\left.\begin{matrix} [Hg_2]'' \\ N\Theta_2 \\ H \end{matrix}\right\} \Theta_2$$

Mercurous mononitrate (colourless soluble rhomboidal prisms: Gerhardt).

$$\left.\begin{matrix} Bi''' \\ N\Theta_2 \\ H_2 \end{matrix}\right\} \Theta_3$$

Soluble subnitrate of bismuth.

The neutral acetates of lead and of copper correspond to the ethylenic diacetate; the bibasic acetates of lead and of copper correspond to the ethylenic monacetate—

$$\left.\begin{matrix} (C_2H_4)'' \\ (C_2H_3\Theta) \\ H \end{matrix}\right\} \Theta_2, \quad \left.\begin{matrix} Pb'' \\ (C_2H_5\Theta) \\ H \end{matrix}\right\} \Theta_2 + aq^*, \quad \left.\begin{matrix} Cu'' \\ (C_2H_3\Theta) \\ H \end{matrix}\right\} \Theta_2 + aq.^\dagger$$

Ethylenic monacetate. Plumbic monacetate. Cupric monacetate.

$$\left.\begin{matrix} (C_2H_4)'' \\ (C_2H_3\Theta)_2 \end{matrix}\right\} \Theta_2, \quad \left.\begin{matrix} Pb'' \\ (C_2H_3\Theta)_2 \end{matrix}\right\} \Theta_2 + 3aq, \quad \left.\begin{matrix} Cu'' \\ (C_2H_3\Theta) \end{matrix}\right\} \Theta_2 + aq.$$

Ethylenic diacetate. Plumbic diacetate. Cupric diacetate.

MM. Maxwell Simpson and Lourenço have described some mixed ethylenic ethers which contain 2 radicals of different acids, each of these radicals replacing 1 atom of the hydrogen in hydrate of ethylene (glycol). Thus there exists an ethylenic acetobutyrate, and this ether may be compared to the barium and strontium acetonitrates which have been described by M. C. de Hauer.‡

$$\left.\begin{matrix} (C_2H_4)'' \\ H_2 \end{matrix}\right\} \Theta_2, \quad \left.\begin{matrix} Sr'' \\ H_2 \end{matrix}\right\} \Theta_2, \quad \left.\begin{matrix} Ba'' \\ H_2 \end{matrix}\right\} \Theta_2.$$

Ethylenic hydrate. Strontium hydrate. Barium hydrate.

* $Aq = H_2\Theta$, formula in equivalents $= C_4H_3\Theta_3, 2PbO + 3HO$.

† Formula in equivalents $= C_4H_3O_3, 2CuO + 3HO$.

‡ *Journal für praktische Chemie*, vol. lxxv., p. 431.

$$\left.\begin{matrix}(\Theta_2H_4)'' \\ (\Theta_2H_3\Theta)' \\ (\Theta_4H_7\Theta)'\end{matrix}\right\} \Theta_2, \qquad \left.\begin{matrix}Sr'' \\ (\Theta_2H_3\Theta)' \\ (N\Theta_2)'\end{matrix}\right\} \qquad \left.\begin{matrix}Ba'' \\ (\Theta_2H_3\Theta)' \\ (N\Theta_2)'\end{matrix}\right\} \Theta_2.$$

Ethylenic acetobutyrate. Strontium acetonitrate. Barium acetonitrate.

We must here remark that the existence of the strontium and barium acetonitrates supplies an argument in favour of the diatomicity of strontium and barium of the same value as that which Liebig has drawn from the existence of Rochelle salt in favour of the bibasicity of tartaric acid. We know that the composition of tartaric acid was formerly represented by the formula $C_4H_2O_5,HO$, and that it was considered as monobasic. M. Liebig was the first who proposed to double this formula and to consider tartaric acid as containing 2 equivalents of basic water.*

In cream of tartar, said he, a single equivalent of water is replaced by potash. In Rochelle salt the first is replaced by potash, the second by soda.

$$C_8H_4O_{10}\left\{\begin{matrix}HO \\ HO\end{matrix}\right.$$

Tartaric acid.

$$C_8H_4O_{10}\left\{\begin{matrix}KO \\ HO\end{matrix}\right.$$

Acid tartrate of potash.

$$C_8H_4O_{10}\left\{\begin{matrix}KO \\ NaO\end{matrix}\right.$$

Anhydrous Rochelle salt.

Thus the existence of the acid tartrates and of the bibasic tartrates led M. Liebig to double the molecular weight and the formula of tartaric acid. In the same way the existence of salts of strontium and barium with two acids may cause the atomic weights of strontium and barium to be doubled.

* *Annalen der Chemie und Pharmacie*, vol. xxvi., p. 154.

SECTION III.

Combination of Multiple Radicals.

In the preceding pages we have called attention to the property possessed by radicals and polyatomic elements of uniting with each other and becoming accumulated in one and the same combination. This property explains the constitution of a great number of compounds, and reveals a certain analogy of structure, and, as it were, a family likeness, between very many groups of bodies.*

* We have already shown how the atoms of oxygen are united together in perchloric acid (page 137). The number of them united together may be more or less great, thus forming with chlorine and hydrogen the whole series of the hydrated acids of chlorine. This series, as Laurent first showed, may be considered as formed, to some extent, by the oxidation of hydrochloric acid in the same way that the series of the phosphorus acids may be looked upon as resulting from the oxidation of phosphoretted hydrogen—

ClH	Hydrochloric acid	PH_3	Phosphuretted hydrogen
$ClH\Theta$	Hypochlorous acid	$PH_3\Theta$	Unknown
$ClH\Theta_2$	Chlorous acid	$PH_3\Theta_2$	Hypophosphorous acid
$ClH\Theta_3$	Chloric acid	$PH_3\Theta_3$	Phosphorous acid
$ClH\Theta_4$	Perchloric acid	$PH_3\Theta_4$	Phosphoric acid

Dr. Odling, who has investigated this subject, has, in fact, shown the formation of hypochlorous acid by submitting hydrochloric acid to the action of oxygen under the influence of platinum black.

Analogous series exist in organic chemistry—

C_2H_4	Ethylene	C_7H_6	
$C_2H_4\Theta$	Oxide of ethylene (aldehyde)	$C_7H_6\Theta$	Hydride of benzoyl
$C_2H_4\Theta_2$	Acetic acid	$C_7H_6\Theta_2$	Benzoic acid (salic)
$C_2H_4\Theta_3$	Glycolic acid	$C_7H_6\Theta_3$	Salicylic acid
$C_2H_4\Theta_4$ [?]	Glyoxylic acid	$C_7H_6\Theta_4$	Carbohydroquinonic acid
		$C_7H_6\Theta_5$	Gallic acid

Let us take as examples those ethylenic compounds which we have just considered. The ethylene radicals possess the property of accumulating themselves in the polyethylenic alcohols, so as to form compounds belonging to more and more complicated types.

Type.	Type.	Type.
$\left.\begin{matrix}H_2\\H_2\end{matrix}\right\}\Theta_2,$	$\left.\begin{matrix}H_2\\H_2\\H_2\end{matrix}\right\}\Theta_3,$	$\left.\begin{matrix}H_2\\H_2\\H_2\\H_2\end{matrix}\right\}\Theta_4,$ &c.
$\left.\begin{matrix}(C_2H_4)''\\H_2\end{matrix}\right\}\Theta_2,$	$\left.\begin{matrix}(C_2H_4)''\\(C_2H_4)''\\H_2\end{matrix}\right\}\Theta_3,$	$\left.\begin{matrix}(C_2H_4)''\\(C_2H_4)''\\(C_2H_4)''\\H_2\end{matrix}\right\}\Theta_4.$
Ethylenic alcohol.	Diethylenic alcohol.	Triethylenic alcohol.

In inorganic chemistry there exist hydrates which may be compared to the polyethylenic alcohols. According to the analyses of MM. Mitscherlich, Payen, and Mulder, plumbic hydrate—a well-defined and crystallised body—contains $3PbO,HO$, which composition is expressed in our notation by the formula—

$$\left.\begin{matrix}Pb''\\Pb''\\Pb''\\H_2\end{matrix}\right\}\Theta_4.$$

In this compound the diatomic atoms of lead and oxygen form a chain, to the extremities of which is attached the monatomic hydrogen; and it may be supposed that the atoms of oxygen are inserted between the atoms of lead, as we may admit that they are between the ethylene groups in the polyethylenic alcohols. (Page 123.)

The normal stannic hydrate contains—

$$\left.\begin{matrix}Sn^{iv}\\H_4\end{matrix}\right\}\Theta_4.$$

By losing $H_2\Theta$ it is converted into another hydrate—or rather into a first anhydride—

$$\left.\begin{matrix} Sn^{iv} \\ H_2 \end{matrix}\right\} \Theta_3$$

which is stannic acid dried in vacuo, analysed by M. Fremy. The composition of the stannates is represented by the formula—

$$\left.\begin{matrix} Sn^{iv} \\ 2R' \end{matrix}\right\} \Theta_3.$$

According to M. Fremy, metastannic acid contains in its molecule 5 atoms of tin. When it has been dried at 100° its composition is expressed by the formula—

$$\left.\begin{matrix} 5Sn^{iv} \\ H_{10} \end{matrix}\right\} \Theta_{15}$$

The metastannates, which contain, according to M. Fremy,

$$\left.\begin{matrix} 5Sn^{iv} \\ R_2H_8 \end{matrix}\right\} \Theta_{15}$$

correspond to this latter hydrate.

Silicium, tetratomic like tin, possesses also, like it, the property of becoming accumulated in those combinations which I have called *polysilicic*,* and which form a very large number of the complex silicates. The following may be considered the mode of generation of these compounds:—

Anhydrous silicic acid contains $Si\Theta_2$. Its hydrate is—

$$\left.\begin{matrix} Si^{iv} \\ H_4 \end{matrix}\right\} \Theta_4$$

By losing $H_2\Theta$, it gives a first anhydride—

$$\left.\begin{matrix} Si^{iv} \\ H_2 \end{matrix}\right\} \Theta_3$$

But several molecules of silicic hydrate can unite and form, by losing water, a series of anhydrides intermediate in composition between the normal hydrated silicic acid and anhydrous silicic acid. We thus obtain

* *Répertoire de Chimie pure*, vol. ii., p. 464.

series of polysilicic acids in which hydrogen may be replaced, completely or partially, by metals. These series are the following:—

POLYSILICIC COMPOUNDS.

$$\left.\begin{matrix}Si\\H_4\end{matrix}\right\}\Theta_4 \quad \left.\begin{matrix}Si_2\\H_8\end{matrix}\right\}\Theta_8{}^* \quad \left.\begin{matrix}Si_3\\H_{12}\end{matrix}\right\}\Theta_{12} \quad \left.\begin{matrix}Si_4\\H_{16}\end{matrix}\right\}\Theta_{16} \quad \left.\begin{matrix}Si_6\\H_{24}\end{matrix}\right\}\Theta_{24}$$

* The following considerations will show that all these polysilicic hydrates cannot exist in a free state. The first hydrate—

$$\left.\begin{matrix}Si\\H_4\end{matrix}\right\}\Theta_4$$

can exist; tetratomic silicium can, in fact, unite with four monatomic groups $(H\Theta)'$. But, in the hydrates which contain several atoms of silicium, part of the affinities of the silicium and the oxygen must be employed to join these atoms together, without which the molecular edifice would fall to pieces. The most probable supposition is to admit that the atoms of silicium are joined to each other by the atoms of oxygen. Now, to join n atoms of silicium, there must be $n-1$ atoms of oxygen. The latter deprive the silicium of $2(n-1)$ affinities; and if we subtract $2(n-1)$ from the sum of the affinities residing in n atoms of silicium (that is to say, from $4n$), the difference $4n-2(n-1)=2(n+1)$ will express the affinities remaining in the chain of n atoms of silicium united by $n-1$ atoms of oxygen. The silicic hydrate, which is the richest in hydrogen, is therefore—

$$Si_n + \Theta_{(n-1)} + (H\Theta)_{2(n+1)}$$

If we make $n=3$, the trisilicic hydrate containing the greatest amount of hydrogen will be—

$$Si_3\Theta_2(H\Theta)_8 = \left.\begin{matrix}Si_3\\H_8\end{matrix}\right\}\Theta_{10}.$$

he following formula expresses the mutual relations existing between he atoms of such a hydrate:—

$$\begin{matrix}Si-(H\Theta)_3\\ | \\ \Theta \\ | \\ Si-(H\Theta)_2 \\ | \\ \Theta \\ | \\ Si-(H\Theta)_3\end{matrix}$$

$$\left.\begin{matrix}Si\\H_2\end{matrix}\right\}\Theta_3 \quad \left.\begin{matrix}Si_2\\H_6\end{matrix}\right\}\Theta_7 \quad \left.\begin{matrix}Si_3\\H_{10}\end{matrix}\right\}\Theta_{11} \quad \left.\begin{matrix}Si_4\\H_{14}\end{matrix}\right\}\Theta_{15} \quad \left.\begin{matrix}Si_6\\H_{22}\end{matrix}\right\}\Theta_{23}$$

$$\left.\begin{matrix}Si_2\\H_4\end{matrix}\right\}\Theta_6 \quad \left.\begin{matrix}Si_3\\H_8\end{matrix}\right\}\Theta_{10} \quad \left.\begin{matrix}Si_4\\H_{12}\end{matrix}\right\}\Theta_{14} \quad ,, \quad ,,$$

$\left.\begin{matrix}Si\\(C_2H_5)_4\end{matrix}\right\}\Theta_4$	$\left.\begin{matrix}Si_3\\H_2\end{matrix}\right\}\Theta_5$	$\left.\begin{matrix}Si_3\\H_6\end{matrix}\right\}\Theta_9$	$\left.\begin{matrix}Si_4\\H_{10}\end{matrix}\right\}\Theta_{13}$	$\left.\begin{matrix}Si_6\\H_{12}\end{matrix}\right\}\Theta_{18}$
Tetrethylic silicate.	Silicic hydrate of Fuchs.	$\left.\begin{matrix}Si_3\\H_4\end{matrix}\right\}\Theta_8$	$\left.\begin{matrix}Si_4\\H_8\end{matrix}\right\}\Theta_{12}$	,, ,,

$\left.\begin{matrix}Si\\2Mg''\end{matrix}\right\}\Theta_4$	Silicic hydrate of M. Fremy.	$\left.\begin{matrix}Si_4\\H_6\end{matrix}\right\}\Theta_{11}$	$\left.\begin{matrix}Si_6\\H_8\end{matrix}\right\}\Theta_{16}$
Peridot			

$\left.\begin{matrix}Si\\2Gl\end{matrix}\right\}\Theta_4$	$\left.\begin{matrix}Si_2\\Al_2^{vi}\\Ca''\end{matrix}\right\}\Theta_8$	$\left.\begin{matrix}Si_3\\H_2\end{matrix}\right\}\Theta_7$	$\left.\begin{matrix}Si_4\\Al_2^{vi}\\Na_2H_6\end{matrix}\right\}\Theta$	$\left.\begin{matrix}Si_6\\2Al_2^{vi}\\6Ca''\end{matrix}\right\}\Theta_{24}$
Phenacite.	Anorthite.	Hydrate of Doveri.	Analcime.	Grossulaire.

$\left.\begin{matrix}Si\\2Zn''\end{matrix}\right\}\Theta_4$	$\left.\begin{matrix}Si_2\\Ca''\\H_4\end{matrix}\right\}\Theta_7$	$\left.\begin{matrix}Si_3\\2Mg''\\H_4\end{matrix}\right\}\Theta_{10}$	$\left.\begin{matrix}Si_4\\Al_2\\2K\end{matrix}\right\}\Theta_{12}$	$\left.\begin{matrix}Si_6\\2Al_2^{vi}\\6Fe''\end{matrix}\right\}\Theta_{24}$
Willemite.				
$\left.\begin{matrix}Si\\\overset{iv}{Zr}\end{matrix}\right\}\Theta_4$ Zircon.	Okenite.	Magnesite.*	Amphigene.	Almandine (Oriental garnet).

$\left.\begin{matrix}Si\\(C_2H_5)_2\end{matrix}\right\}\Theta_3$	$\left.\begin{matrix}Si_2\\Ca''\\Mg''\end{matrix}\right\}\Theta_6$	$\left.\begin{matrix}Si_3\\Al_2^{vi}\\Ca''\end{matrix}\right\}\Theta_{10}$	$\left.\begin{matrix}Si_4\\Al_2^{vi}\\H_2\end{matrix}\right\}\Theta_{12}$	$\left.\begin{matrix}Si_6\\Al_2^{iv}\\3Gl''\end{matrix}\right\}\Theta_{18}$
Diethylic silicate.	Diopside.	Labradorite.	Pyrophyllite.	Emerald

$\left.\begin{matrix}Si\\Mg''\end{matrix}\right\}\Theta_3$	$\left.\begin{matrix}Si_2\\(C_2H_5)_2\end{matrix}\right\}\Theta_5$	$\left.\begin{matrix}Si_3\\Fe_2^{vi}\end{matrix}\right\}\Theta_9 + 12aq.$	$\left.\begin{matrix}Si_4\\3Mg''\\H_2\end{matrix}\right\}\Theta_{12}$	$\left.\begin{matrix}Si_6\\Al_2^{vi}\\K_2\end{matrix}\right\}\Theta_{16}$
Enstatite.	Diethylic disilicate.	Chlorophæite.	Talc.	Orthose felspar.

It is clear that this theory allows us to conceive, and even to predict, the existence of innumerable silicates. Their constitution and the formulæ which represent them are not always very simple, and, in a large number of

* Or, $\left.\begin{matrix}Si_3\\2Mg\end{matrix}\right\}\Theta_8 + 2\ aq\ (Aq = H_2\Theta).$

We may similarly decompose the formulæ of okenite, pyrophyllite, analcime, talc, &c.

cases, cannot be so. One thing, however, is simple and
rational—viz., their mode of generation, which is based
on the one hand upon the principle of *the accumulation
of the polyatomic radicals*, and on the other hand upon
the *successive dehydration* which may be undergone by
hydrates containing polyatomic radicals. These principles, which govern the constitution of a crowd of organic
compounds, are susceptible of a great number of appli-
cations in inorganic chemistry and in mineralogy. We
will give some new examples of them :—

1st. Glycerine contains—

$$\left. \begin{array}{c} (C_3H_5)''' \\ H_3 \end{array} \right\} O_3$$

It may form, by losing H_2O, glycide—

$$\left. \begin{array}{c} (C_3H_5)''' \\ H \end{array} \right\} O_2$$

whose curious combinations were made known by M.
Reboul.*

The hydrates of aluminium, of iron, and their analogues may similarly suffer a partial decomposition—

$$\left. \begin{array}{c} Al_2^{vi} \\ H_6 \end{array} \right\} O_6 \qquad \left. \begin{array}{c} Al_2^{vi} \\ H_4 \end{array} \right\} O_5 \qquad \left. \begin{array}{c} Al_2^{vi} \\ H_2 \end{array} \right\} O_4 \qquad Al_2^{vi}O_3$$

Gibbsite.   Diaspore.   Corundum.

$$\left. \begin{array}{c} Fe^{vi} \\ H_6 \end{array} \right\} O_6 \qquad\qquad\qquad '' \qquad\qquad \left. \begin{array}{c} Fe_2^{vi} \\ H_2 \end{array} \right\} O_4$$

Ferric hydrate   Goethite.

$$\left. \begin{array}{c} Mn_2^{vi} \\ H_2 \end{array} \right\} O_4$$

Manganite.

$$\left. \begin{array}{c} Ur_2^{vi} \\ H_2 \end{array} \right\} O_4$$

Uranic hydrate.

There exist salts corresponding to these different
hydrates. Such are disthene and the spinels—

$$\left. \begin{array}{c} Al_2^{vi} \\ Si^{vi} \end{array} \right\} O_5 \qquad\qquad \left. \begin{array}{c} Al_2^{vi} \\ Mg'' \end{array} \right\} O_4$$

Disthene.   Spinel.

* *Annales de Chimie et de Physique*, 3rd series, vol. lx., p. 5, 1860.

2nd. M. Lourenço* has shown that several molecules of glycerine may unite with elimination of water, and form polyglyceric combinations—

$$2\left[\left.\begin{matrix}C_3H_5\\H_3\end{matrix}\right\}\Theta_3\right] = \left.\begin{matrix}C_3H_5\\C_3H_5\\H_4\end{matrix}\right\}\Theta_5 + H_2\Theta.$$

Pyroglycerine.

$$2\left[\left.\begin{matrix}C_3H_5\\H_3\end{matrix}\right\}\Theta_3\right] = \left.\begin{matrix}C_3H_5\\C_3H_5\\H_2\end{matrix}\right\}\Theta_4 + 2H_2\Theta.$$

Pyroglycide.

$$3\left[\left.\begin{matrix}C_3H_5\\H_3\end{matrix}\right\}\Theta_3\right] = \left.\begin{matrix}3(C_3H_5)\\H_5\end{matrix}\right\}\Theta_7 + 2H_2\Theta.$$

$$3\left[\left.\begin{matrix}C_3H_5\\H_3\end{matrix}\right\}\Theta_3\right] = \left.\begin{matrix}3(C_3H_5)\\H_3\end{matrix}\right\}\Theta_6 + 3H_2\Theta.$$

The bodies thus formed constitute, in a manner, basic hydrates. Similarly limonite constitutes a basic ferric hydrate—

$$2\left[\left.\begin{matrix}Fe_2^{vi}\\H_6\end{matrix}\right\}\Theta_6\right] = \left.\begin{matrix}2Fe_2^{vi}\\H_6\end{matrix}\right\}\Theta_9 + 3H_2\Theta.$$

Limonite.

It is evident that in such hydrates the basic hydrogen may be replaced by radicals of acids. We thus obtain basic salts, of which the polyethylenic and polyglyceric ethers are the representatives in organic chemistry, and of which very numerous examples are known in inorganic chemistry.

Let us first take the constitution of the basic ethers in question—

$$\left.\begin{matrix}C_2H_4\\C_2H_4\\(C_2H_3\Theta)_2\end{matrix}\right\}\Theta_3 \qquad \left.\begin{matrix}C_2H_4\\C_2H_4\\C_2H_4\\(C_2H_3\Theta)_2\end{matrix}\right\}\Theta_4 \qquad \left.\begin{matrix}C_2H_4\\C_2H_4\\C_2H_4\\C_2H_3\Theta\\H\end{matrix}\right\}\Theta_4$$

Diethylenic diacetate. Triethylenic diacetate. Triethylenic monacetate.

It is evident that the basic acetates of lead and copper are the analogues of these ethers—

* *Comptes Rendus*, vol. lii., p. 369.

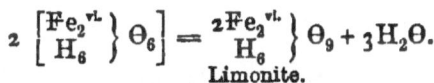

$$\left.\begin{matrix}Cu'' \\ Cu'' \\ (C_2H_3\Theta)_2\end{matrix}\right\}\Theta_3 + 3aq.$$

Dicupric diacetate.*

$$\left.\begin{matrix}Cu \\ Cu \\ Cu \\ (C_2H_3\Theta)_2\end{matrix}\right\}\Theta_4$$

Tricupric diacetate.

$$\left.\begin{matrix}Pb \\ Pb \\ Pb \\ (C_2H_3\Theta)_2\end{matrix}\right\}\Theta_4 + 3aq.$$

Triplumbic diacetate.

$$\left.\begin{matrix}Pb \\ Pb \\ Pb \\ C_2H_3\Theta \\ H\end{matrix}\right\}\Theta_4.$$

Triplumbic monacetate (called sexbasic acetate).

Many other basic compounds of inorganic chemistry possess an analogous constitution. We will mention some from the different kinds of salts. We must first remark that these basic salts always contain a polyatomic metal; the well-defined monatomic metals—such as potassium, sodium, and even silver—not forming basic salts properly so called.

Basic Nitrates.

$$\left.\begin{matrix}Pb_3 \\ (N\Theta_2)_2\end{matrix}\right\}\Theta_4$$

Triplumbic dinitrate. (Berzelius.)

$$\left.\begin{matrix}Hg_3 \\ (N\Theta_2)_2\end{matrix}\right\}\Theta_4$$

Trimercuric dinitrate. (Kane.)

$$\left.\begin{matrix}(Hg_2)_2 \\ (N\Theta_2)_2\end{matrix}\right\}\Theta_3 + aq.$$

Dimercurous dinitrate; yellow crystalline salt. (Kane).†

$$\left.\begin{matrix}Pb_2 \\ N\Theta \\ N\Theta_2\end{matrix}\right\}\Theta_3$$

Nitrosonitrate of lead. Basic hyponitrate of lead of M. Peligot.

Basic Sulphates.

$$\left.\begin{matrix}Cu_4 \\ S\Theta_2\end{matrix}\right\}\Theta_5 + 4\ aq.$$

Brochantite.

$$\left.\begin{matrix}Hg_3 \\ S\Theta_2\end{matrix}\right\}\Theta_4.$$

Turbith mineral.

Basic Carbonates.

Carbon being a tetratomic element, like silicium, the composition of the normal carbonic hydrate should be—

$$\left.\begin{matrix}C^{iv.} \\ H_4\end{matrix}\right\}\Theta_4,$$

* It is possible that this salt may be a monocupric monacetate—

$$\left.\begin{matrix}Cu \\ (C_2H_3\Theta)' \\ H\end{matrix}\right\}\Theta_2 + H_2\Theta.$$

† Polymere of the soluble mercurous nitrate of Gerhardt (p. 153).

and the normal carbonates should contain—

$$\left.\begin{matrix} C^{iv.} \\ 4R' \end{matrix}\right\} \Theta_4 \quad \text{or} \quad \left.\begin{matrix} C^{iv.} \\ 2R'' \end{matrix}\right\} \Theta_4.$$

These carbonates Dr. Odling has called *orthocarbonates*;* but we know that the most numerous and best defined carbonates belong to the type—

$$\left.\begin{matrix} C^{iv.} \\ 2R \end{matrix}\right\} \Theta_3;$$

or, in other words, that in these carbonates the ratio of the oxygen of the acid to that of the oxide is 2 : 1. It seems then natural to consider these latter carbonates as neutral or normal. Their constitution may be expressed by the formula—

$$\left.\begin{matrix} (C\Theta)'' \\ 2R' \end{matrix}\right\} \Theta_2;$$

and the orthocarbonates may be considered as basic carbonates of the formula—

$$\left.\begin{matrix} 2R'' \\ (C\Theta)'' \end{matrix}\right\} \Theta_3,$$

derived from the type

$$\left.\begin{matrix} 2R'' \\ H_2 \end{matrix}\right\} \Theta_3$$

That being laid down, we may admit the existence of basic carbonates belonging to several types, and in which the oxygen of the oxide Oo is to the oxygen of the acid Oc in the following ratios :—

Oo : Oc : : 2 : 2 bibasic carbonates.
Oo : Oc : : 3 : 4 sesquicarbonates.
Oo : Oc : : 3 : 2 carbonates of the sesquioxides.

Bibasic Carbonates.	*Sesquicarbonates.*	*Carbonates of the Sesquioxides.*
$\left.\begin{matrix} 2Cu \\ C\Theta \end{matrix}\right\} \Theta_3 + aq.$†	$\left.\begin{matrix} 3Cu \\ 2C\Theta \end{matrix}\right\} \Theta_5 + aq.$	$\left.\begin{matrix} Fe_2^{vi.} \\ C\Theta \end{matrix}\right\} \Theta_4$
Malachite.	Azurite.	Ferric carbonate. (Parkmann.)

* *Philosophical Magazine*, vol. xviii., p. 368.

† $Aq = H_2\Theta$.

Bibasic Carbonates.	*Sesquicarbonates.*	*Carbonates of the Sesquioxides.*
$\left.\begin{matrix}2\text{Cu}\\ \text{C}\Theta\end{matrix}\right\}\Theta_3$	$\left.\begin{matrix}{}_3\text{Cu}\\ {}_2\text{C}\Theta\end{matrix}\right\}\Theta_5+\text{aq.}$	$\left.\begin{matrix}\text{Ur}_2{}^{\text{vi.}}\\ \text{C}\Theta\end{matrix}\right\}\Theta_4$
Mysorine?	Azurite.	Uranic carbonate. (Ebelmen.)
$\left.\begin{matrix}2\text{Pb}\\ \text{C}\Theta\end{matrix}\right\}\Theta_3+\text{aq.}$	$\left.\begin{matrix}3\text{Pb}\\ 2(\text{C}\Theta)\end{matrix}\right\}\Theta_5+\text{aq.}$	$\left.\begin{matrix}\text{Cr}_2{}^{\text{vi.}}\\ \text{C}\Theta\end{matrix}\right\}\Theta_4$*
Subcarbonate of hydrated lead. (Bounsdorff.)	Dutch whitelead. (Hochstetter.)	Chromic carbonate (Parkmann.)
$\left.\begin{matrix}\text{Zn}_2\\ \text{C}\Theta\end{matrix}\right\}\Theta_3+2\text{aq.}$	$\left.\begin{matrix}2\text{Bi}'''\\ 2\text{C}\Theta\end{matrix}\right\}\Theta_5+\text{aq.}$	
Subcarbonate of hydrated zinc. (Schindler.)	Carbonate of bismuth.	

There exist basic silicates. Thus staurotide may be looked upon as a basic compound of the form—

$$\left.\begin{matrix}4\text{Al}_2{}^{\text{vi.}}\\ 3\text{Si}\end{matrix}\right\}\Theta_{18},$$

in which the sixth part of the aluminium is replaced by ferricum.

In the inorganic compounds that we have just reviewed we see polyatomic elements accumulate in one and the same combination, uniting one with another doubtless by the intervention of atoms of oxygen (page 156). We find this property in other organic and inorganic compounds, in which we see the radicals of polyatomic acids accumulated in one and the same combination. Let us investigate this point.

* The chromic dicarbonate analysed by M. Parkmann (*Bulletin de la Société Chimique*, vol. v., p. 551)—

$$\left.\begin{matrix}\text{Cr}_2{}^{\text{vi.}}\\ 2\text{C}\Theta\end{matrix}\right\}\Theta_5 \quad \text{or} \quad \left.\begin{matrix}\text{C}_2\\ \text{Cr}_2\end{matrix}\right\}\Theta_7$$

may be compared to a disilicate (p. 159). In general the carbonate may be referred to the type

$$\left.\begin{matrix}\text{C}^{\text{iv.}}\\ 2\text{R}'\end{matrix}\right\}\Theta_3$$

which corresponds to the first carbonic anhydride—

$$\left.\begin{matrix}\text{C}^{\text{iv.}}\\ \text{H}_2\end{matrix}\right\}\Theta_3 = \left.\begin{matrix}\text{C}^{\text{iv.}}\\ \text{H}_4\end{matrix}\right\}\Theta_4-\text{H}_2\Theta.$$

By the oxidation of diethylenic alcohol there is formed a compound which I have called diglycolic acid,[*] and in which the two ethylene radicals of the alcohol are replaced by two glycolyl radicals.

$$\left. \begin{array}{l} 2(C_2H_4) \\ H_2 \end{array} \right\} \Theta_3, \qquad\qquad \left. \begin{array}{l} 2(C_2H_2\Theta) \\ H_2 \end{array} \right\} \Theta_4.$$

Diethylenic alcohol.   Diglycolic acid.

M. Friedel and I have described the ethers of a dilactic and of a trilactic acid which possess a constitution analogous to that of diglycolic acid.[†]

$$\left. \begin{array}{l} 2(C_3H_4\Theta) \\ H_2 \end{array} \right\} \Theta_3, \qquad\qquad \left. \begin{array}{l} 3(C_3H_4\Theta) \\ H_2 \end{array} \right\} \Theta_3.$$

Dilactic acid   Trilactic acid.

In a very important article, M. H. Schiff[‡] has lately made known a ditartaric acid—

$$\left. \begin{array}{l} 2(C_4H_4\Theta_4)'' \\ H_2 \end{array} \right\} \Theta_3.$$

Analogous combinations exist in inorganic chemistry. I may mention disulphuric (Nordhausen acid), dichromic, and diphosphoric acids, whose salts are represented by the following formulæ:—

$$\left. \begin{array}{l} 2(S\Theta_2) \\ K_2 \end{array} \right\} \Theta_3 \qquad \left. \begin{array}{l} (Cr\Theta_2)'' \\ (Cr\Theta_2)'' \\ K_2 \end{array} \right\} \Theta_3 \qquad \left. \begin{array}{l} (P\Theta)''' \\ (P\Theta)''' \\ Na_4 \end{array} \right\} \Theta_5$$

Disulphate of potassium (anhydrous).   Dichromate of potassium.   Pyrophosphate of sodium.[§]

We know that MM. Maddrell,[||] Fleitmann, and Henneberg have described a series of acids polymeric with metaphosphoric acid, and which may be looked upon, in common with all the compounds here referred

[*] *Annales de Chimie et de Physique*, 3rd series, vol. lxix., p. 344.

[†] *Annales de Chimie et de Physique*, 3rd series, vol. lxiii., p. 112.

[‡] *Ibid.*, vol. lxix., p. 257.

[§] *Annalen der Chemie und Pharmacie*, vol. lxi., p. 53.

[||] *Ibid.*, vol. lxv., p. 304, and vol. lxxii., p. 232.

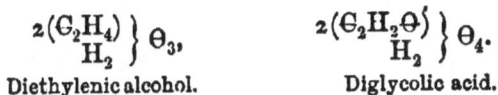

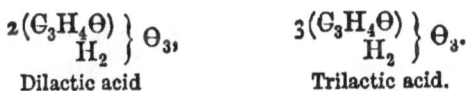

to, as anhydrides formed by the condensation of several molecules of phosphoric acid with elimination of water.

$$2\left[\left.\begin{matrix}(P\Theta)'''\\ H_3\end{matrix}\right\}\Theta_3\right] = \left.\begin{matrix}2(P\Theta)'''\\ H_2\end{matrix}\right\}\Theta_4 + 2H_2\Theta$$

Phosphoric acid. Dimetaphosphoric acid.

$$3\left[\left.\begin{matrix}(P\Theta)'''\\ H_3\end{matrix}\right\}\Theta_3\right] = \left.\begin{matrix}3(P\Theta)'''\\ H_3\end{matrix}\right\}\Theta_6 + 3H_2\Theta$$

Trimetaphosphoric acid.

$$4\left[\left.\begin{matrix}(P\Theta)'''\\ H_3\end{matrix}\right\}\Theta_3\right] = \left.\begin{matrix}4(P\Theta)'''\\ H_4\end{matrix}\right\}\Theta_8 + 4H_2\Theta, \text{ \&c.*}$$

Tetrametaphosphoric acid.

M. Friedel and I† have made known the ether of a mixed acid formed by the union of one molecule of lactic acid with one molecule of succinic acid, with elimination of water—

$$\left.\begin{matrix}(\Theta_3H_4\Theta)''\\ H_2\end{matrix}\right\}\Theta_2 + \left.\begin{matrix}(\Theta_4H_4\Theta_2)''\\ H_2\end{matrix}\right\}\Theta_2 = \left.\begin{matrix}(\Theta_3H_4\Theta)''\\ (\Theta_4H_4\Theta_2)''\\ H_2\end{matrix}\right\}\Theta_3 + H_2\Theta$$

Lactic acid. Succinic acid. Lacto-succinic acid.

Lacto-succinic acid, whose ether we have analysed—

$$\left.\begin{matrix}(\Theta_3H_4\Theta)'\\ (\Theta_4H_4\Theta_2)''\\ (\Theta_2H_5)_2\end{matrix}\right\}\Theta_3$$

contains both the radical of lactic acid and that of succinic acid, and these radicals are probably united one to the other by an atom of oxygen. A certain number of other organic and inorganic acids are formed in a like manner, and possess an analogous constitution. Thus M. Bolley's chromosulphuric acid contains—

$$\left.\begin{matrix}(Cr\Theta_2)''\\ (S\Theta_2)''\\ H_2\end{matrix}\right\}\Theta_3$$

* We may foresee the existence of anhydrides

$$\left.\begin{matrix}3(P\Theta)\\ H\end{matrix}\right\}\Theta_5 \quad\text{and}\quad \left.\begin{matrix}4(P\Theta)\\ H_2\end{matrix}\right\}\Theta_7$$

formed according to the principle of *successive dehydrations*, as shown at page 158 and the following pages.

† *Annales de Chimie et de Physique*, 3rd series, vol. lxiii., p. 122.

M. Friedel and I have compared sphene, or silico-titanate of calcium, to the lacto-succinate of ethyl—

$$\left.\begin{matrix}(Si\Theta)'' \\ (Ti\Theta)'' \\ Ca''\end{matrix}\right\}\Theta_3{}^*$$

Other inorganic kinds are formed by the condensation of the elements of two acids with elimination of water. This is the case with the borosilicates. The hydrate corresponding to datholite would be formed by the combination of 2 molecules of boric acid and 2 molecules of silicic acid, with elimination of 5 molecules of water—

$$2\left[\left.\begin{matrix}Bo''' \\ H_3\end{matrix}\right\}\Theta_3\right] + 2\left[\left.\begin{matrix}Si^{iv.} \\ H_4\end{matrix}\right\}\Theta_4\right] = \left.\begin{matrix}2Si^{iv.} \\ 2Bo'' \\ H_4{}'\end{matrix}\right\}\Theta_9 + 5H_2\Theta$$

$$\left.\begin{matrix}Si_2 \\ Bo_2 \\ Ca_2\end{matrix}\right\}\Theta_9 + aq.$$

Datholite.

* Or,

$$\left.\begin{matrix}Si^{vi.} \\ Ti^{vi.} \\ Ca''\end{matrix}\right\}\Theta_5$$

Annales de Chimie et de Physique, 3rd series, vol. liii., p. 124.

SECTION IV.

Inorganic and Organic Chlorides, Bromides, &c.

In the preceding pages we have made apparent the analogies of structure, and even of reactions, that exist between the organic oxides, hydrates, and ethers, and the inorganic oxides, hydrates, and salts. These analogies may be traced in other classes of compounds. We have already compared the inorganic with the organic chlorides. Let us confine ourselves to this short remark, that it is not a question here of purely symbolic relations, but that the analogies expressed by the typical formulæ are founded upon the similitude of the reactions. Let us compare, in this respect, the chloride of sulphuryl with the chloride of succinyl. Both chlorides contain a radical of a bibasic acid. Both are decomposed in the same way under the influence of water, the one forming sulphuric acid, the other succinic acid.

$$S\Theta_2,Cl_2 + \left.\begin{matrix}H_2\\H_2\end{matrix}\right\}\Theta_2 \quad = \quad \left.\begin{matrix}S\Theta_2\\H_2\end{matrix}\right\}\Theta_2 + 2HCl$$

Chloride of sulphuryl. — Sulphuric acid.

$$C_4H_4\Theta_2,Cl_2 + \left.\begin{matrix}H_2\\H_2\end{matrix}\right\}\Theta_2 \quad = \quad \left.\begin{matrix}C_4H_4\Theta_2\\H_2\end{matrix}\right\}\Theta_2 + 2HCl$$

Chloride of succinyl. — Succinic acid.

Similarly the chlorides, bromides, and iodides of the alcohol radicals may be compared to the metallic chlorides, bromides, and iodides. The analogy of the following reactions cannot be mistaken:—

$$(C_2H_5)'I \quad + \quad \left.\begin{matrix}C_2H_3\Theta\\Ag\end{matrix}\right\}\Theta \quad = \quad AgI \quad + \quad \left.\begin{matrix}C_2H_3\Theta\\(C_2H_5)'\end{matrix}\right\}\Theta$$

Iodide of ethyl. — Acetate of silver. — Acetate of ethyl.

$$KI \quad + \quad \left.\begin{matrix}C_2H_3\Theta\\Ag\end{matrix}\right\}\Theta \quad = \quad AgI \quad + \quad \left.\begin{matrix}C_2H_3\Theta\\K\end{matrix}\right\}\Theta$$

Iodide of potassium. — Acetate of potassium.

$$(C_2H_4)''I_2 + 2\left[\left.\begin{matrix}C_2H_3\Theta\\ Ag\end{matrix}\right\}\Theta\right] = 2AgI + \left.\begin{matrix}2(C_2H_3\Theta)\\ (C_2H_4)''\end{matrix}\right\}\Theta_2$$

Diniodide of ethylene. — Dinacetate of ethylene.

$$Ca''I_2 + 2\left[\left.\begin{matrix}C_2H_3\Theta\\ Ag\end{matrix}\right\}\Theta\right] = 2AgI + \left.\begin{matrix}2(C_2H_3\Theta)\\ Ca''\end{matrix}\right\}\Theta_2$$

Iodide of calcium. — Dinacetate of calcium.

It seems to me useless to insist upon these relationships, which are evident and accepted by all chemists. I will give some others that are newer and more remarkable.

There exists, independently of M. Regnault's dichloride of sulphuryl, a compound intermediate between the latter and sulphuric acid. This is chlorosulphuric acid, obtained by Dr. Williamson* by treating concentrated sulphuric acid with perchloride of phosphorus.

$$\left.\begin{matrix}(S\Theta_2)''\\ H_2\end{matrix}\right\}\Theta_2 \qquad \left.\begin{matrix}(S\Theta_2)''\\ H\end{matrix}\right\}\Theta \atop Cl \qquad (S\Theta_2)''Cl_2$$

Sulphuric acid. — Chlorosulphuric acid. (Sulphuric chlorhydrine.) — Dichloride of sulphuryl.

Chlorosuccinic acid—

$$\left.\begin{matrix}(C_4H_4\Theta_2)''\\ H\end{matrix}\right\}\Theta \atop Cl$$

corresponding to chlorosulphuric acid, has not yet been obtained, to my knowledge, although theory foresees the existence of such a compound. But in the lactic acid series we know of compounds intermediate between the dichlorides and the acids.

$$\left.\begin{matrix}(C_2H_2\Theta)''\\ H_2\end{matrix}\right\}\Theta_2 \qquad \left.\begin{matrix}(C_2H_2\Theta)''\\ H\end{matrix}\right\}\Theta \atop Cl \qquad (C_2H_2\Theta)''Cl_2$$

Glycolic acid. — Chloroglycolic acid (monochloracetic). — Dichloride of glycolyl.

$$\left.\begin{matrix}(C_3H_4\Theta)''\\ H_2\end{matrix}\right\}\Theta_2 \qquad \left.\begin{matrix}(C_3H_4\Theta)''\\ H\end{matrix}\right\}\Theta \atop Cl \qquad (C_3H_4\Theta)''Cl_2$$

Lactic acid. — Chlorolactic acid (monochloropropionic). — Dichloride of lactyl.

* *Annales de Chimie et de Physique*, 3rd series, vol. xli., p. 486.

Such intermediate compounds exist also in the series of the polyatomic alcohols. The first were obtained by M. Berthelot,* who described, under the name of monochlorhydrine and dichlorhydrine, compounds intermediate between glycerine and trichloride of glyceryl (trichlorhydrine)—

$$\left.\begin{array}{r}(\text{Ꞓ}_3H_5)''' \\ H_3\end{array}\right\}\Theta_3 \qquad \begin{array}{c}\left.\begin{array}{r}(\text{Ꞓ}_3H_5)''' \\ H_2\end{array}\right\}\Theta \\ Cl\end{array} \qquad \begin{array}{c}\left.\begin{array}{r}(\text{Ꞓ}_3H_5)''' \\ H\end{array}\right\}\Theta \\ Cl_2\end{array} \qquad (\text{Ꞓ}_3H_5)'''Cl_3$$

Glycerine.	Monochlorhydrine.	Dichlorhydrine.	Trichloride of glyceryl.

With glycol I have similarly obtained an intermediate compound, which I have called chlorhydric glycol, or monochlorhydrine of glycol.

There are some metallic compounds which possess an analogous constitution, and which may be considered as intermediate between the hydrates and the chlorides, bromides, and fluorides.

Berzelius has described, under the name of oxyfluoride of copper, a well crystallised body, whose composition he expressed by the formula $CuFl,CuO,HO$. If we adopt for oxygen and copper, atomic weights double their equivalents, this formula becomes—

$$\text{Ꞓ}u''\Theta.HFl.$$

Fluorhydrate of oxide of copper.

Now, it is easy to see that there exist between hydrate of copper, fluoride of copper, and this body, the same relations as those which exist between chlorhydric glycol, glycol, and chloride of ethylene.

$$\left.\begin{array}{r}\text{Ꞓ}u'' \\ H_2\end{array}\right\}\Theta_2 \qquad \begin{array}{c}\left.\begin{array}{r}\text{Ꞓ}u'' \\ H\end{array}\right\}\Theta, \\ Fl\end{array} \qquad \text{Ꞓ}u''Fl_2$$

Hydrate of copper.	Cupric monofluorhydrine.	Cupric difluoride.

* *Annales de Chimie et de Physique*, 3rd series, vol. xli., p. 296.

$\left.\begin{matrix}(C_2H_4)''\\H_2\end{matrix}\right\}\Theta_2$	$\left.\begin{matrix}(C_2H_4)''\\H\end{matrix}\right\}\Theta$ Cl	$(C_2H_4)''Cl_2$
Glycol.	Monochlorhydric glycol.	Ethylenic dichloride.

M. Debray* observed this important fact, that when molybdic acid is heated in a current of hydrochloric acid gas to 150° or 200°, it forms a white, crystalline, and very volatile substance. This is a chlorhydrate of molybdic acid, the composition of which he expresses by the formula MoO_3,HCl. I look upon this body as being a molybdic chlorhydrine, and I should define in the following manner its connexion with molybdic hydrate. Molybdenum may be considered as hexatomic in molybdic acid

$$Mo\Theta_3.$$

Normal molybdic hydrate would be—

$$\left.\begin{matrix}Mo^{vi}\\H_6\end{matrix}\right\}\Theta_6.\dagger$$

M. Debray described the first anhydride of this normal hydrate, viz., the dihydrate—

$$\left.\begin{matrix}Mo^{vi}\\H_4\end{matrix}\right\}\Theta_5.\ddagger$$

The molybdic chlorhydrine, described by M. Debray, is derived from this dihydrate—

$\left.\begin{matrix}Mo^{vi}\\H_4\end{matrix}\right\}\Theta_5,$	$\left.\begin{matrix}Mo^{vi}\\H_2\end{matrix}\right\}\Theta_3$ $Cl_2.$
Molybdic dihydrate.	Molybdic dichlorhydrine.

We may similarly consider the fluoxytungstates of M. Marignac. This chemist has described a fluoxytungstate of ammonia,§ the composition of which he represents in equivalents by the formula—

$$NH_4,WO_2Fl_2.$$

* *Comptes-Rendus*, vol. xlvi, p. 1093.

† Mo = 96.

‡ $MoO_3 + 2HO$ in the old notation.

§ *Annales de Chimie et de Physique*, 3rd series, vol. lxix., p. 66.

In our notation, adopting for tungsten the atomic weight 184, this formula becomes—

$$2(NH_4)\overline{W}\Theta_2Fl_4.$$

The substance in question forms, according to M. Friedel, a tungstic fluorhydrine—

$$\left.\begin{array}{c}\overset{vi}{\overline{W}}\\(NH_4)_2\\Fl_4\end{array}\right\}\Theta_2$$

derived from the hydrate—

$$\left.\begin{array}{c}\overset{vi}{\overline{W}}\\H_6\end{array}\right\}\Theta_6$$

As to the other fluoxytungstates described by M. Marignac, they are derived from a ditungstic hydrate.

There are chromic chlorhydrines and ferric chlorhydrines. In an important article, M. H. Schiff* justly remarked that the hydrated oxychlorides of chromium, obtained by M. Moberg by the desiccation of the hydrated perchloride, are derived from chromic hydrate by the substitution of several atoms of chlorine for several groups of HΘ.

$$\left.\begin{array}{c}\overline{C}r_2\\H_6\end{array}\right\}\Theta_6, \quad \left.\begin{array}{c}\overline{C}r_2\\H_4\\Cl_2\end{array}\right\}\Theta_4 \quad \left.\begin{array}{c}\overline{C}r_2\\H_2\\Cl_4\end{array}\right\}\Theta_2 \quad \left.\begin{array}{c}Cr_2\\H\\Cl_5\end{array}\right\}\Theta+4aq. \quad \overline{C}r_2Cl_6$$

| Chromic hydrate. | Chromic dichlorhydrine. | Chromic tetrachlorhydrine. | Chromic pentachlorhydrine. | Chromic chloride. |

We know, on the other hand, that ferric hydrate dissolves freely in a solution of ferric chloride. The oxychlorides which are thus formed, and to which M. Béchamp† has called attention, are doubtless ferric chlorhydrines, or rather mixtures of ferric chlorhydrines.

Metastannic hydrate dissolves in hydrochloric acid, and the solution thus obtained differs notably, according to H. Rose,‡ from the aqueous solution of stannic chlo-

---

* *Ibid.*, 3rd series, vol. lxvi., p. 142, October, 1862.

† *Ibid.*, vol. lvii., p. 286.

‡ Poggendorff's *Annalen*, vol. cv., p. 564.

ride. We may, in fact, imagine that by the action of hydrochloric acid upon metastannic hydrate there may be formed polystannic chlorhydrines (see page 157).

Condensed chlorhydrines exist, derived from the poly-ethylenic or polyglyceric alcohols. Thus diethylenic alcohol may give birth to two derived bodies of this class viz.:—

$$\left.\begin{matrix}C_2H_4\\C_2H_4\\H_2\end{matrix}\right\}\Theta_3 \qquad \begin{matrix}\left.\begin{matrix}C_2H_4\\C_2H_4\\H\end{matrix}\right\}\Theta_2\\Cl\end{matrix} \qquad \begin{matrix}\left.\begin{matrix}C_2H_4\\C_2H_4\end{matrix}\right\}\Theta\\Cl_2\end{matrix}$$

Diethylenic alcohol. — Monochlorhydrine of diethylenic alcohol. — Dichlorhydrine of diethylenic alcohol.

The second may be looked upon as a combination of oxide of ethylene and of chloride of ethylene. By heating for a long time bromide of ethylene with oxide of ethylene, I obtained a small quantity of a bromised liquid whose composition was sensibly that of a brom-oxide of ethylene.*

$$C_2H_4Br_2 + 2C_2H_4\Theta = \begin{matrix}\left.\begin{matrix}C_2H_4\\C_2H_4\\C_2H_4\end{matrix}\right\}\Theta_2\\Br_2\end{matrix}$$

The chlorides or bromides of oxides of inorganic chemistry have a constitution analogous to that of this latter body. The following examples will make this analogy evident.

Hydrate of lime dissolves in a solution of chloride of calcium, and the alkaline liquid properly concentrated deposits on cooling hydrated crystals, to which H. Rose assigns the composition,

$$3CaO,CaCl + 16HO.$$

In our notation this formula becomes—

$$3Ca\Theta,CaCl_2 + 16aq.\dagger$$

* *Annales de Chimie et de Physique*, vol. lxix., p. 342.
† aq. $= H_2\Theta$.

and may be written—

$$\left.\begin{matrix}Ca\\Ca\\Ca\\Ca\end{matrix}\right\}\Theta_3 + 16 \text{ aq. analogous to } \left.\begin{matrix}C_2H_4\\C_2H_4\\C_2H_4\\C_2H_4\end{matrix}\right\}\Theta_3$$
$$Cl_2 \qquad\qquad\qquad\qquad Cl_2$$

Dichlorhydrine of tetrethylenic alcohol.

There are oxychlorides of lead possessing an analogous constitution. Thus *mendipite*, which is a well-crystallised mineral, contains—

$$2Pb\Theta.PbCl_2 = \left.Pb_3\right\}\Theta_2$$
$$Cl_2$$

Atacamite is an oxychloride of hydrate of copper the composition of which is expressed in equivalents by the formula—

$$CuCl + 3CuO + HO.$$

By adopting for copper an atomic weight double the equivalent, this formula becomes—

$$\left.\begin{matrix}2Cu''\\H\end{matrix}\right\}\Theta_2 \text{ derived from the hydrate } \left.\begin{matrix}2Cu''\\H_2\end{matrix}\right\}\Theta_3.$$
$$Cl$$

Dicupric monochlorhydrine.

In all the chlorhydrines which still contain one or more atoms of typical hydrogen, this hydrogen may be replaced by radicals of acids. M. Berthelot * has described, under the name of benzochlorhydrine, a glyceric compound which may be looked upon as chlorhydrine in which 1 atom of typical hydrogen has been replaced by the benzoyl radical.

$$\left.\begin{matrix}(C_3H_5)'''\\H_2\end{matrix}\right\}\Theta_2, \qquad \left.\begin{matrix}(C_3H_5)'''\\H.(C_7H_5\Theta)\end{matrix}\right\}\Theta_2.$$
$$Cl \qquad\qquad\qquad Cl$$

Monochlorhydrine. Benzochlorhydrine.

* *Annales de Chimie et de Physique*, 3rd series, vol. xli., p. 301.

Mr. Maxwell Simpson* has likewise prepared an analogous ethylenic compound—viz., acetochlorhydrine of glycol, or acetochlorhydric glycol; he obtained it by submitting glycol to the simultaneous action of hydrochloric and acetic acids. This body represents chlorhydric glycol, whose typical hydrogen has been replaced by the acetyl radical.

$$\begin{matrix}\left.\begin{matrix}(\mathrm{C_2H_4})'' \\ \mathrm{H}\end{matrix}\right\}\Theta, \\ \mathrm{Cl}\end{matrix} \qquad \begin{matrix}\left.\begin{matrix}(\mathrm{C_2H_4})'' \\ \mathrm{C_2H_3\Theta}\end{matrix}\right\}\Theta, \\ \mathrm{Cl}\end{matrix} \qquad \text{or} \qquad \left.\begin{matrix}(\mathrm{C_2H_4})'' \\ \mathrm{C_2H_3\Theta}\end{matrix}\right\}\begin{matrix}\Theta \\ \mathrm{Cl}\end{matrix}$$

Chlorhydric glycol. Acetochlorhydric glycol. Ethylenic acetochlorhydrine.

We know a certain number of inorganic compounds that possess an analogous constitution.

When we evaporate an aqueous solution of equivalent quantities of acetate of lime and of chloride of calcium, we obtain large crystals permanent in the air, which contain, according to the analysis of M. Fritzsche—

$$\mathrm{CaCl + C_4H_3CaO_4 + 10HO}.$$

This substance is a calcic acetochlorhydrine,

$$\begin{matrix}\left.\begin{matrix}\mathrm{Ca}'' \\ \mathrm{C_2H_3\Theta}\end{matrix}\right\}\Theta + 5\mathrm{H_2\Theta} \\ \mathrm{Cl}\end{matrix}$$

Calcic acetochlorhydrine.

M. Carius† has lately described some plumbic compounds anologous to the preceding, and has perfectly ascertained and defined their constitution. These compounds are formed by the direct addition of chloride, bromide, or iodide of lead to a solution of acetate of lead made acid with acetic acid. Their composition may be expressed by the following formulæ:—

$$\begin{matrix}\left.\begin{matrix}\mathrm{Pb}'' \\ \mathrm{C_2H_3\Theta}\end{matrix}\right\}\Theta, \\ \mathrm{Cl}\end{matrix} \qquad \begin{matrix}\left.\begin{matrix}\mathrm{Pb}'' \\ \mathrm{C_2H_3\Theta}\end{matrix}\right\}\Theta, \\ \mathrm{Br}\end{matrix} \qquad \begin{matrix}\left.\begin{matrix}\mathrm{Pb}'' \\ \mathrm{C_2H_3\Theta}\end{matrix}\right\}\Theta, \\ \mathrm{I}\end{matrix}$$

Plumbic acetochlorhydrine. Plumbic acetobromhydrine. Plumbic aceto-iodhydrine.

* *Proceedings of the Royal Society*, vol. ix., p. 725.

† *Annales de Chimie et de Physique*, 3rd series, vol. xviii., p. 207.

Let us here remark that the existence of these calcic and plumbic compounds furnishes a good argument in favour of the diatomicity of calcium and of lead, which may be compared in this respect to ethylene.

By dissolving the basic tetrachloride of chromium in ammonia (page 172), M. Hugo Schiff* obtained a salt which he calls acetotetrachloride of chromium, and whose composition he represents by the formula—

$$\left.\begin{matrix}[Cr_2]^{vi}\\ 2C_2H\Theta\end{matrix}\right\}\Theta_2 + 4aq.$$
$$Cl_4$$

He also describes a sulphodichloride—

$$\left.\begin{matrix}(Cr)^{vi}\\ 2(S\Theta_2)''\end{matrix}\right\}\Theta_4 + 2aq.$$
$$Cl_2$$

and a nitrotetrachloride—

$$\left.\begin{matrix}[Cr_2]^{vi}\\ 2N\Theta_2\end{matrix}\right\}\Theta_2$$
$$Cl_4$$

which possesses an analogous constitution.

Further, he justly proposes to consider the ferric acetochloride described by M. Scheurer-Kestner† as an acetochlorhydrine—

$$\left.\begin{matrix}[Fe_2]^{vi}\\ 3C_2H_3\Theta\\ H\end{matrix}\right\}\Theta_4 + 3aq.$$
$$Cl_2$$

There are a certain number of minerals which possess a constitution analogous to that of the acetochlorhydrines just mentioned. Thus there are wagnerite and apatite, well-defined kinds of minerals. Their composition is usually represented by the formulæ—

$$PO_5, 3MgO + MgFl; \text{ and } 3(PO_5, 3CaO) + CaFl;$$

and they are looked upon as double compounds of phos-

* *Annales de Chimie et de Physique*, 3rd series, vol. lxvi., p. 147.

† *Ibid.*, 3rd series, vol. lxiii., p. 422.

phates and of fluorides or of chlorides. If we adopt for oxygen, magnesium, and calcium, atomic weights double their equivalents, the preceding formulæ become, in the typical notation—

$$\left.\begin{matrix}(P\Theta)''' \\ 2Mg''\end{matrix}\right\}\Theta_3 \qquad\qquad \left.\begin{matrix}3(P\Theta)''' \\ 5Ca''\end{matrix}\right\}\Theta_9$$

$$Fl \qquad\qquad\qquad Fl$$

Magnesian phosphofluor-hydrine (wagnerite). Calcic triphosphofluor-hydrine (apatite).

Here there is an important remark to be made. Ordinary phosphoric acid

$$\left.\begin{matrix}(P\Theta)''' \\ H_3\end{matrix}\right\}\Theta_3$$

requires, to saturate it, more than 1 molecule of magnesia—

$$Mg''\Theta. \quad (Mg=24),$$

for

$$Mg'' \text{ only equals } H_2;$$

but 2 molecules of magnesia, which contain 2 atoms of magnesium, are too much for saturation—in fact,

$$2Mg'' \text{ equals } H_4$$

and phosphoric acid only contains H_3. Now, wagnerite contains exactly 2 atoms of magnesium : it would then be supersaturated if the fourth unit of combination of the group

$$2Mg''$$

was not saturated by fluorine. The same reasoning applies to apatite and to the calcium which it contains. We see that, when looked at from the dualistic point of view, the fluorine or chlorine plays an important and necessary part in these compounds, whose composition appears at first so strange. I may add that the presence of such a monatomic element in these compounds furnishes an argument in favour of the diatomicity of magnesium and calcium. If magnesium were monatomic, the fluorine would be useless, for

$$3Mg(Mg=12)$$

could replace 3H in ordinary phosphoric acid $PH_3\Theta_4$. But this metal, together with calcium, being diatomic, and therefore of even atomicity, the presence of a monatomic element is necessary to complete the uneven atomicity of the phosphoryl $(P\Theta)'''$.*

We may extend this point of view to other compounds. There is a chlorophosphate of lead whose composition is exactly analogous to that of apatite. It is pyromorphite—

$$\left.\begin{matrix} 3(P\Theta)''' \\ 5Pb'' \end{matrix}\right\} \Theta_9 \atop Cl$$

Pyromorphite.

a mineral in which calcium and fluorine may replace a certain quantity of lead and chlorine. Mimetese offers an analogous constitution, except that a certain quantity of phosphoric acid is replaced by arsenic acid.

* My friend, Dr. Odling, has called my attention to a salt described by M. Briegleb (*Annalen der Chemie und Pharmacie*, vol. xcviii., p. 95), and represented by the formula $3NaO,PO_5+NaFl+24HO$. Without attempting to deny that the existence of this salt weakens the argument drawn from the constitution of wagnerite in favour of the diatomicity of magnesium, I would, however, point out:—

1. That this salt is very unstable, for boiling water decomposes it into a phosphate and a fluoride. We know, on the other hand, that wagnerite and apatite possess great stability, and that, when they contain chlorine, boiling water never extracts from them chloride of magnesium or calcium.

2. That it is impossible to obtain the corresponding fluophosphate of potassium.

3. That the salt in question contains water of crystallisation, and that, even in this respect, it is not comparable to wagnerite.

We owe to M. Cannizzaro another argument in favour of the diatomicity of calcium and barium. This is it—There is neither a quadroxalate of calcium nor a quadroxalate of barium, whilst there is a quadroxalate of potassium. In fact, an atom of hydrogen may be replaced in two molecules of oxalic acid by an atom of potassium, but not by a diatomic atom of calcium—

$$(Ca'' = 40).$$

As the latter displaces two atoms of hydrogen, the product of the substitution can be only a binoxalate or a neutral oxalate.

Cerasine, or horn lead, forms a chlorocarbonate of the form—

$$\left.\begin{array}{l} 2Pb'' \\ \Theta\Theta \\ Cl_2 \end{array}\right\} \Theta_2 \qquad \begin{array}{c} \text{derived from the hypo-} \\ \text{thetical hydrate} \end{array} \qquad \left.\begin{array}{l} 2Pb \\ H_4 \end{array}\right\} \Theta_4$$

I should likewise point out that this formula may be written—

$$\left.\begin{array}{l} 2Pb'' \\ \Theta\Theta \end{array}\right\} \begin{array}{l} \Theta_2 \\ Cl_2. \end{array}$$

And the same remark applies to the formulæ of all the organic and inorganic chlorhydrines. The notation I have hitherto preferred to employ* shows more clearly than the preceding formula the relations of these chlorhydrines to the corresponding hydrates.

Gerhardt has analysed a mercurous nitrophosphate which contains one molecule of mercurous phosphate united to one molecule of mercurous nitrate. This compound, represented in equivalents by the formula—

$$NO_5, Hg_2O + PO_5, 3Hg_2O + 2HO,$$

may be considered as a kind of wagnerite in which the magnesium is replaced by mercurosum ($Hg_2 = 400$) and the fluorine by nitrous gas—

$$\left.\begin{array}{l} (P\Theta)''' \\ 2[Hg_2]'' \end{array}\right\} \begin{array}{l} \Theta_3 \\ (N\Theta_2)' \end{array} + H_2\Theta.$$

* M. Weltzien proposed this notation the same time that I did.

SECTION V.

Inorganic and Organic Nitrides.

It remains for us, lastly, to pursue the analogies which may exist between the nitrides of inorganic chemistry and those of organic chemistry. Since the discovery of the compound ammonias has shown the evident relations that exist between the organic bases and ammonia, and has, so to say, formed the ammonia type, chemists have sought to connect the metallic nitrides with this type. On this point we will remind the reader of the ingenious views advocated by M. Weltzein* and by M. H. Schiff.†

The compounds in which metals are partially or wholly substituted for the hydrogen in ammonia have been called *metallic amines.*‡

As the metals differ from each other in their equivalence, or, in other words, as their atoms possess a different value of substitution, it is evident that they cannot be substituted in the same way for the hydrogen of ammonia. The monatomic metals—potassium, sodium, silver, &c.—may replace one atom of hydrogen in ammonia; the results are monamines.

Thus the compounds known by the name of amidides of potassium and of sodium may be compared to ethylamine; nitride of potassium, and perhaps fulminating silver, may be compared to triethylamine.

$$\left.\begin{matrix}K\\H\\H\end{matrix}\right\}N \qquad \left.\begin{matrix}Na\\H\\H\end{matrix}\right\}N \qquad \left.\begin{matrix}C_2H_5\\H\\H\end{matrix}\right\}N$$

Amidide of potassium. Amidide of sodium. Ethylamine.

* *Annalen der Chemie und Pharmacie*, vol. xcvii., p. 19.

† *Ibid.*, vol. cxxiii., p. 1.

‡ Or metallic ammoniums, if the substitution is considered as taking place in ammonium.

$$\left.\begin{matrix}K\\K\\K\end{matrix}\right\}N \qquad \left.\begin{matrix}Ag\\Ag\\Ag\end{matrix}\right\}N(?) \qquad \left.\begin{matrix}C_2H_5\\C_2H_5\\C_2H_5\end{matrix}\right\}N$$

Nitride of potassium. Fulminating silver. Triethylamine.

The diatomic metals—copper, cobalt, mercury, &c.—can replace two atoms of hydrogen. We have compared them to ethylene, and there exist a certain number of metallic amines which may be compared to the ethylenic bases so well studied by Dr. Hofmann.

We know ammoniacal combinations of cobalt, copper, mercury, and platinum in which these metals replace 2 atoms of hydrogen in 2 molecules of ammonium, as ethylene is substituted for 2 atoms of hydrogen in 2 molecules of ammonium.

$$\left.\begin{matrix}Co''\\H_2\\H_2\\H_2\end{matrix}\right\}N_2 \quad \left.\begin{matrix}Cu''\\H_2\\H_2\\H_2\end{matrix}\right\}N_2 \quad \left.\begin{matrix}[Cu_2]''\\H_2\\H_2\\H_2\end{matrix}\right\}N_2 \quad \left.\begin{matrix}Pt''\\H_2\\H_2\\H_2\end{matrix}\right\}N_2 \quad \left.\begin{matrix}(C_2H_4)''\\H_2\\H_2\\H_2\end{matrix}\right\}N_2$$

Cobaltosonium. Cupriconium. Cuprosonium. Platosonium. Ethylene-ammonium.

Thus, to take some examples, acetate of cupriconium (ammoniacal acetate of copper), which crystallises in oblique rhomboidal prisms, contains:—

$$\left.\begin{matrix}Cu''\\H_2\\H_2\\H_2\end{matrix}\right\}N_2.2(C_2H_3O.O)'.$$

The green salt of Magnus (ammoniacal protochloride of platinum) is the dichloride of platosonium,

$$\left.\begin{matrix}Pt''\\H_2\\H_2\\H_2\end{matrix}\right\}N_2.Cl_2.$$

We must observe that it is produced by the fixation of 2 molecules of ammonia upon 1 molecule of protochloride of platinum,

$$Pt''Cl_2,$$

as bromide of ethylene-ammonium,

$$\left.\begin{matrix}(C_2H_4)''\\ H_2\\ H_2\\ H_2\end{matrix}\right\} N_2.Br_2,$$

is formed by the fixation of 2 molecules of ammonia upon 1 molecule of bromide of ethylene $(C_2H_4)''Br_2$.

The white precipitate which is formed when an aqueous solution of corrosive sublimate is treated with ammonia, and which is known by the name of chloramidide of mercury, is a dichloride of dimercurammonium :—

$$\left.\begin{matrix}Hg''\\ Hg''\\ H_2\\ H_2\end{matrix}\right\} N_2.Cl_2,$$

analogous to the dibromide of diethylene-ammonium,

$$\left.\begin{matrix}(C_2H_4)''\\ (C_2H_4)''\\ H_2\\ H_2\end{matrix}\right\} N_2.Br_2.$$

All these ammonio-metallic compounds are formed by the fixation of the elements of ammonia upon chlorides, bromides, &c., or upon metallic salts. But it often happens that an excess of ammonia is retained in these circumstances. Thus, when ammonia is made to act upon cuprous iodide, $[Cu_2]''I_2$, there are 4 molecules of ammonia, $4NH_3$, retained, and not 2 only, as is the case with protochloride of platinum, for example. We thus obtain a well-defined compound crystallised in large prisms, and to which the analyses of M. Rammelsberg assign the composition $Cu_2I_2,4NH_3$.

We may look upon this compound, and upon its numerous congeners, as containing an ammonium in the molecule of which a certain quantity of hydrogen has been replaced by an equivalent quantity of the ammonium radical $NH_4 = Am$. In this hypothesis, first suggested by M. Hofmann, and adopted by MM. Weltzien, Hugo Schiff, and other chemists, the iodide in question appears as the diiodide of a diamicuprosonium—that is to say, of the cuprosonium (page 181), in which 2 atoms of hydrogen have been replaced by $2NH_4 = Am_2$.

$$\left.\begin{array}{r}[Cu_2]'' \\ H_2 \\ H_2 \\ H_2\end{array}\right\}N \qquad \left.\begin{array}{r}[Cu_2]'' \\ (NH_4)_2 \\ H_2 \\ H_2\end{array}\right\}N_2\,I_2 \text{ or } \left.\begin{array}{r}[Cu_2]'' \\ Am_2 \\ H_2 \\ H_2\end{array}\right\}N_2.I_2.$$

Cuprosonium. Iodide of diamicuprosonium.

Similar remarks apply to the other ammoniacal combinations of copper, cobalt, and platinum. According to the analysis of Berzelius, the composition of ammoniacal sulphate of copper is expressed, in equivalents, by the formula—

$$CuO,SO_3,2NH_3,HO.$$

This body may be regarded as a sulphate of diamicupriconium—

$$\left.\begin{array}{r}Cu'' \\ Am_2 \\ H_2 \\ H_2\end{array}\right\}N_2.SO_4 + aq.$$

Similarly, Henry Rose has analysed a combination of ammoniacal chloride of cobalt, which forms the chloride of diamicobaltosonium—

$$\left.\begin{array}{r}Co'' \\ Am_2 \\ H_2 \\ H_2\end{array}\right\}N_2.Cl_2.$$

Reiset's salt, which is formed when Magnus's salt or chloride of platosonium is digested with an excess of ammonia, may be regarded as the dichloride of diamiplatosonium—

$$\left.\begin{array}{r}Pt'' \\ Am_2 \\ H_2 \\ H_2\end{array}\right\}N_2.Cl_2.^*$$

These examples, which might be greatly multiplied, will suffice to show that the capacity of saturation of the

* Hofmann.

ammoniaco-metallic bases is not always in proportion to the quantity of nitrogen which they contain. Thus, the ammonium of Reiset's salt contains 4 atoms of nitrogen, two of which are in Am_2, and unites only with 2 atoms of chlorine.

We know, by the valuable researches of Dr. Hofmann, that it is the same with the polyamines or organic poly-ammonias. Thus the ethylenic triammonias or ethylenic triamines* can form three kinds of salts, which are as follows, for the diethylenic triamine, which we will take as an example—

$$\left.\begin{matrix}(C_2H_4)_2\\H_5\end{matrix}\right\}N_3,3HCl.$$

$$\left.\begin{matrix}(C_2H_4)_2\\H_5\end{matrix}\right\}N_3,2HCl.$$

$$\left.\begin{matrix}(C_2H_4)_2\\H_5\end{matrix}\right\}N_3,HCl.$$

The second of these salts is a diacid triamine, the third a monacid triamine. In accordance with the system of notation adopted above, the diacid salt may be formularised in the following manner:—

$$\left.\begin{matrix}(C_2H_4)_2\\NH_4\\H_3\end{matrix}\right\}N_2.Cl_2 \quad \text{or} \quad \left.\begin{matrix}(C_2H_4)_2\\Am\\H_3\end{matrix}\right\}N_2.Cl_2$$

Inversely, nothing prevents us from considering the cuprous, cobaltous, and platinous ammoniacal combinations in question as diacid tetramines—that is to say, incompletely saturated:—

$$\underset{\text{Ammoniacal cuprous iodide.}}{\left.\begin{matrix}[Cu_2]''\\H_{10}\end{matrix}\right\}N_4,H_2I_2,} \quad \underset{\text{Ammoniacal chloride of cobalt.}}{\left.\begin{matrix}Co''\\H_{10}\end{matrix}\right\}N_4,H_2Cl_2,} \quad \underset{\text{Reiset's salt.}}{\left.\begin{matrix}Pt''\\H_{10}\end{matrix}\right\}N_4,H_2Cl_2}$$

I do not put forward these formulæ as being preferable to those before given; my aim is merely to show that we know, in inorganic and organic chemistry, of combinations formed by the fixation of ammonia upon a

* Hofmann, *Comptes Rendus*, vol. lii., p. 947.

chloride, a bromide, &c., and whose capacity of saturation is not in proportion to the quantities of ammonia retained.

But there are other analogies which we meet with without going out of the group of compounds that we have been considering. Dr. Hofmann has proved that trimethylamine, Me_3N, may unite with dibromide of ethylene, $C_2H_4Br_2$, to form a bromide

$$\left.\begin{matrix}(C_2H_4Br)' \\ Me_3\end{matrix}\right\} N.Br.$$

In this body we see the group

$$C_2H_4Br = C_2H_4Br_2 - Br$$

takes the place of 1 atom of hydrogen in a compound ammonium. Similarly the group

$$[PtCl_2]'' = Pt^{iv}Cl_4 - Cl_2$$

may replace 2 atoms of hydrogen.

When a current of chlorine is directed upon the green Magnus's salt (chloride of platosonium), it is changed by absorbing 2 atoms of chlorine into chloride of chloroplatammonium (Gerhardt).

$$\left.\begin{matrix}[Pt_2Cl_2]'' \\ H_2 \\ H_2 \\ H_2\end{matrix}\right\} N_2.Cl_2$$

There also exists a chloride of diamichloroplatammonium—

$$\left.\begin{matrix}(PtCl_2)'' \\ Am_2 \\ H_2 \\ H_2\end{matrix}\right\} N_2.Cl_2$$

It is formed by the union of chlorine with chloride of diamiplatosonium or Reiset salt.

All the formulæ we have given above in which diatomic metals enter are double those which M. H. Schiff has adopted in his remarkable work. It appears to us, in fact, that these metals may unite several molecules of ammonia, as ethylene does in the ethylenic ammonias.

Oxygenised groups, inorganic and organic, may replace the hydrogen of ammonia to form compound ammonias or amines. I have shown the existence of oxyethylenic bases, which may be looked upon as ammonia, in which 1, 2, or 3 atoms of hydrogen are replaced by 1, 2, or 3 oxyethylic groups $ϴ_2H_5Θ$. This group acts the part of a monatomic radical; it may be looked upon as formed of an ethylene group joined to the residue $(HΘ)'$.*

$$[(ϴ_2H_4)''(HΘ)]'.$$

The atomicity of the ethylene group is lowered one degree by the addition of the monatomic group $(HΘ)'$.

The following formulæ express the relations of these bases with ammonia:—

$$\left.\begin{matrix}ϴ_2H_5Θ\\H\\H\end{matrix}\right\}N, \qquad \left.\begin{matrix}ϴ_2H_5Θ\\ϴ_2H_5Θ\\H\end{matrix}\right\}N, \qquad \left.\begin{matrix}ϴ_2H_5Θ\\ϴ_2H_5Θ\\ϴ_2H_5Θ\end{matrix}\right\}N.$$

Oxethylenamine. Dioxethylenamine. Trioxethylenamine.

There are oxycobaltic, oxymercuric, and oxyplatinic bases.

We know that the ammoniacal solutions of the salts of cobaltosonium absorb the oxygen of the air and change into ammoniacal bases corresponding to cobaltic oxide. These bases have been studied (within the last few years) by M. Fremy and by MM. Gibbs and Genth. M. H. Schiff rightly admits the existence in them of a group $[ϹoΘ]'$. He considers this group as monatomic, and formed by the combination of diatomic oxygen with cobalt ($Ϲo=59$), which is triatomic in the cobaltic salts (cobalticum). Here we see the atomicity of the triatomic

* The group $[ϴ_2H_4.HΘ]'$ represents glycol $ϴ_2H_4.2HΘ$ minus $(HΘ)'$.

metal lowered two degrees by the addition of oxygen, which saturates 2 affinities:—

$$[Co'''\Theta'']'.$$

We know that there are oxygenised salts corresponding to the combinations of chloroplatammonium and of amichloroplatammonium. These are formed when the chlorised combinations are boiled with an excess of nitrate of silver (Gerhardt, Kolbe). The chlorine of the chloroplatinum radical is then replaced by oxygen.

$$\left.\begin{matrix}[PtCl_2]'' \\ H_2 \\ H_2 \\ H_2\end{matrix}\right\} N_2 \qquad \left.\begin{matrix}(Pt\Theta)'' \\ H_2 \\ H_2 \\ H_2\end{matrix}\right\} N_2$$

Chloroplatammonium. Oxyplatammonium (Gerhardt).

$$\left.\begin{matrix}(PtCl_2)'' \\ Am_2 \\ H_2 \\ H_2\end{matrix}\right\} N_2 \qquad \left.\begin{matrix}(Pt\Theta)'' \\ Am_2 \\ H_2 \\ H_2\end{matrix}\right\} N.$$

Amichloroplatammonium. Amoxyplatammonium (Kolbe).

In these bases the group

$$Pt\Theta$$

acts as a diatomic radical formed by the combination of diatomic oxygen with tetratomic platinum.

M. Millon some years ago discovered a remarkable base, to which he gave the name of *ammonio-mercuric oxide*. This body is formed by the action of ammonia upon oxide of mercury. Its composition is usually represented by the formula

$$3HgO,HgH_2N + 3HO.$$

When anhydrous it contains—

$$3HgO,HgNH_2.$$

In our notation this formula becomes

$$3Hg\Theta,HgN_2H_4.$$

The base itself may be locked upon as the oxide of an ammonium—

$$\left[\left.\begin{matrix}(Hg.H\Theta) \\ Hg'' \\ H\end{matrix}\right\} N \;\Theta\right]_2$$

in which the diatomic mercury would be joined to the $H\Theta$ group, as, in the oxyethylammoniums, ethylene is joined to the same group.

Conclusion.

I MUST now stop, for my task is completed. I have tried, in the most diverse compounds and in the most varied reactions, to pursue this alliance between organic and inorganic chemistry, which all have proclaimed, but which few have hitherto tried to establish in a definite manner. In the preceding pages I have pointed out many analogies, and I have sought to express them in that typical notation which is so clear when we have to represent the ties of relationship existing between bodies. I have laid stress upon some of the fundamental data of that which is now called the *new chemistry*. But it may be wrong to call it so. For this chemistry is simply that of Lavoisier, and if during ninety years the science he created has received a magnificent development, it owes it not to a revolution but to a continuous progress; the chain of this progress has never been broken.

At the end of last century the facts concerning the composition of acids, of oxides, and of salts, composed almost the whole domain of chemistry.

Theoretical ideas relative to the composition of compound bodies in general were founded upon the study of the reactions which give rise to the oxygenised compounds, particularly to salts.

We can sum them up thus: All chemical compounds are formed by the addition of two simple or compound elements; all compound bodies have a binary constitution. This is what was called dualism.

Berzelius adopted this doctrine, and sought to strengthen it by basing it upon the facts relating to the electrolytic decomposition of salts. The electro-chemical hypothesis became the support of the dualistic hypothesis. "You see plainly," said this master, "that salts contain the elements of the acid side by side with those of the oxide, and not confounded with them; for when we submit to electrolysis such a salt as sulphate of soda, the sulphuric acid, or the electro-negative element, goes to the positive pole, and the soda, or electro-positive element, goes to the negative pole." Thus the dualistic formulæ of sulphate of soda

$$SO_3 + NaO,$$

and of salts in general appeared strengthened, not only by the facts relating to the synthesis of these compounds and their most ordinary mode of formation, but also by the decomposition which the electric current causes in some among them. We now know that the argument is bad, and that it may be turned against the hypothesis which has been so long in vogue as to the constitution of salts. We know that in the electrolysis of sulphate of soda, as in that of sulphate of copper, it is not the oxide but the metal which goes to the negative pole, and that the free alkali only appears as the result of a secondary action — namely, the decomposition of the water by the metal around the negative electrode.

But that was not known in 1834, and since this epoch have been discovered the facts which should ruin the dualistic hypothesis of the constitution of compound bodies. M. Dumas proved that chlorine can unite with organic bodies otherwise than by addition—that is to say, by substitution; that chlorine, an electro-negative element, can there replace hydrogen, an electro-positive element.

Berzelius rejected the most natural interpretation of these facts, and sought to express the composition of the chlorised organic bodies by dualistic formulæ. Thus trichloracetic acid was looked upon as a combination of chloride of carbon and of oxalic acid—

$$C_2Cl_3 + C_2O_3 + HO.$$

Trichloracetic acid.

Formulæ analogous to the preceding, and often more complicated, were attributed to the numerous products of substitution with which the labours of Laurent and of MM. Regnault and Malaguti had enriched the science. Berzelius had never before shown himself so fertile in hypotheses, and the resources of his powerful mind were wasted on this thankless task; by torturing facts to adapt them to his theory, he hastened the ruin of his ideas.

The French school has reacted against these exaggerations. M. Dumas, Laurent, and, later still, Gerhardt, entered into an energetic and victorious conflict with the author of the electro-chemical theory. Organic bodies are formed by groups of atoms united together by the bonds of affinity, and forming a whole; M. Dumas first stated this fact; Laurent and Gerhardt, adopting and developing this idea, made it the foundation of their theoretical conceptions; it is the basis of the *unitary system.*

But, as always happens, some have gone too far in this reaction. By saying, about ten years since, that simple or compound bodies can only react upon each other by exchanging their atoms, and by summing up chemistry in these words—All is double decomposition—Gerhardt himself exaggerated.

Yes, all is double decomposition in a large number of reactions, when molecules, which we may look upon as saturated, come into conflict with each other. In each of them, taken separately, the affinities of all the atoms are satisfied, and the forces which unite them are exhausted. But when they are put in contact, this state of equilibrium may be broken, and exchanges of atoms may take place, by virtue of that elective affinity of which Bergmann spoke a century ago.

But all is not double decomposition when we have to do with reactions between bodies which have not arrived at the state of saturation. A combination which contains one or more polyatomic elements whose affinities are not satisfied, may unite with new elements by virtue of the tendency which atoms possess to manifest and exert to their full extent the chemical forces which reside in them. Here it is not an exchange of atoms which forms the reaction—it is an addition of atoms. New affinities have revealed themselves and have been satisfied; the molecular edifice has increased.

Such reactions show that the combining power of the atoms is not exhausted at once, but that it is exerted by degrees. This combining power is now called atomicity. It is the basis of the modern theoretical ideas. If we wish to express in general terms the relations existing between bodies, shall we still say with Gerhardt that all should be compared with three or four substances chosen as types and able to be modified indefinitely by means of substitution? No; we can turn to a higher principle and say—

That the quantities of matter which act in chemical phenomena, and which have been called atoms, are not endowed to the same extent with the force which governs combinations.

That the diversity in the manifestation of this force, sometimes simple, sometimes multiple, gives rise to different forms of combination.

That in a given compound representing some one of

these forms, all the atoms are united by a part or by the whole of the affinities which reside in them.

Finally, that this affinity is exerted not only between heterogeneous atoms, but also between atoms of the same nature.

In the diversity of forms of combination we again see the typical idea, but this idea is now only of secondary importance; it is subordinate to a more general principle.

The theory of types, suggested by an attentive study of a large number of metamorphoses, confined itself to comparing bodies together, and represented them as being derived the one from the other by substitution. We now go further, and determining in what manner affinity joins the atoms together in a given compound, we endeavour to define the relationships which exist between these atoms. But who does not also see that this theory of atomicity which we have endeavoured to explain is only the invigorated and developed expression of the law of multiple proportions? Who does not see that contemporaneous chemistry, by considering so attentively the action of affinity in combinations, and especially in those molecular additions which Gerhardt had neglected, has made in a manner a return towards the past? We may thus say that the ideas which now tend to prevail stand midway between the ancient theories and those developed by Laurent and by Gerhardt.

London: Benjamin Pardon, Printer, Paternoster Row.

www.ingramcontent.com/pod-product-compliance
Lightning Source LLC
Chambersburg PA
CBHW030833270326
41928CB00007B/1027
* 9 7 8 3 3 3 7 0 7 0 2 2 9 *